D0945266

WOMEN'S LIVES INTO PRINT

Women's Lives into Print

The Theory, Practice and Writing of Feminist Auto/Biography

Edited by

Pauline Polkey

First published in Great Britain 1999 by
MACMILLAN PRESS LTD
Houndmills, Basingstoke, Hampshire RG21 6XS and London
Companies and representatives throughout the world

A catalogue record for this book is available from the British Library.

ISBN 0–333–68410–9

 First published in the United States of America 1999 by
ST. MARTIN'S PRESS, INC.,
Scholarly and Reference Division,
175 Fifth Avenue, New York, N.Y. 10010

ISBN 0–312–22352–8

Library of Congress Cataloging-in-Publication Data
Women's lives into print : the theory, practice and writing of
feminist auto/biography / edited by Pauline Polkey.
p.   cm.
Includes bibliographical references and index.
ISBN 0–312–22352–8 (cloth)
1. Women's studies—Biographical methods.   2. Women—Biography–
–Methodology.   3. Autobiography—Women authors.   I. Polkey,
Pauline, 1958–   .
HQ1185.W67   1999
808'.06692—dc21   99–18158
                                                                  CIP

This book is printed on paper suitable for recycling and made from fully managed and sustained forest sources.

10   9   8   7   6   5   4   3   2   1
08   07   06   05   04   03   02   01   00   99

Printed and bound in Great Britain by
Antony Rowe Ltd, Chippenham, Wiltshire

Contents

List of Illustrations

Acknowledgements

Since its inception in 1993, this book has evolved from a variety of influences and motivations. It would certainly not have been possible without the groundbreaking work that has been produced by feminist scholars working on auto/biography during the past two decades. The support and encouragement of dear friends and colleagues has been a vital lifeline, and my thanks to all those who have offered their time, practical help and intellectual stimulation. Pam Lilley's diligent attention to detail in the final stages of the book's production has been exemplary, and I am indebted to her assistance. I am particularly grateful to Sonia Lawson for permission to reproduce her 'Homage to Emily Brontë, Night Writing' on the jacket. Heartfelt thanks to David Taylor and Tom Polkey, whose support has been unending; and to Elizabeth Ellis, who always makes me think twice before I put pen to paper.

But this book has been a *collaborative* project, and my gratitude goes to all the contributors for their patience and co-operation in bringing this book into print.

Notes on the Contributors

Catherine Byron grew up in Belfast and read medieval literature at Somerville College, Oxford. Her poetry and prose have been published widely in Ireland, Britain and North America. Her most recent poetry collection is *The Fat-Hen Field Hospital* (1993). In 1997 she received an Arts Council of England Writer's Award.

Alison Donnell teaches postcolonial literatures at Nottingham Trent University. Her specialist research interests are Caribbean writing, postcolonial women's writing and postcolonial theory. She is co-editor of *The Routledge Reader in Caribbean Literature* and joint-editor of *Interventions: the International Journal of Postcolonial Studies*.

Elizabeth Edwards is a senior research associate at Homerton College, Cambridge, and was formerly the College's librarian and archivist. She has published several articles on women's experience in teacher training Colleges, and is currently working on a book to be entitled *Women in Teacher Training Colleges: A Culture of Femininity 1900–1960* (UCL Press).

Mary Evans was educated at the London School of Economics and the University of Sussex. She has taught sociology and women's studies at the University of Kent since 1971, and is the author of *A Good School*, *the Women Question*, *Jane Austen and the State* and an *Introduction to Contemporary Feminist Thought*. She is currently writing a book on love.

Lesley Forrest originally trained as a teacher, and completed her MA in women's studies at the University of Bradford. She now teaches women's studies and sociology at the University College of Ripon and York St John. She is currently engaged on research with young female students who are studying women's studies at undergraduate level.

Katherine Frank is the author of three biographies: *A Voyager Out: The Life of Mary Kingsley* (1986), *Emily Brontë* (1990) and *Lucie Duff Gordon: A Passage to Egypt* (1994). She is currently working on a biography of Indira Gandhi which will be published by

HarperCollins. She has published numerous articles on biographical writing, women writers and the lives of women.

Judy Giles is Senior Lecturer at the University College of Ripon and York St John. She teaches women's studies, cultural studies and literature. She is the author of *Women, Identity and Private Life in Britain, 1900–50*, and 'Second Chance, Second Self' in *Gender and Education*, which deals with the experience of being a mature student.

Julia Hallam trained and worked as a nurse before undertaking a PhD in Women's Studies at Warwick University. She currently teaches in the Communication Studies Department at Liverpool University, and is working on a book on realism and popular cinema for Manchester University Press.

Christine Kenny is senior lecturer at South Bank University, in the School of Health and Social Care. Her research and hobby interests include women's history, gender and care, thanatology, autobiography and local history. As a member of the Lancashire Authors' Association, much of Christine's leisure time is spent researching the local history of Bolton, particularly women's history, and writing popular local history books.

Pauline Polkey is lecturer in women's writing and feminist theory at Nottingham Trent University. Her research focuses on politically active women's autobiographies 1880–1920. She is currently working on several projects: Edith Simcox's *Autobiography of a Shirt Maker*, a co-edited collection, with Alison Donnell, *Representing Lives: Women and Auto/Biography*; and a book on *Passionate Landscapes of Selfhood: Women, Politics and Autobiography*.

Jo Stanley is a writer and creative historian. Specialising in women's work on liners, she is the Co-ordinator of the National Maritime Museum's Women and the Sea Network. With an arts background, her writing includes poems, plays, short stories and novels as well as non-fiction books, reviews and articles.

Liz Stanley is a feminist sociologist by conviction, lives in the north of England by choice, is a lesbian by luck, and enjoys the earthly pleasures of (in changing permutations of this order) books, food, wine, cats, music. Her current books are *Knowing Feminisms: On*

Academic Borders, Territories and Tribes (Sage, 1997) and *Olive Schreiner: Imperialism, Labour and the 'New Woman'* (Sage, 1998).

Julia Swindells teaches at Homerton College, Cambridge. She is author of *Victorian Writing and Working Women, the Other Side of Silence*, co-author with Lisa Jardine of *What's Left? Women in Culture and the Labour Movement*, and, most recently, editor of *The Uses of Autobiography*. Currently, she is writing about the theatre and auto-biography in the period 1789 to 1832.

Bogusia Temple is a Senior Research Lecturer in the Ethnicity and Health Unit at the University of Central Lancashire. Her interests outside of her employment include research with Polish communities. This centres on issues of ethnicity, gender and identity. She is at present carrying out research with second generation Poles.

Val Walsh is a freelance writer, researcher, editor and tutor. She trained as an artist and teacher, before qualifying in sociology and women's studies, and was a full-time academic for many years, first as an art tutor, then as an interdisciplinary communication studies and women's studies tutor and course leader. She is editor of the new series on *Gender and Higher Education*, published by Taylor & Francis.

Joss West-Burnham is Subject Leader in Cultural Studies, Department of Humanities and Applied Social Studies, Crewe and Alsager Campus, Manchester Metropolitan University. She is also a member of the Management Group of the Development of University English Teaching (DUET) Project. Her most recent research has been on the relationship between religious denomination and identity formation in a selection of nineteenth-century women writers.

Introduction

One of the most significant contributions that feminist scholarship has made to academia over the past two decades concerns autobiography and biography, and the way in which we now engage with life-writing has perceptibly shifted. Theoretically, practically and creatively, the parameters of life-writing have been reshaped, interest in its various representations has been substantially reinvigorated, and the sheer quantity of work produced by feminists is evidence of a very full larder indeed.

This book offers a collection of essays by researchers and writers who are intent upon exploring the various ways in which women's lives are 'put into print' – that is to say, placed into the public domain – and upon formulating methods and strategies for interpreting those lives. Our use of 'feminist' in the book's subtitle – *The Theory, Practice and Writing of Feminist Auto/biography* – denotes a politically-enshrined focus that is both propelled and sustained by theoretical debates concerning matters of selfhood, identity and subjectivity. Crucially, our emphasis is upon grappling with and problematising the *workings* of theory – its uses and formulations – and the ethical and methodological implications that arise from those workings. The term 'auto/biography' aligns itself to contemporaneous interventions within feminist critical theory (see Stanley, 1992; Marcus, 1994), which 'involves the insistence that accounts of other lives influence how we see and understand our own and that our understandings of our own lives will impact upon how we interpret other lives' (Stanley, 1994: i). Not only does this approach have far-reaching consequences about the way in which we position the lives we read and/or represent, but it also opens up a vigorous and incisive challenge to the conventional – 'unique subject' – critical model.

Each of the contributors avers the principle of participating in a continuum of ideas taking place within feminist theory about ways of reading, interpreting, researching and writing women's lives. In so doing, we raise questions about various configurations of life-writing,[1] looking, for example, at the webbed connectedness of lives; the significance of, and differences between, auto/biographical forms – letters, diaries, published works, oral history, fictional autobiography; and the proximity between autobiography and biography, hence: auto/biography. Narratological facets of tone, mood, shifting focus, atmosphere and ambience are also considered, as are representations of 'voice' and authentication. Issues of 'truth' and probity are explored, wherein 'a realist version of "truth" as something single and unseamed is jettisoned' in favour of a contextured analysis wherein 'perspective is all' (Stanley, 1992: 14). As the Personal Narratives Group (eds) explain:

> Only by attending to the conditions which create these narratives, the forms that guide them, and the relationships that produce them are we able to understand what is communicated in a personal narrative. These angles not only provide different perspectives but reveal multiple truths of a life ... Therefore, rather than focus on the objective Truth, [it is important to] focus on the links between women's perspectives and the truths they reveal. (1989: 262)

We do not intend to confound the reader with abstruse altercations, nor do we wish to confine our analysis to rudimentary either/or solutions. Rather, our aim is to open up debate, stimulate discussion and extend analysis further.

Women's Lives into Print works within and across subject disciplines of history, media and communication studies, women's studies, sociology, health and social care, English studies and writing. While this yields varied and diverse interpretations about life-writing, certain broad-based commonalities unite them together in terms of interest and approach. On the basis of such commonalities, the book is divided into three distinct Parts, each focusing, in turn, on the theory, practice and writing of auto/biography.

PART I THEORY – PUTTING WOMEN'S LIVES INTO PRINT:
FEMINIST ETHICS, METHODOLOGIES
AND EPISTEMOLOGIES

Part I contains four essays, and deals with the varied and combined use of theory, methodology and ethics in pursuit of a life/lives. Liz Stanley's opening essay interrogates the provisionality of a realist – 'everybody knows' – methodological framework, and invites us to critically self-determine and evaluate the bases on which we construe and represent lives. There is affirmation here, not only of the intellectual 'risks' we take in pursuance of a life-story, but also of the self-reflexive processes whereby the researcher becomes bound up with that project. Crucially, her discussion is underpinned by a discerning caveat, urging us to 'use our minds in intellectually challenging ways, by making our analytic procedures open to others for scrutiny, and possibly also for rejection, by providing our evidences, by detailing our interpretations, and by justifying our conclusions'.

Like Liz Stanley, Bogusia Temple, in her discussion of 'Terrible Times: Experience, Ethnicity and Auto/Biography', sets out to explore the webbed connections between researcher and research project, and their auto/biographical manifestations. Herself a second-generation Pole, Temple reflects on work she has undertaken on Polish emigrants, from which a series of intricate debates unfold concerning issues of selfhood and identity, experience and truth. Temple's agenda lies not only in assessing how far the individual 'voice' of oral testimony is coterminous with, and representative of, collective historical memory, but she is also intent on scrutinising herself as conveyor of those testimonies.

In 'Memory, Truth and Orality: The Lives of Women Textile Workers', Christine Kenny offers a self-reflexive and retrospective account of the processes she went through in writing and researching her book *Cotton Everywhere: Recollections of Northern Women Textile Workers* (1994). Her essay reveals a troubled story, both in terms of having to negotiate and redefine her role as interviewer of family and friends, and in relation to the way in which her book was adjudged by academia. Because Kenny's research is auto/biographically framed – her own life-story is intertextually entwined within the stories of the women she writes about – questions of ethics and responsibility are self-reflexively foregrounded. This discussion both attests to the crucial importance of life-history projects and offers a salutary evaluation of the impact that academic marginalisation can have; it is also a testimony to the possibility of working through the problematics of academic marginalisation.

Bringing this Part to its conclusion, Lesley Forrest and Judy Giles's collaborative essay on 'Feminist Ethics and Issues in the Production and Use of Life History Research' also examines the relationship between interviewer and interviewee. Forrest looks back on her interviews with groups of young women aged between 14 and 15 years, and Giles reflects on her interviews with individual, older women aged between 70 and 80 years. Each evaluates the process of life-history research, and provides a comparative discussion about their expectations, discoveries, performance and conclusions. While recognising that their conclusions differ considerably, they each acknowledge the role that class and cultural experience play in shaping a life. What unites both projects is the (feminist) paradigm of reciprocity: for the researcher to 'give back' to the community what that community has shared with the researcher.

PART II PRACTICE – RECOVERING AND READING WOMEN'S LIVES: INTERPRETIVE ISSUES

All of the essays in Part II are contingent upon a practical objective, namely to read, recover and interpret women's lives. It opens with my essay on the love-passions of Edith Simcox. Making detailed reference to Simcox's *Autobiography of a Shirt Maker*, I evaluate 'what happens' when the lives of women whom we recover become entangled in a recuperative process. Rebuttal is only one aspect of this discussion. More importantly, I am intent upon providing a new perspective on Simcox that emerges from an assiduous and attentive reading of her *Autobiography*: a reading that is motivated by a theoretical perspective that is auto/biographically shaped, and which insists on the webbed connections that impinge on all lives. I conclude by holding up three 'time-framed' versions of Simcox – past, present and future – and invite the reader to partake in the processes and challenges of archival research.

Joss West-Burnham's 'Travelling Towards Selfhood: Victorian Religion and the Process of Female Identity' travels across various academic and intellectual boundaries – of literary, historical and religious studies – and gauges the implications this might have for reading past lives. In so doing, West-Burnham offers a contextual analysis of three women's lives – Grace Aguilar (1816–47), Harriet Martineau (1802–76) and George Eliot (1819–90) – each discursively framed within the phenomenon of religion. Like Polkey, West-Burnham provides an interchange of knowledge, and seeks out the points of intersection between 'perceived' and 'alternative' versions of selfhood.

Julia Swindells's discussion of Mary Somerville's *Personal Recollections* also insists on a historically-contextured reading of life-writing, but whereas West-Burnham was concerned with religion, Swindells focuses on science. What this essay contemplates is the problems that beset interpretational procedures with regards to autobiography. More specifically, Swindells is concerned with opening up debate about how we decode editorial interventions that prevail in Somerville's (published) autobiography; the methods we might use to evaluate two apparently disparate formulations of a 'domestic' and 'professional' self; and the constraints that operate in controlling and restraining self-expression.

In her examination of Alice Havergal Skillicorn's life, Elizabeth Edwards is also concerned with exploring discourses of gendered subjectivity alongside the alternating modalities of masculine/feminine, public/private. Basing her evaluation on archival records – including letters written by students who attended Homerton College, Cambridge, where Skillicorn was Principal, and Skillicorn's autobiographical testimonies – Edwards focuses on the intricate and complex relationship between sexuality and gender. In particular, she examines the uneasy crossing-over between Skillicorn's unorthodox sexual orientation and a gendered identity that was deeply conservative.

Alison Donnell turns to questions of ethnicity, and her discussion hinges upon a central question: how can we speak for an 'other'? Working within feminist and post-colonial theoretical paradigms, this essay examines the politics of selfhood and identity in Jamaica Kincaid's *The Autobiography of My Mother*, and argues that we can, and should, engage with women's auto/biographies in insightful and contentious ways. Fundamentally, this is a discussion that explores with vigour the intertextual/intra-subjective dimensions of mother–daughter relations, and which provides an approach to the reading of women's auto/biography that is both persuasive in its eloquence and revealing in its explication.

Like Donnell, Julia Hallam raises important questions about the ways in which we 'speak for' others. Basing her discussion on interviews she made with ten black women nurses who work for the NHS, Hallam sets out to 'throw light on what happens to self-image when dominant discourses do not correspond to lived experience'. Whereas Donnell was concerned with interpreting a published autobiography within a non-realist framework, Hallam focuses on oral testimonies in order to reveal a history that runs against – and is in 'deep conflict' with – the 'official interpretive devices of [our] culture'. Like Temple, Hallam's reading of lives has a distinct and practical purpose, namely: to revise and reshape our perception of individual and communal identities via life-writing.

Katherine Frank's 'The Lives of Indira Gandhi' is unique in this collection, in that it is specifically concerned with the writing and reading of biography. In pursuit of her thesis that 'gender' is the decisive factor in biographical coverage of women politicians, Frank offers a detailed and absorbing assessment of the interpretations that have been made about Indira Gandhi's life. Not only does this essay convey a scholarly and discerning analysis of biography, it also questions the way in which we construe female subjectivity within the realms of iconography, in Gandhi's case: Freedom's Daughter, Mother India, the Hindu Goddess Durga, Warrior Queen, Iron Lady and Joan of Arc martyr. Using her critique of Gandhi's biographers as leverage against conventional models of biography wherein the crushing simplification of life all too often occurs, Frank contends that we should seek out the complexities, intrigues and subtleties of a life.

PART III WRITING – REPRESENTING WOMEN'S LIVES:
THE LIFE-HISTORY PROJECT

The four contributors to this final Part are concerned with narrating their own journeys towards selfhood: narratives that find succour in the *experience* of travelling forth, the *expectation* of arrival, and in the *endless* gratification that is found in the written word. In 'A Good School Revisited', Mary Evans recalls the privileges of her grammar-school education during the 1950s, and the unassailable interest in books, reading and knowledge that this experience encouraged. But Evans is intent upon explication: in particular, a vigorous examination of the mediocrity – as well as enormous self-confidence – that a privileged education brings about. What sustains Evans in her narratological journey of selfhood, are the values and insights she gained in spite of her education. Two key themes thus emerge: on the one hand, a belief in the dynamics of female agency, and, on the other hand, optimism about the endless possibility of intellectual and imaginative survival that is derived from the books we read.

Like many other essays in this collection, Catherine Byron's 'The Most Difficult Door' critically interrogates the Woolfian paradigm of 'thinking back through mothers'. But for Byron, matrilineality is indubitably *engagée*. Mother Ireland/Motherland, and the identity of a nation – its history, landscape and cultural idiosyncracies – become synonymous with subjectivity. In her episodic journey towards selfhood, Byron wrenches herself from the enthralling contiguity of

Introduction

Mother/Ireland, and explores another, perhaps more controversial lineality: the patrilineality of England and Englishness. Here, the version of selfhood comprises a uniquely different landscape of history and identity; and it is the fundamental demarcation between two places, cultures and peoples that this essay so evocatively explores.

If Byron's journey was from mother/land to father/land, Val Walsh's is antipodean: her journey traces a perplexing and distressing move from father to feminism. Thinking back through her father – working-class, Socialist and the hinge-point of her development from child to adult – Walsh proffers a therapeutic *Künstlerroman*. On the one hand, this journey traces an attempt to theorise and make sense of her desire to 'cut-and-run' from all that she once shared with her father, while on the other hand, it explicates her need to unravel and resolve the 'tangled roots' from whence she came. There is no easy synthesis; and it is only through a recognition of untenable difference that the journey forward can proceed.

Jo Stanley's 'The Swashbuckler, the Landlubbing Wimp and the Woman in Between: Myself as Pirate(ss)' brings this book to its auto/biographical conclusion. Expressive, creative and fluently self-scrutinising, this chapter traces the way in which a life-history project – focusing on the lives of women pirates – can become auto/biographically framed. It asks how the lives of those that we variously recover and reconfigure can impinge – intertextually – upon our own; and evaluates how far that process can formulate intellectual development and self-renewal. Perhaps most significantly, this essay asserts the need to take responsibility for the research we undertake, and makes cognisance of our indebtedness to women whose lives we put into print.

Pauline Polkey

Note

1. Acknowledgements to the Personal Narrative Group, eds, (1989) *Interpreting Women's Lives: Feminist Theory and Personal Narratives*, Bloomington and Indianapolis: Indiana University Press, for their insightful and groundbreaking discussion about the significance context, form, voice and truth in relation to women's life-writing.

References

Marcus, L. (1994) _Auto/biographical Discourses_, Manchester: Manchester University Press

Personal Narratives Group, eds (1989) _Interpreting Women's Lives_, Bloomington and Indianapolis: Indiana University Press

Stanley, L. (1992) _The Auto/biographical I_, Manchester: Manchester University Press

—— (1994) 'Introduction', _Auto/Biography_, 3:1 and 3:2, pp. i–ii

Part I
Theory

Putting Women's Lives into Print: Feminist Ethics, Methodologies and Epistemologies

1

How Do We Know about Past Lives?

Methodological and Epistemological Matters Involving Prince Philip, the Russian Revolution, Emily Wilding Davison, My Mum and the Absent Sue

LIZ STANLEY

INTRODUCTION

This chapter explores a number of issues concerning the claims that feminist and other researchers make about lives in the past. These can be summarised as claims about 'expert knowing', that is, knowing about people or events with a certainty which can be convincingly demonstrated to others by a variety of accepted expert means. Such claims rest upon a 'method for knowing', a method which is typically unexplicated and used implicitly; and in explicating aspects of it here, I shall discuss some of the concrete issues involved in deciding what evidence, what tests of this evidence, used in what ways, to support what kinds of interpretations, 'will do' for satisfactorily establishing expert knowing. In doing so, I look at how these issues arise both generally, and in a number of case studies involving, as the subtitle of my chapter notes, 'Prince Philip, the Russian Revolution, Emily Wilding Davison, my Mum and the absent Sue'. These are epistemological as well as methodological matters – they are 'about knowledge', and so involve the methods of inquiry used in the production of knowledge as well as 'knowledge itself'; and there are aspects of it which are distinctly, if not uniquely, feminist.

This chapter is about 'not knowing', as well as about 'knowing'. However, before I look at issues in 'not/knowing' through examining these case studies, I shall discuss some more general themes, beginning with some of the issues involved in producing expert knowledge-claims about sexuality in the past but also the present, for this can entail moving beyond what the existing evidence supports into ungrounded interpretational supposition (Stanley, 1992b). I shall argue that this is not just 'a historical problem'. In fact it throws up general issues in knowing, knowing about the present as well as about the past. To illustrate the complexity of such matters, I begin with the apparently self-evident question: is Prince Philip heterosexual? and, relatedly, if so, then how can this be known with certainty?

WHAT WE KNOW AND HOW WE KNOW IT: PRINCE PHILIP AND THE RUSSIAN REVOLUTION

We all know that Elizabeth II is the Queen of England, Wales, Scotland and Northern Ireland. There are a large variety of external proofs of this, from the annual 'Opening of Parliament', to the Queen's Christmas message broadcast on Christmas Day, to her occupancy of various 'royal' residences such as Buckingham Palace and Balmoral. In addition, we know this 'for fact' for another important reason – the vast majority of denizens of the British Isles treat it as a fact; that is, they believe it to be true, and this includes even those who disapprove of the moral or political or other basis of the notion of royalty. In more formal terms, this can be summarised as the existence of: (1) external material evidence about her being the Queen – 'this is fact'; and (2) the coherence of public beliefs about this – 'everybody knows'.

In addition, we also know that the Queen has four children. That is, we know that there are four children who have always been treated as siblings, and also as all the 'natural born' children of this woman. Doubtless there are a variety of certain 'factual' proofs as well, such as reside in medical records and the testimony of witnesses to births, which may not be readily available but which are likely to exist somewhere and 'in the last resort' be available to some licensed person to consult and assess. Again, there is: (1) external material evidence – 'the facts'; and (2) the coherence of public beliefs about this – 'everybody knows'.

We also all know that Prince Philip is the husband of Queen Elizabeth: again, there is external evidence and a coherent set of supporting beliefs about this. We know, but in a different sense, that Prince Philip, as the husband of Queen Elizabeth, is the father of her four children; that is, this is the kind of knowing that rests upon beliefs and conventions, what I termed above the coherence of beliefs – 'everybody knows that!'. But what material external evidence is there? that is, how could we 'prove' that Prince Philip is their father? indeed, beyond this, how could we know with certainty, how could we prove, that Prince Philip is heterosexual?

Regarding parentage, there are family resemblances to be sure, but these can also exist between people who are more distant kin – and Prince Philip's family line is intertwined with that of most of the 'Royal Houses' of Europe. While there are likely to be no witnesses to the actual moments of the four conceptions beyond the Queen and her partner, nor to be any evidential proofs of fathering in the way there are for mothering, still these could be made available given the current state of scientific knowledge (that is, if one accepts the claims-making of science itself in relation to genetic testing, something I will discuss later). However, proving heterosexuality is another and much more troublesome matter: marriage is no proof, parentage is no proof, sexual involvement with 'the other sex' is no proof: gay-identified people can and do all these without being 'really' heterosexual.

A recent example of the biographical relevance of the role that scientific tests and proofs about genetic inheritance can play involves the family, and thus genetic, relationship between Prince Philip and the former 'royal house' of Russia (Klier and Mingay, 1995). Anna Anderson, the woman who claimed to be the Grand Duchess Anastasia and the only child of the Tsar and Tsarina to survive the murders carried out by Bolsheviks in Ekaterinburg in 1918, died in 1984. Throughout her adult life, her claims to this status were subject to a wide variety of tests: legal, historical and relational (through 'tests' against collective family memory). However, after her death, these claims have become subject to new forms of scientific testing. While living in America following her marriage, Anna Anderson had undergone an operation many years before her death; tissue samples taken at this time were found by friends supporting her claim still to be lodged in the archives of an American hospital. Some of this was brought to Britain in 1994 to be tested against a sample from Prince Philip, the nearest surviving relative of the

Grand Duchess for these genetic purposes. What these tests 'proved' was that Prince Philip's genetic structure was not the same as that of the claimant, but that another similar test showed that hers was sufficiently close to prove a close genetic relationship to the young male relative of a woman munitions worker who had vanished – and with the same injuries – at the same time that Anastasia had first appeared in a German hospital.

This is interesting enough for those concerned with 'the fate' of the former Russian royal family. It is more interesting with regard to a scholarly concern with notions of evidence and proof in researching past lives more generally. The scientific claim 'to know' here, in accepting or rejecting that Anna Anderson could have been the Grand Duchess, rests on the following procedural method which has both highly general and also case specific elements:

i.   the sample located in America is 'known' to be that of the claimant, that is, its provenance is taken to be certain;
ii. the sample tested in Britain is assumed to be 'the same' as the sample located in the American hospital;
iii. the tests that are now available are regarded, if carried out properly, as providing satisfactory enough 'findings' to make definite claims about the presence and absence of genetic relationships; that is, they are taken to be scientifically adequate and sufficient for the purposes claimed;
iv. the interpretation of these particular test results is assumed to be sufficient, indeed precisely certain.

However, disputes can arise even when science is involved. Although science may claim indisputable certainty, its claims are rarely so absolute as popularly assumed, and can frequently be shown to rest upon actually rather shaky science. Four kinds of disputes can occur, two of them about provenance and probity, and two of them concerned with 'science itself' concerning its methodology and its interpretative role. Again, these have both general and also case specific elements.

Dispute 1   This dispute concerns the provenance of the evidence, assumed in this case to be 'a sample' from the claimant. Provenance here rests upon the probity of the particular persons ('friends of the claimant', 'a doctor' and so on) involved and on whether there is incontrovertible evidence about the original sample in the form of certain medical records; and constant tracking of the 'uncontaminated' sample from being taken to being tested is by no means clear. Certainly there are questions to be asked about why, and how, obscure tissue samples some thirty years old were ever kept, then found, and then released. The provenance of the evidence here must be seen as 'not proven' in any absolute sense.

Dispute 2   This dispute concerns the claimed synonymy of the evidence scrutinised with that for which provenance is claimed, here the tested sample as synonymous with the sample located in the American hospital. It may not be likely that samples would be switched; however, this is certainly not beyond the bounds of possibility, particularly so in this case where passions continue to run very high even 75 years after the Russian Revolution and where every such claim has been met by vigorous resistance on the part of 'legitimate' royal survivors of those times. The issue here is that claims about the interpretation of results from the evidence – procedural item (iv) above – actually rests upon an assumption of the indisputable probity of those persons involved in evaluating it, that is, it postulates a possible 'gap' between procedural items (i) and (ii).

Dispute 3   This dispute concerns the sufficiency as well as the reliability of the available means for evaluating the evidence. In this case, this is not merely whether such tests are *reliable* (in the sense of always producing the same results from the same samples), but also whether they are *sufficient* to prove what they claim to be able to prove. This is a difficult issue, for generally speaking evaluating such claims can only be done by other scientists, and disputes here tend to be concerned with the conduct of such tests on the one hand and the interpretation of their results on the other. However, in science as in life, contrary opinion can always be found, and a typical means of producing such disputes is to involve 'contrary science': the cross-examination of one set of 'expert witnesses' by using the testimony of other experts with different but equally creditable views and professional credentials.

Dispute 4   This dispute concerns the specific 'tests' or means of interpreting the evidence, including whether these were conducted with probity, whether the evidence was sufficient to bear the particular interpretational weight put upon it, and what margin of doubt or lack of certainty there might be about any conclusion drawn. In this particular case, it also includes whether the scientific tests actually prove what they claim to provide. Apples plummeting to the ground may convincingly demonstrate gravity, but only rarely are there such satisfyingly incontrovertible certainties regarding the historical past and particular lives within it.

Even if the questions about provenance and probity raised in disputes 1 and 2 are settled, then questions can still arise around the role of experts in evaluating and interpreting evidence and the methodologies they use in doing so which have been outlined in disputes 3 and 4. This is because these disputes about provenance, probity, interpretation and methodology are general ones that characterise all areas of scholarly inquiry. They have been formulated here around a particular historical and biographical case, but the underlying elements are common to 'inquiry' as such.

In addition, although 'science itself' may seem a long way from the activities of the jobbing feminist historian or biographer, still, as the Anastasia case demonstrates, science and biography are increasingly likely to come together regarding particular current as well as historical issues or problems. For example, regarding the 'genetic finger-printing' associated with rape cases involving sperm and genetic testing, there was a period in which such scientific tests and proofs were taken as absolutely certain, but more recently such evidence has been increasingly disputed in court, including by other scientists suggesting that the original claims about these tests and the conclusions which could be drawn from them were too sweeping and too certain. The overlapping of science and historical and biographical investigations is likely to continue and indeed increase; thus, for instance, in the USA feminist historians have been involved as expert witnesses on *both* 'sides' of the Sears Roebuck legal case regarding how to interpret gender issues around the employment practices of this organisation (Farganis, 1994), as well as in a number of other legal cases.

Returning to the role of science regarding the parentage of Queen Elizabeth's children: certainly there are tests available to examine the genetic relationship between a putative father and a child or children, but such tests are by no means indisputable, not least because fatherhood is only one of a number of genetic relationships 'demonstrated' by such tests. But of course, in most historical and biographical instances, such 'tests' and 'proofs' are not available for use at all, or, even if they were, they would not address the intellectual problem at hand. Thus, even though Prince Philip could 'scientifically' be shown to be the father of the Queen's children, this would still provide no proof of his sexual *identity*, only of a number of instances of his sexual *behaviour*. Certainly, circumstantial evidence could suggest or emphasise his heterosexuality in the form of the coherence of beliefs about this, what 'we all know'. However, what *certain* proofs there could be about such matters is by no means clear, for the coherence of beliefs can be based on false premises and false evidence, as demonstrated in the case of the recent posthumous 'outing' of the playwright John Osborne, about whom 'everybody knew' that he was absolutely heterosexual, even though it now transpires he certainly wasn't.

The kinds of problems of not/knowing outlined above, and the various disputes that arise in connection with inquiry into them, are fundamental ones concerned with the very basis for making knowledge-claims. Moreover, there is no final answer to these disputes and no certain means of preventing them from existing by, for example, more rigorous scholarship and more stringent means of training, because any and all knowledge-claims, however meticulously and scrupulously constructed and presented, can be subject to dispute by someone at some time. This is how it should be: knowledge, after all, becomes closed and indisputable in the kind of political circumstances most antithetical to feminism; and, anyway, it is through such intellectual mechanisms that ideas and social practices come to change, through their very permeability.

Feminist interventions in academia have been determinedly epistemological: feminism entered the doors of the academy disputing what passed for 'knowledge' therein, and it remains centrally and definitionally concerned with remaking knowledge by disputing canonical knowledge-claims. Initially, this was carried out by feminists advancing disputes of the kind outlined above, in particular disputes 1, 2 and 4: that is, by critiquing the provenance of evidence, the probity of researchers, and the unacceptability of mainstream frameworks for constructing and interpreting evidence; and later by making positive claims to have produced new knowledge. However, feminist scholars have used largely the same 'method for knowing' that was previously under feminist critique. Recently, criticisms have been made of this, for example by feminist poststructuralists and postmodernists; at basis, the 'successor science' stance of much feminist inquiry, its implicit claims to be able to produce 'real science, this time', are being rejected, along with the similar claims of 'science itself'. This seems to me a move in the right direction, one which will recognise the openness of 'knowledge', who claims it and how they do so. Feminist scholarship should in my view make intellectual virtue of the complexities of knowledge production and promote such epistemological inquiries to the forefront of feminist debate. It is this provisionality of knowledge production, its always 'for now' quality, that I move on to discuss in more specific detail.

THE LIMITS OF KNOWING: EMILY WILDING DAVISON, MY MUM AND THE ABSENT SUE

I now look at a number of 'issues in not/knowing' by using case studies, which derive from some of the historical and biographical research I have been involved with. As I shall discuss, each, albeit in rather different ways, raises different aspects of this provisional and 'for now' quality of research in what have been taxing, as well as challenging, ways.

Emily Wilding Davison

Accounts of the suffragette period often announce with complete certainty that Emily Wilding Davison 'committed suicide' by 'throwing herself under the King's horse' at the June 1913 Derby (see Banks, 1985, and more recently Byrne, 1995). With Ann Morley, I undertook research on 'the life and times' of Emily Davison and her closest friends and comrades in Edwardian feminist politics and this resulted in a book which explored the mythologies surrounding Emily Davison (Stanley, 1988). Our research concluded that Emily Davison had certainly not 'committed suicide' in 1913, and nor had she 'attempted suicide' earlier when, in Holloway during a time of mass forced-feeding of suffragette prisoners, she had thrown herself off a high prison stairwell and been seriously injured.

Regarding the incident in Holloway, in an essay published posthumously Emily Davison had placed this act firmly in the context of mass force-feeding. She had been in prison and routinely force-fed over a period of months, when a large demonstration resulted in large-scale arrests, imprisonments, hunger strikes, and then, in an action on the part of the prison authorities calculated to inspire terror and thus obedience, there took place the force-feeding of over a hundred women at once. Emily Davison clearly expressed her act as one designed to stop such calculated brutality: better that she should die if this would stop the prison authorities from torturing and harming so many women; and such an act on the part of, say, an IRA prisoner, would have been seen as the antithesis of anything that 'attempted suicide' conjures up.

Regarding the Derby and Emily Davison's death in 1913, there was more than a sufficiency of circumstantial evidence to conclude that her action here was equally political – an attempt to pin a suffragette flag on Anmer, the King's racehorse. Emily Davison would have known that the act was risky but, we concluded, she expected that it would be neither fateful nor even necessarily injurious. The evidence here was mainly that used at the inquest on Emily Davison's death in 1913 which reached a similar conclusion: she had bought a return rail ticket from London to Epsom; she had been betting on the races immediately before the Derby race; and, most compellingly, she had in her bag a helper's pass card to work at a Kensington suffragette bazaar which didn't open until late afternoon, well after the Derby was over.

The coherence of present-day beliefs in this case is contrary to contemporary beliefs – and it was the contemporary view which the interpretational conclusions of our research supported. The provenance of the evidence here was certain, but it didn't, and indeed couldn't, be used to prove one way or another what Emily Davison's intentions might have been. Rather than intention, my concern is instead with whether, and to what extent, there is evidence that Emily Davison was planning for future events 'after' that which supposedly saw her suicide. There are two pieces of evidence for an 'after' which are already in the public domain: the return rail ticket from Epsom to London, and the pass card to attend a suffragette event later that day. A few years after the book was published, at a seminar on archival work in historical sociology, I was challenged by a critic who insisted, firstly, that these evidences could permit no such conclusion to be drawn from them, for there was no proof inherent in them; and, secondly, that documentary film evidence I had wilfully ignored existed which proved the suicide.

In a sense, the critic was right regarding the first point, for there certainly isn't any final proof in these evidences, and, indeed, it is difficult to see what absolute proof could consist of. But my argument was actually different, and was instead that there was sufficient 'absence of a proof to suicide' to permit these circumstantial evidences to provide the basis of a contrary interpretation; and I would still insist that this argument is valid. I also think the critic was wrong regarding the second point, for Ann and I had found and discussed in the book the various documentary film evidence which 'shows' different things because it was shot from different angles. The film which 'proves suicide' was taken from a position ahead of the race and shows a welter of horses into which a woman moves and is immediately bowled over; while, as the book discusses in some detail, the film shot from immediately opposite where Emily Davison waited shows one group of horses galloping past, then a wide gap into which she moves, waits and draws out a flag, then another horse up to which she reaches with the flag, and only then is she bowled over. The two films do not 'prove' suicide or its absence; but the second film does support the other circumstantial evidence, and thus my interpretation that Emily Davison was carrying out a political act designed to have an 'after' which was not death.

A coda here: At the time the critic made these points, in summer 1994, I had just returned from Paris and a visit to Madame Stuart de Becker, Emily Davison's niece and daughter of her much loved elder sister. I produced my trump card against the critic: there was the evidence, still in private family hands, of the almost daily letters Emily Davison sent to her sister, which included early June letters planing for a family holiday in France in mid and late June and also a letter posted on Derby day itself in which Emily had written that she would arrive a few days hence. 'No proof' replied the critic; and, again, this is right in the sense this is still not incontrovertible proof. However, it seems to me there is so much circumstantial evidence upon circumstantial evidence to support the 'political act, not suicide' interpretation that dismissing it looks like intransigence, not scholarly scrupulousness.

In this case, then, it is the acts that constitute 'interpretation' which are completely central. The main evidence is known and certain and exists in the form of the death of Emily Wilding Davison; but the intellectual action here concerns what kind of a death hers was, and what evidence, interpreted in what way, supports particular conclusions about this.

My Mum

'Auto/biography' is concerned with the intertextuality of biography and autobiography, and also of fact and fiction, the spoken and the written, and the past and the present (Stanley, 1992a). My third case study concerns its first and most simple aspect, the intertextuality of biography and autobiography, and, in particular, the intertextuality of my concerns as a biographer with my own autobiography and the autobiographies of others. The particular other autobiography of concern here is that of my Mum. I have written elsewhere (see Stanley, 1989) about some aspects of the problematic (a problem and methodological procedures for investigating if not solving it) discussed here, focusing on, variously, my mother's constructions of her life as a working-class woman between the wars; issues concerned with my father's strokes, brain damage and compulsory hospitalisation; my changing understandings of my mother's 'self' when she too suffered a massive stroke; and the ways in which my mother proficiently theorised her own 'self' and its relationship to the group of others composed by her friends and relatives – her particular age-cohort; while more recently I have focused upon the epistemological and ethical dilemmas involved (Stanley, 1995, 1996).

The oral history model of how 'lives' are produced has in-built ethical comfort: the researcher decides upon a project; the people interviewed give their consent to being interviewed; the ethical interviewer tapes their accounts, transcribes these, then writes with probity and sensitivity about these other lives; and such writings are used as part of an 'underdog' project in which previously submerged voices speak. I engaged in a project with my mother which in a sense might be called oral history: many hours of tapes were made of my mother speaking about her life, particularly between the wars and concerning the impact of the second war in producing what she perceived as massive social change in the lives of working-class people. It is, however, the differences, not the similarities, between this project and the oral history model that strike me. My project was not researcher-originated; instead, it was my mother who requested, indeed insisted, both that these conversations took place and that they were taped. Consent was less 'given' than insisted upon by her in the aftermath of my father's decline and death, and these conversations started out as many hours of her talking about these tragic events. However, this was consent to the events that were the conversations themselves, and not to any articulated 'after' or 'beyond' them; what might be done with the tapes was never discussed between us, although the taping itself was requested, indeed almost demanded, by her, for the balances of power in this 'research' context were such that my mother firmly controlled what was spoken about – and what was not. Consequently I was never sure whether it would be ethically proper to use these tapes or not; and, at the point at which I might have broached the matter, my mother had a devastatingly damaging stroke which removed her ability to comprehend spoken language, and consequently also her ability to speak it.

There are questions and dilemmas which have arisen subsequently from this: what did my mother want these tapes made for? what, if anything, did she want them used for? what should I do with 'her voice' after she herself was silenced? and then what after her death? and should my being able to speak about these events of decline and death, which after all involved me as well as my mother, be predicated upon her giving express consent? These are not 'research' questions in any simple sense: they are about research and writing, and they do involve issues concerning privacy, vulnerability, consent, all important research matters; but they are also questions about my relationship and emotional as well as intellectual relationship with my mother, how I understand her life and my own, and also the points of intersection and departure between our two lives. The basic dilemma here was and is 'what shall I do?', that is, what I feel I can legitimately, with probity and sensitivity, do with this body of evidence.

There is no public coherence of beliefs to be consulted here, for there is nothing external to my memory and some of my fieldwork diary entries beyond the tapes and transcriptions themselves. The material evidence is clear, and its provenance known and certain, but its existence doesn't speak to the problems in hand. In this case study, as a researcher as well as a daughter, I am constrained to focus upon ethical debates and issues which the circumstances of death have removed any possibility of a resolution from; consequently, thus far my engagement with the evidence has dealt with such issues rather than 'historical content'.

The Absent Sue

This last case is different from those discussed thus far, for it consists in what has *not* been done and recorded auto/biographically. One of the bugbears that confronts the researches of feminist biographers can be summed up using the words of Victorian feminist Frances Power Cobbe (1904), that when a relationship such as hers with Mary Lloyd became one of love then it stopped being something she would comment upon or even mention in any public pronouncements. In my career as a feminist researcher, I have on occasion written of 'private' things, often things that have painful associations as well as interesting intellectual problematics, but never of those which give central meaning to my emotional life and well-being on a daily basis. In this connection it is useful to confront how anyone in the future would (re)construct 'my life' and in particular how they would 'prove' that I was a lesbian as well as a feminist. Key issues here involve the relationship between discretion, privacy and silence with knowledge (Stanley, 1992b).

In various of my published work, I have written about myself in a social structural sense, as a woman, a feminist, an academic, working class, and also as a lesbian. The first four indicators here are available to future scrutiny via publicly available material evidences: parental and other marriages, birth certificates, occupational evidence, employers' records, educational records, and after a hundred years there will also be census enumeration data. However, for any relationship 'outside the law' – friendship and enmity as well as other emotional and also sexual ties – researchers depend upon largely private evidences: diaries, letters and other personal papers, possibly also accounts from friends and relatives if the investigation takes place before or soon after the death of the subject. When these ties are those which people keep either secret or private, then demonstrating even the mere existence of such relationships can range between difficult and impossible.

Those people who as it were inhabit the social categories of stigma such as 'the (male) homosexual' and 'the lesbian', but who do not 'pass' as heterosexual and have chosen to 'come out' in the political and not merely the socio-sexual sense – like Edward Carpenter and to a lesser extent Edith Lees among the late nineteenth century 'sexual radicals' whose lives and work I have researched (see Stanley, 1992b) – can act as reference points for assessing the lives and relationships and sexual allegiances of those who knew them. But establishing these connections to make even tentative statements about love and sex is often hard work, even with these for their time very open and frank people. There is a simple lesson to be learned here: if we now do not 'name names' and preferably on paper – public paper – then our relationships and allegiances too will vanish in the future as much as theirs have done.

However, I experience a quandary here. Although I agree with this broad argument about public knowledge and political statement, with my own close relationships I want to maintain privacy with all the protectiveness of a Frances Power Cobbe. The result is that my lover, 'the absent Sue', does not appear in, for example, my published work concerned with feminist auto/biography even where this might seem relevant – such as in exploring the intertextuality of biography and autobiography – and nor do the other people who are close to me. Within academic and feminist circles for the past 25 years I have been a 'public lesbian' and in the political sense 'out' in the rest of my life as well. Nevertheless, the methods I have used regarding the sexual radicals of the past would in my own case yield little of what is most important regarding the importance and longevity of either this central relationship or those others of love and friendship in my life.

There is very little 'material evidence' in this case, and nor is there any public coherence of belief. Or rather – the point I have been making – here as in the case of John Osborne people will assume 'normality' and conformity unless there are incontrovertible reasons for doing otherwise. Thus, on the one hand, it is clear that feminist researchers and biographers in the future are as likely to experience the same 'problems of not/knowing' with regard to the emotional and sexual lives of their 'subjects' as those of us in the present have done. But on the other, there are also good reasons why we should not want to inscribe the details of our lives, in the sense of wanting to live as private a life as other people, and leaving the future after death to take care of itself, as well as eschewing inappropriate self-importance. However, there are also additional and perhaps more important reasons connected with the nature of reflexivity in the research process, and I shall return to these in the conclusion.

METHODOLOGICAL MATTERS AND EPISTEMOLOGICAL CONCLUSIONS

The case studies I have discussed here have both methodological and epistemological aspects, and they illustrate what I referred to earlier as feminist social theory's emphasis on the provisionality of knowledge, it's always 'for now' character. I have deliberately discussed these epistemological matters in a very grounded way, because typically they are discussed in highly abstract, not to say arcane, terms. I want to emphasise the relevance of these ideas for all researchers, not just for self-styled 'Theorists'. Indeed, more than this, it is because I want to insist that such matters only really make sense when looked at in a grounded and down-to-earth-way – after all, there is more than irony involved in discussing situated knowledges and open accountable texts in a removed and impenetrable fashion, as many feminist theorists do.

The fact that 'knowledge about past lives' is being problematised and investigated within a feminist framework demonstrates that such questions and arguments *matter* to feminism. However, I have also proposed, via my case studies, that there are distinctly feminist forms that such epistemological inquiries take; and I now want to look at this argument a little more closely. This is because the influential epistemologist Susan Haack has dismissed the very idea that there can be any such thing as a feminist epistemology (Haack, 1993a; see also 1985, 1991, 1993b). Her grounds for doing so appear to be her conviction that, if there are general problems in knowing, then there must be general responses to these – knowledge should be single and unseamed; and thus, at basis, Haack advances a foundationalist position.

The most influential strand of feminist thinking proposes, as I have done, that there are distinct features to feminist epistemology (see Whitford and Lennon, 1994; Alcoff and Potter, 1993), even though there is dissent concerning the precise parameters of this. Certainly there is agreement that there are general issues in knowing, and it has been a number of these which I have discussed in the first part of my chapter, regarding historical and biographical knowledge-claims. However, the grounds for arguing that there is a distinct feminist epistemology (or rather, epistemologies) do not lie in denying that general issues are in fact general, as Haack presupposes, but rather whether there are specifically or particularly feminist kinds of response to such general problems.

Feminist thinking has proposed three related, and immensely influential, arguments concerning knowledge which have underpinned feminist ideas about epistemology. While these can only be sketched out in this chapter, it is clear that they give a distinct cast to resultant feminist epistemological discussion. The first is the insistence that all knowledge is situated and is in fact knowledges – plural rather than unitary and each marked by the politics of location, including the time, place, cast of mind and circumstances of the particular knower/s who produce them; succinctly, 'objective knowledge' is a logical impossibility, an oxymoron (Rich, 1986; Haraway, 1988). The second is that knowledge derives from thinking, researching and writing processes and necessarily relies upon the reflexivity of the researcher/theo-rist, in the sense that they actively engage with, and think about, these processes so that a constant dialectic is involved; therefore feminist epistemology should acknowledge the centrality of reflex-ivity (Stanley, 1990; Fonow and Cook, 1991). And the third is that for political and ethical, but also intellectual, reasons femin-ism should be concerned with producing accountable knowledge, including through writing open texts which can be investigated and reworked by active readers (Smith, 1990).

These arguments result in very different kinds of response to 'problems in not/knowing' than Haack's 'general answers to gen-eral problems' approach. I have endeavoured to show something of this in presenting case studies embodying some of the general 'problems of not/knowing' that I introduced earlier in the chapter. I conclude by briefly reviewing my case studies in the context of the above three feminist epistemological arguments, for each has sought to show aspects of these arguments, including by pointing out that none of them is quite so straightforward as more abstract and 'theo-retical' expositions of them may suggest.

On two occasions (the Derby film from 'sideways on', and from her niece about her 1913 holiday plans), I gained new information about Emily Wilding Davison. Consequently, changes in, or rather confirmations of, a point of view here were not the result of rethink-ing, but rather from the accretion of information. However, in spite of this, there was still not sufficient 'proof' without doubt that her death was not suicide. Demonstrating the 'null hypothesis' can only consist in the ambiguous arena of the circumstantial: evidence which supports or fails to support an argument, rather than actually 'proving' it. Moreover, the circumstantial evidence here consisted of various elements, made significant because they could be related to a possible 'after' to Derby day 1913 for Emily Davison. The evi-dence here was a subset of what exists: things seen as significant for the analytic purposes in hand. That is, it was pieced together around a point of view constructed over the course of this research that underpinned what was deemed relevant and what was not.

In many feminist discussions of research, issues of consent and accountability are presented as though self-evident: the researched give their consent, the researcher is accountable to them. As I have proposed in relation to the tapes of conversations with my Mum, life is rarely so comfortingly simple. How to distinguish 'the researched' from 'the researcher' was by no means straightforward here, for it was my mother who controlled the interaction between us, insisted that the research took place, determined the shape that it took. Indeed, much feminist and pro-feminist research is carried out under similarly complex circumstances, for a combination of political and ethical reasons that the researcher shares with the researched often underpins its conduct. In addition, 'the researched' are not always either living, or ethically or politically right-on. How are issues of consent to be handled when the people concerned, like Emily Davison, are dead? Or when, like my Mum, they are incapable of either giving or withholding consent? Or when, like Peter Sutcliffe, the serial sexual murderer whose trial and press coverage I have researched and written about (Stanley, 1992a, ch.5), they are not the kind of people one would want to be accountable to in any way, indeed rather the reverse?

Many feminist researchers have interpreted reflexivity in terms of the politics of location: as the provision to the reader as description about the researcher's social, political, class, ethnic and sexual location as a kind of general guide to their point of view. However, for me reflexivity is something that moves away from descriptive although well-intentioned provision of personal information. When researching the life and death of Emily Wilding Davison, for instance, my class and my politics may have had some broad general impact, but of far greater importance for providing readers with an open text were the reasoning procedures involved in my making sense of events and people and drawing conclusions about these. That is, 'reflexivity' does not merely consist in a litany of personal characteristics provided at the start of an article or book or in a footnote to demonstrate political credibility. Reflexivity can be, should be in feminist terms, a matter of intellectual accountability, and this form of it lies in providing analytic details of the relationship between evidence, interpretation and conclusion within the knowledge production process. Analytical reflexivity, unlike descriptive reflexivity, brings matters of epistemology and methodology to the heart of feminist texts as they are at the heart of actual research processes. Analytical reflexivity requires us to use our minds in intellectually challenging ways, by making our analytic procedures open to others for scrutiny, and possibly also for rejection, by providing our evidences, by detailing our interpretations, and by justifying our conclusions. In considering the major feminist contributions to epistemological debates, it is the notion of analytical reflexivity that draws together these together into a powerful whole.

The epistemological concerns and problematics I have raised and explored – issues in not/knowing – are indeed general ones, and common to inquiry as such. They take a particular turn in relation to biographical and historical matters, but this is because they are thereby made clearer, more easily perceived, and they exist in all practical forms of inquiry. However, as I have argued, there are specific and particular feminist responses to these general issues which, taken together, can justifiably claim to form a distinct epistemological position which other scholars should take as seriously and as scrupulously as we take theirs.

References

Alcoff, Linda and Potter, Elizabeth, eds (1993) *Feminist Epistemologies*, London, New York: Routledge

Banks, Olive (1985) *Biographical Dictionary of British Feminists*, vol. 1 1800–1930, Brighton: Wheatsheaf

Byrne, Lavinia (1995) *The Hidden Voice: Christian Women and Social Change*, London: SPCK

Cobbe, Frances Power (1904) *Life of Frances Power Cobbe As Told By Herself*, London: Swan Sonnenschein

Farganis, Sondra (1994) *Situating Feminism: From Thought To Action*, Thousand Oaks, California: Sage Publications

Fonow, Mary and Cook, Judith, eds (1991) *Beyond Methodology*, Buckingham: Open University Press

Haack, Susan (1985) 'Review of Harding and Hintikka, eds, Discovering Reality', *Philosophy*, 60:230, pp. 265–70

——(1991) 'Critical notice of Code *Epistemic Responsibility*', *Canadian Journal of Philosophy* 21:1, pp. 91–108

——(1993a) 'Epistemological reflections of an old feminist', *Reason Papers*, 18, fall 1993

——(1993b) *Evidence and Inquiry: Towards Reconstruction in Epistemology*, Oxford: Blackwell

Haraway, Donna (1988) 'Situated knowledges: the science question in feminism and the privilege of partial perspective', *Feminist Studies*, 14, pp. 575–99

Klier, John and Mingay, Helen (1995) *The Quest for Anastasia: Solving the Mystery of the Lost Romanovs*, London: Smith Gryphon

Rich, Adrienne (1986) *Blood, Bread and Poetry*, New York: W.W. Norton

Smith, Dorothy (1990) *Texts, Facts and Femininity: Exploring the Relations of Ruling*, London: Routledge

Stanley, Liz (1989) 'Our Mother's Voices' unpublished paper given at the Dublin International Congress on Women, Ireland

——(1988) *The Life and Death of Emily Wilding Davison*, London: The Women's Press

——ed., (1990) *Feminist Praxis: Research, Theory and Epistemology in Feminist Sociology*, London: Routledge

——(1992a) *The Auto/Biographical I: Theory and Practice of Feminist Auto/Biography*, Manchester: Manchester University Press

——(1992b) 'Epistemological issues in researching lesbian history: the case of "romantic friendship" ' in H. Hinds, A. Phoenix and J. Stacey, eds, *New Directions for Women's Studies in the 1990s*, London: Falmer Press, pp. 161–73

——(1995) 'My mother's voice?: on "going native" ' in J. Walsh and L. Morley, eds, *Feminist Academics as Agents of Change*, London: Taylor Francis, pp. 182–93

——(1996) 'The mother of invention: Necessity, writing and representation', *Feminism & Psychology*, 6:2 & 3, pp. 45–51 (repr. in S. Wilkinson and C. Kitzinger, eds, *Representing the Other*, London: Sage Publications, pp. 43–50)

Whitford, Margaret and Lennon, Kathleen, eds (1995) *Knowing the Difference: Feminist Perspectives on Epistemology*, London: Routledge

2

Terrible Times: Experience, Ethnicity and Auto/Biography

BOGUSIA TEMPLE

We will remember the tenth of February.
When the Soviets came we were still sleeping
And they put our children onto sledges.
Us they took to the main station.
O terrible moment, O terrible hour ...

(author's translation)

INTRODUCTION

The terrible times referred to in this song are the events of 1940 when Soviet troops took over parts of Poland and transported any likely opposition to Siberia. The song was written by someone who had been made to leave everything they had. As such, it has resonance for many now living all over the world. Moreover, the events have formed part of a legacy for those who never actually experienced them. As a child growing up in a Polish community in Britain, I did not appreciate the significance of these events both for individuals and communities, those who had experienced them directly and those who had not. In this chapter, I discuss how I came to conceptualise what being Polish meant for me and for others. I point, in particular, to recent developments in auto/biography as valuable ways to approach questions of gender, ethnicity and class. I concentrate here on ethnicity, but argue that being Polish is different for women and men, and again is different for different women and men according to factors such as class and age. I do not abandon terms such as 'Polish', or 'woman' or 'working class', since they are used by people as ways of describing their connection to the social world. These ascriptions are, however, occasioned and purposeful and can be challenged.

When I carried out my interviews with people who went to a Polish Club in the North of England (Temple, 1992) as part of my PhD, I saw the accounts they gave me of their journey to England after the Second War as interesting background information. However, as I wrote up my PhD, I began to realise that they were more than background, since they formed a part of the sense of identity of those relating them, as well as of a sense of community generally. The effects of living through such times were far-reaching: emotional as well as intellectual. Trying to compare the daily lives of people I spoke to with academic accounts of Polish community life, left me puzzled. What happened to the emotional, the everyday practical accomplishments of keeping alive a tradition? What the academic literature described were the formal organisations set up by Poles since the War (see, for example, Patterson, 1977; and for a fuller critique of the literature on Poles, see Temple, 1995). The descriptions of Polish life did not match well with anything I had experienced. They did describe my father's role in Polish organisations. However, the almost clinical accounts of organisations set up by Poles missed the intense emotional connections with 'the Home Country', and the painful histories of Poles all over the world. They also missed the hard work of keeping everyday traditions alive in a foreign country, the backstage work usually carried out by women.

After I had finished the interviews for my PhD, I began to collect stories of journeys to England. I have subsequently used them to discuss questions of self and identity (Temple, 1995, 1996). More recently, I have begun to collect the accounts of people who settled in America after being expelled from Poland.

WINDOW ON THE WORLD?

While doing research for my PhD, I started to become increasingly drawn to writing about the influence of the researcher on the research. I have come to see my research, and that of other researchers, as to some extent autobiographical in nature. My research is an autobiographical product. I have selected areas I am interested in, here ethnicity, and I have used my perspective to select parts of the lives of others in order to produce an account. There are obvious links between my research and my life outside of my academic interests. However, I feel that although these links are obvious in my case, they apply equally to other academics. Liz Stanley has used the term 'intellectual autobiography' to describe how researchers can use their life experiences to make their position explicit. She describes this as:

> an analytic (not just descriptive) concern with the specifics of how we come to understand what we do, by locating acts of understanding in an explication of the grounded contexts these are located in and arise from. (1990: 62)

Using others' accounts of their lives also makes research biographical, so that the final research product is both autobiographical and biographical. The linkages between autobiography and biography and the process of knowledge construction have been described by Stanley (1992), using the concept of 'the auto/biographical I'. The connections between autobiography and biography are denoted by the term 'auto/biography', and the 'I' denotes a process of knowledge construction in which the researcher is active. Using these concepts enables me to analyse my experiences and to think about concepts such as 'Polish' or 'woman'. They also help me to understand how others experience such categorisations.

Using a researcher's intellectual autobiography re-admits and values the role of experience, but used hand-in-hand with the notion of the 'auto/biographical', it does not automatically prioritise the researchers' account over the experiences and accounts of others. Claiming experience as the basis of knowledge, does not automatically validate a claim to 'truth'. Others may use their experiences to challenge. Experience is itself never 'pure'; rather, it is a product of social constructions and theorisations. I see the value of analytically engaging with our own lives to lie in Fuss's words in the 'window onto the complicated workings of ideology' (Fuss, 1989: 114) that it allows. We need both to value experience and to deconstruct it.

Moreover, acknowledging research as interpretation from a social and material position involves acknowledging the power relations involved in the research process. I have used my experiences to construct a category 'Polish' and the people I spoke to constructed an alternative, which did not involve a feminist perspective on the position of women in Polish communities. However, it is my interpretation that is privileged in my writing. Although both researcher and subject are active in what is constructed, they are active in different ways. The people in my research were not power-less, they only told me what they wanted me to know. My account was dependent on what they were willing to discuss. Another researcher may well have been treated differently and produced a different account. Who the researcher is matters in that it affects the dynamics of the encounter. As a second generation Polish woman, people assumed that I knew about, and would be sympathetic to, certain aspects of Polish life such as the history of betrayal of Poland by her neighbours and did not need these spelling out. Phrases such as 'you've grown up hearing this' or 'you know, the same as you' were common. What could be left unsaid was important.

TIME, NARRATIVE AND AUTO/BIOGRAPHY

Growing up in a Polish community, then, helps me to juxtapose my experiences with the accounts of Polish communities written by other academics and non-academics. Much academic writing focuses on the role of men and the work of the formal organisations they are part of (for a more detailed review of previous work see Temple, 1995). Non-academic work, such as accounts in Polish newspapers, include descriptions of the work of Polish organisations, but they include much more besides. In these latter accounts, being Polish is more than public display. It was this sense of being Polish that peo-ple wanted to talk to me about, not just the narrower, more formal, aspects. Their experiences were often recounted in informal get-togethers and formed an important aspect of their sense of self and community.

The 'story' of the expulsion from Poland, the trek to Siberia, and the release to life in another country, is one that is familiar to any-one bought up in a Polish community. The song at the beginning of this chapter has been sung and told many times, and the signifi-cance of that period for the definition of self and community for Poles all over the world is inescapable. However, the nature of that significance is not the same for everyone. For second and third gen-eration British-Poles, the 'home country' has changed. Although the events of that period have effected my life, emotionally and intel-lectually, I have not felt what it means to be thrown out of my home. Nor have I seen my friends and relatives die of starvation and

disease. I have been able to grow up free of these experiences, but I
would argue not free of some of their effects. Second generation
Poles have grown up and made lives for themselves in their 'home
country', but growing up has involved for many of us being part of
a community that has felt a sense of loss and pain. My experiences
differ from those of my parents because I have been bought up as
'Polish' in a different country. What 'being' Polish is, is very much
time and place specific. Looking at my parents lives, and my own,
illustrates this for me. Moreover, comparing their experiences with
those of people living in Poland today makes the point again.

Recent academic literature on narrative has given me a way of
tackling the issue of time and place in concepts of ethnicity. For
example, Margaret Somers (1994: 606) incorporates what she calls the
'categorically destabilizing dimensions' of space, time and relational-
ity. Social life, she argues, is storied, and narrative is a way of being
in the social world. Identity and self are something one becomes:

> From this angle of relational membership, identities are not
> derived from attributes imputed from a stage of societal develop-
> ment … or by 'experience' imputed from a social category … but
> by actors' places in the multiple (often competing) symbolic and
> material narratives in which they are embedded or with which
> they identified. (Somers, 1994: 606)

For many, the importance of the narrative of the journey from
Poland lies in its contribution to a tale of self over time and of a
community of Poles over time. The narrative can be a pivot for
identities built over time but also across place.

THE ROYAL WE

The past can be used both by the individual and by the group to
build accounts of self and nation. Nadia Valman (1995) argues that
Anglo-Jewish women's evangelical autobiography was written:

> not as a testimony of subjectivity, but as argument and evidence
> for universal truth, evidence which is strengthened by every
> addition to the genre. They are not about the search for a nar-
> rative of the self, but the submission of the self to an already-
> written narrative. Thus, I would suggest, these texts effectively

write autobiography against itself, the individual voice dissolving easily into the universal story. (Valman, 1995: 102)

In the narratives I collected, and in written accounts in the *Dziennik Polski* (Polish daily newspaper), for example, it is impossible to separate out the story of the self from that of the wider one of the Polish people. The individual voice does dissolve easily because it is also a social voice. There is room in the wider narrative for the individual voice, and it is the fact that each subjective account seems to fit into this grand narrative that makes it so unquestionably true for those involved.

The importance of personal testimony as a way of confirming Polish identity is illustrated by looking at the comments of Mr Baranowski who was born in Poland in 1927, and who now lives in America. Although being Polish in America is different to being Polish in England or in Poland, the need to reaffirm the subjective as social can be seen in his statements. Mr Baranowski spent a long time preparing a written account of his life in English, since he insisted that the account was not only his and had to be just right. He then read the written account into a tape recorder:

> This is my true life memory that I wish to share with my family. This day is also intended for my dear cousin who went through the same ordeal in Russia…February 10th is a day I can never forget. There was a knock at the door and my mother opened and two Russians walked in. They told my mother we must get ready in twenty minutes. Take some food and clothing and move to another county…My family went down on their knees and started praying…About four hundred were arrested in our village…Neighbours were ringing bells, all of us were crying. This was the last time I saw my village…I want you to know this story…People in the history of Poland have been through things you would not believe…My cousin's story is not the same as mine but some things are the same for all of us.

The work of Elizabeth Tonkin (1992) illustrates the problems in trying to separate out the I and the 'We' in accounts. She discusses the 'I's continuity' with reference to accounts given by people who were not present during the events they described (Tonkin, 1992: 134). She argues that they are presentations of self that do not subscribe to 'the ideological character of the Western belief in an autonomous bounded self, unique and coterminous with a body's life'. I will illustrate this point with a quote from a woman born in Poland and now living in a Midlands town who experienced the events of 1940, but not all the events she alludes to:

> We have always suffered. Poland is in a difficult location. We have often been betrayed. Nobody has helped us. We need to talk about how it feels to live with such neighbours and we need to remember the pain of our people all over the world. We have died of starvation and hidden in the forests to avoid being murdered. We will not forget.
>
> (author's translation)

Paul Thompson (1993) argues that life stories are themselves a form of transmission, but also that they can indicate in a broader sense what is passed down in families, for example, values and ways of looking at events that may be different to prevailing accounts. For the woman quoted above, her narrative of self is inextricably intertwined with her narrative of nation and what she has passed down is similarly a sense of 'we' that is more than an individual experience.

I have been arguing that who we are matters. It is only by identifying our perspectives and 'intellectual autobiographies' that we can understand where people are 'coming from'. However, as Dorothy Sheridan (Thomson, 1995) states, what people say is as important as who they are. She argues that people who write for the Mass-Observation Archive do so both for themselves and for others. Accounts are for both the writers and for 'historical others'. Moreover, writing is 'negotiated and shaped in relation to those perceived audiences' (quoted in Thomson, 1995: 166). In the accounts, both written and oral, of Polish peoples' lives since the Second World War, the I and the We are shaped by the sometimes competing needs of both.

The narratives I have collected describe a collective sense of 'we', but also an individuality that makes them very much a 'testimony of subjectivity' and a search for a narrative of self. They are, as Mr Baranowski asserts, true because they have been witnessed by individuals of the group involved, they are both subjective and universal. As Paula Black argues (1996), the subjective is not something that gets in the way of a study of society, but is actually expression of the social within the individual. Using the debates in the

literature on auto/biography and narrative to discuss ethnic categorisations can demonstrate the importance of change over time
and place, but also it gives us a glimpse into the nature of 'the
social'.

ESSENCE AND EXPERIENCE

As I have argued above, events are continually integrated into an
ongoing story about self. However, there can be more than one
story. The self has a history of experiences and reflections on those
experiences: an autobiography. The journey though life is in some
ways as important as the point at which you have arrived. These
experiences differ according to who you are, and when I began to
use my experiences to unpack categories such as 'Polish' I rediscov-
ered what I had learnt growing up being Polish: belonging to the
category means different things to different people.

Feminist writing has led me to question the ways in which one
can experience belonging (see for example, Grosz, 1990; Fuss, 1989).
Similar issues have to be addressed by students of autobiography
and biography: the need to call up a 'self' around which to focus
writing, while denying any essence to categorisations. For example,
some of the writings in the collection edited by Julia Swindells
(1995) deal directly with this issue, as do articles in the journal
Auto/Biography. Such writing has led me to ways of thinking in
which self, author and reader could 'be' without denying their
social location. Both sets of literature (which sometimes overlap)
discuss the ways in which it is possible to belong to a category
whilst at the same time allowing for difference.

Moreover, it is possible to be 'Polish' at times, while denying that
you are at others. During my research I am occasionally treated as
'one of them', a daughter of a prominent member of a Polish community. I am also seen as 'not one of them': I am a feminist academic, married with a son and husband who speak no Polish. I am
both 'same' and 'other'. My treatment is not a result solely of my
status as researcher. The people I spoke to were ambivalent about
who was 'Polish'. For example, looking at material from my research
for my PhD (Temple, 1992), Mrs Nurewicz's description of herself
swung from denial that she was 'Polish' to asserting her right to
be considered as such. She spoke of her commitment to the Polish
Saturday School as a means of passing on her 'Polish' way of life.

However, she socialised with English friends, and was not Polish in this respect. In contrast, Mrs Noble, from the same research, talked of being part of something which, for her, involved the social life of a group of people with common backgrounds, but not sending them to Saturday School, which involved teaching a way of life which had died. Mrs Noble was born in Poland, but did not see this as a marker of her 'Polishness'. She now spoke no Polish. Both women considered they belonged, and did not belong, in different ways. There was no 'core' to being Polish.

Moreover, for these women it was clear that they were part of a community in different ways from their husbands: the nature of belonging to their community was gender differentiated. They were responsible for child-care, for the education of their children, and for the housework: only women and cats, a Polish proverb states, belong in the kitchen. Looking at my life, and those of other women in the communities I had researched and grown up in, pointed to the influences of both gender and class on the category Polish. Attributing a core characteristic to the category such as language proficiency or involvement in formal Polish organisations is limiting. It is a process of naming which is political – a process of inclusion and exclusion – and the standards set, are generally defined by men. Such exclusionary practices hide the premises upon which they are built: they privilege a particular group (men) who define women as solely mothers and wives. The masculine nature of prevailing definitions of Polish communities can be see by looking at what is hidden from sight: the exhausting accumulation of the work of child rearing, teaching children both Polish and English, taking on the back-stage work of keeping Polish traditions alive and often going out to work as well. There has been no discussion, to date, in the literature about Polish communities of the evenings women spend sewing sequins on to Polish national costumes, cooking time-consuming Polish dishes, or organising productions of Polish plays. There has been debate on the role of organisations of Polish people, usually represented by the men. Moreover, the Polish community I grew up in was very class conscious. Intellectual life was valued, and professionals had status denied to working-class Poles, the 'intelligentsia' seemed to set the agenda, mainly, it appeared to me from London, in the shape of a Government in Exile. There was a stigma attached to manual work, particularly to women manual workers, who often as a result of having to go out to work, had little time or energy to devote to helping at the Polish Club, but some of whom still spent the little free time they had ensuring their children could take part in traditional Polish activities.

DISCUSSION

The narratives of second and third generation Polish inevitably differ from those of their parents and grandparents. They tell of different ways of being Polish or they (sometimes, never or always) deny the relevance to them of the category. Stating that one belongs to a category is a political act, and so is excluding oneself. Whether I say I am Polish, or British-Polish, or British, depends on who I am talking to and the context. Similarly, recent arrivals from Poland tell of their attempts to leave a country run by Communists and what being Polish means for them. Men and women tell overlapping but different stories. Being Polish is neither undifferentiated nor unchanging.

The main advantages for me of engaging with feminist and autobiographical/biographical debates include the following. First, such approaches allow questioning from a position using the researcher's own and others' experiences. Second, they encourage an examination of the nature of the relationship between researcher and researched. The relative positions of both are not straightforward. These two points are linked in that specifying who the researcher is, makes it possible to discuss the power relationships at play in research. For example, the dynamics of my interviews with women for my PhD differed from those with men. How people saw me inevitably influenced the kinds of information they gave me. Women could more easily understand my desire to talk about everyday life. I found men less sympathetic to some of the topics I wanted to include, and less understanding of my desire to get my PhD. Establishing the 'rapport' advocated in research methods texts proved easier with some than with others.

Third, such auto/biographical approaches enable the researcher to illustrate the time and place specific nature of ethnic categorisations. The nature of 'Polish' communities throughout the world varies and changes over time. Fourth, the individual and social can be related via the examination of the specifics of everyday life without devaluing either individuality or 'the social'. And finally, the complexity and diversity of ways of experiencing can be demonstrated without denying the value of categorisation such as 'Polish', 'woman' or 'working class'. It is by looking at the lives of British-Poles, as of others categorised as belonging to other groups, that it is possible to show the diversity of ways in which people can belong without having to name one characteristic as a qualification for inclusion. Closing ranks is a political act, one that can be challenged by outsiders.

I would like to finish by giving a flavour of what it means to me to be a British-Pole. The scene is a gathering for a fortieth wedding anniversary. Some of the people there were born in Poland, some in England. There is a lot of traditional food that has been made by the women and a lot of drink. There is much laughter. Then the atmosphere changes and a man stands up to give a speech in Polish. It is his wedding anniversary but, he feels, as a time for family it is also a time to remember two of his children who died of starvation in Russia. The story is told again. Others in the room have also lost family in this way, including my father who lost a sister. Those of us who weren't part of these events cry for those who were. Then the laughter returns and we enjoy being Polish.

References

Black, P. (1996) 'Sex, Class and Subjectivity: a Sociologist Revisits the Black Country', *Auto/Biography*, 4:105–10

Fuss, D. (1989) *Essentially Speaking*, London: Routledge

Grosz, E. (1990) 'A Note on Essentialism and Difference', in S. Gunew, ed., *Feminist Knowledge: Critique and Construct*, London: Routledge

Patterson, S. (1977) 'The Poles: an Exile Community in British Society', in J. Watson, ed., *Between Two Cultures: Migrants and Minorities in Britain*, Oxford: Basil Blackwell

Somers, M. (1994) 'The Narrative Construction of Identity: a Relational and Network Approach', *Theory and Society*, 23:605–49

Stanley, L. (1990) 'Moments of Writing: Is There a Feminist Auto/biography?', *Gender and History*, 2:58–67

——(1992) *The Auto/biographical I: the Theory and Practice of Feminist Auto/biography*, Manchester: Manchester University Press

Swindells, J. (1995) *The Uses of Autobiography*, London: Taylor & Francis

Temple, B. (1992) *Household Strategies and Types: the Construction of Social Phenomena*, unpublished PhD thesis: University of Manchester

——(1995) 'Telling Tales: Accounts and Selves in the Journeys of British-Poles', *Oral History*, 23:60–4

——(1996) '"Gatherers of Pig-Swill" and "Thinkers": Gender and Community amongst British-Poles', *Journal of Gender Studies*, 4:63–72

Thompson, P. (1993) 'Family Myth, Models, and Denials in the Shaping of Individual Life Paths', in D. Bertaux and P. Thompson, eds, *Between*

Generations: Family Models, Myths and Memories, Oxford: Oxford University Press

Thomson, A. (1995) 'Writing about Learning: Using Mass-Observation Educational Life-Histories to Explore Learning through Life', in J. Swindells, ed., *The Uses of Autobiography*, London: Taylor & Francis

Tonkin, E. (1992) *Narrating Our Pasts: the Social Construction of Oral History*, Cambridge: Cambridge University Press

Valman, N. (1995) 'Speculating upon Human Feeling: Evangelical Writing and Anglo-Jewish Women's Autobiography', in J. Swindells, ed., *The Uses of Autobiography*, London: Taylor & Francis

3

Memory, Truth and Orality: the Lives of Northern Women Textile Workers

CHRISTINE KENNY

This chapter traces the auto/biography of a book that began its life as an 'academic' project, but became instead a popular book: *Cotton Everywhere* (1994).[1] Or did it? During the process of writing this personal narrative, I will be exploring some of the ethical, theoretical and experiential issues that led to the book changing the course of its 'career' in the way that it did. I begin by relating the research process, telling the story of my own increasing awareness of my responsibilities as a researcher and the decision-making process this caused. I then turn to a discussion about what counts as an 'academic' text. As a challenge to the post-modernist notion of the 'death of the author,' I discuss how, during the process of writing the book, aspects of my own memories, intersubjectivity and changing sense of self became woven into its fabric.

WHAT IS AN ACADEMIC TEXT?

Schon (1993) distinguishes between reflection *in* action (that which is on-going), and reflection *on* action (a process of 'summing up'), both of which take place after the completion of a project. During the time I was conducting the research for *Cotton Everywhere*, I kept a reflective diary. This section of the discussion provides a synthesis of the reflections recorded in the diary, and gives account of the way these influenced my increasing commitment to the use of data from the research in order to produce a popular book about Northern women's experiences of working in the textile industry, rather than the 'academic' thesis I had initially intended producing for my MSc. This decision was influenced by writers who have questioned the value of Social Science research (Oliver, 1991; Reason and Rowan, 1981), and who have promoted the principle that research should be used in order to develop less oppressive theories (Miles, 1993). By the time this decision had been made, my ideas about research had become more complex and, I suppose, idealistic, and included the following principles:

1. A research project should amount to more than a 'hoop jump-ing' exercise to further the careers of academics, since it has the potential to benefit society.
2. Research is an ethical project and, as such, has the potential not just to do good, but also harm (see for example, Jenkins, 1971; Oliver, 1991). Thus, researchers should not ignore the fact that their research can have consequences that can be detrimental to individuals and collectives (Finch, 1993).
3. If research is an ethical project, then researchers have a debt to their informants that goes beyond some of the guidelines outlined by professional bodies such as the BPS (1993).
4. Research is both reflexive and self-reflexive; and the starting-point for investigation should be the researcher herself.

Taking into account the principles outlined above, and my increasing commitment to the idea that researchers are accountable to those who take part in their research, my aims when I produced *Cotton Everywhere* were threefold. First, to provide a medium through which the voices of the women who took part in the study could be represented. I attempted to do this by presenting the book in the way that the women (during the interviews) had given their life-stories in a 'chatty' form. *Cotton Everywhere* was written as a semi-autobiographic piece of work. The decision to write the book in this form was partly influenced by theoretical considerations; but it also reflected a desire to present the book in the way that the women of Bolton (in my experience) tend to tell a story. Typically, this involves a relationship with the storyteller's experience and, in particular, her connection with others involved in the scenario described. In other words, I tried to represent a 'voice' that I believed most women of Bolton could relate to. At the time I wrote *Cotton Everywhere*, I had considered this narrative style to be a characteristic specific to Bolton women, but other researchers (Brown and Gilligan, 1992; Mann, 1995) have reported that women generally tend to tell stories in this way.[2]

The second aim concerns my desire to write a feminist-based 'herstory' of the women of Bolton. Many groups have been denied a history (see Miller, 1976) which, to me, is one of the deadliest forms of oppression: namely, to 'kill' people's stories. There is much evidence to suggest that when people are allowed to reclaim their life-stories, this does much to promote feelings of pride and self-esteem (Frisby and Tucker, 1993; Coakley, 1992). Indeed, there is a great deal of evidence to suggest that in some cases, participation in interviews alone can have a therapeutic effect (Norman, 1990; Viney and Benfield, 1991). I therefore hoped that *Cotton Everywhere* might make a useful addition to other local histories that have been written about the town.

Thirdly, I wished to put something back into the community I had investigated. This was achieved by the production of a book written in a style that would be accessible to a very wide audience, while, at the same time, not wishing to alienate the reader by appearing to be patronising. I aimed to make the book enjoyable, relatively cheap and attractive. The book's completed form was influenced by Usherwood's (1992) discussion of the various ways in which people can be denied access to information due to inequalities caused by such things as lack of money, disability and a lack of formal education. I was concerned that people with sight problems should have access to *Cotton Everywhere* and luckily Michael Tatman, the manager of a local charity, 'Newstalk', approached me about the possibility of having the book produced on tape. This has since been done.

Usherwood (1992) distinguishes between books *about* communities and books *for* communities. I wanted *Cotton Everywhere* to fulfil both of these criteria. Crucially, *Cotton Everywhere* was not a completely individual project. Drafts of the book were proof-read and finally approved by some of the women who took part in the study, and also by two of my academic colleagues, Alec Bagley and Phil Goodman. The production of the book concluded a process of discussion and co-operation with my publisher Dawn Robinson and, in the case of the taped version of *Cotton Everywhere*, Michael Tatman. Although academic work tends to be presented in a very individualistic way, the best work, in my mind, is produced in collaboration with others.

Reflecting on the aims I set out to achieve when I wrote *Cotton Everywhere*, it could be said that, given the local popularity of the book when it became available, the project was successful.

However, viewing it from the perspective of 'academia' the question of success is another matter. Which texts are regarded as academic in Higher Education is very much restricted by criteria set out by the Research Assessment Exercise rather than the contribution a piece of work makes to the wider community. However, it could be argued that an academic piece of work, no matter what form it takes, is creative, reflects some individuality, and informs and touches people's emotions in some way. Most of all, an academic text should show evidence of the writer having taken account the work of other writers, as a token of respect for the ways the latter has inspired him or her. In relation to the last criteria, I hope that I have fulfilled this obligation, at least in part, by the writing of this paper.[3]

INTERVIEWING AND THE
(DE/RE)CONSTRUCTION OF SELVES

The politics and complexity of woman-to-woman interviews have been explored by a number of writers (see Oakley, 1991; Finch, 1993; Ribbins, 1989; Miles, 1993). It was partly my agreement with such authors that influenced many of the issues discussed in the last section. However, I found that when I attempted to put abstract principles – such as accountability and empowerment – into practice, the work I had read only partly prepared me for the complexities and difficulties I encountered.

At the time I was writing *Cotton Everywhere*, I was gradually changing my own perspectives and, because of this, sometimes found myself disagreeing with some of the principles my participants held very dear. Moreover, the theoretical discussions of the writers cited, did not prepare me for the nostalgic impact the interviews would have on me. My relationship with the participants also had an impact on the overall 'flow' of the interactive interviews I conducted for *Cotton Everywhere*, so that fluctuations occurred, and hierarchies sometimes evolved – generally with myself placed as 'subordinate' or 'novice'. This was particularly relevant when interviewing my Grandmother and Great Aunts, because my relationship with them had been established before the interviews began. My placement as 'novice' and 'subordinate' during these interactions was most likely to occur when some incident, such as my wanting a cigarette (some of my older relatives strongly disapproved of women smoking), brought out the parent–child interaction (Berne, 1966) which had been established during our lives outside the interview setting. I was also placed as 'novice' when the older women spoke of aspects of the textile industry that were outside my experience.

It was also interesting for me to find that many of the older women's stories were also mine. The conversations brought back recollections of my own childhood and life experiences in connection with the textile industry, and I became increasingly aware of the fact that I was gathering collective auto/biography(ies). Like Temple (1995), I was also struck by the variety of media used in order to construct and convey accounts of lives. 'Christine the child' and her relationship with others had her (their) authenticity recorded and symbolised in various family artefacts and photographs, each serving to inspire further discussion, which in turn validated *even further* the 'truth' of the stories recalled (Coles, 1989). But despite the abundance and variety of such media, it was never enough! It seemed that the lives recalled during my interviews were so 'excessive' in their complexity of experience, that the nearer the conversations *appeared* to bring us to uncovering them, the more distant and inaccessible they became. When I read through my transcripts now, I do not uncover linear, chronological accounts but, rather, fragments of recall which defy any attempt to constrain them within measurable 'chunks' of time: the illusion of linear time is something *I* imposed on the data in order to write a cohesive text.

In the opening chapter of *Cotton Everywhere*, I wrote that I wanted the reader to engage in a conversation with the book and to find themselves saying 'oh yes I remember that'. However, relating this to my experiences of interviewing, I found myself thinking very much the same thing. Comments such as 'How was it for you?' and 'was that all right?' were frequently made by my interviewees, and this has been reported by others (see Hutchinson, 1994). Perhaps because I was interviewing older members of my family who had known me as a child, the conversations went on long after the formal taped interview ended: indeed, my informants often 'turned the tables' around and started interviewing *me*. It seemed to me that there was a general consensus of agreement on what the child 'Christine' had been like – and she not so very different from the 'good' Catholic woman she became! This was (is) a persona with whom I strongly identify. At the same time, it was (is) an identity that I was (am) rejecting and trying hard to rebel against.[4]

The idea that there exists deep within each individual an authentic self is a popular one, both within and outside academia, and it forms the basis of many counselling models (Parker, 1989). But the notion of a fluctuating, constructed self seems to me a very interesting one (Riley, 1980; James, 1994). In one sense it is quite empowering because (I suppose) it means that, providing we have access to the appropriate discourses, we can be whatever we want (or are allowed) to be. However, is this idea really very much different from that proposed by Role Theorists – that we have many selves. If we have many selves, then what about conditions such as multiple personality disorder – is this indeed a disorder or simply a way of being? This raises further questions. If the self is constructed, then to what degree is the 'child' recalled during reminiscence unchanging and authentic? And to what degree do such recollections vary throughout the life-span? To what degree are recollections of the 'child' variable and situational (Riley, 1980; Temple, 1995)? Who was the little girl who 'spoke' of her life from the pages of *Cotton Everywhere*? Did she really exist? She certainly seems/seemed very real. Indeed, in some uncanny way she appears at times to be still there. But when I think of her now, she seems to live an independent existence both inside and outside of me. The experience of 'the child within' has been reported by others some, arguing that this phenomenon may be linked in some way to women's socialisation into the role of carer (see Hancock, 1990).

Perhaps the selves recalled during reminiscence actually lose aspects of their authenticity during the act of 'giving voice', causing them to become detached and alienated from the (present) self who constructs them. And, since the self is caught in a permanent flow of time, perhaps reminiscing is a process of losing, rather than finding, one's self. Could it be that this might be the essence of the success (in *some* cases) of the talking therapies, such as psychoanalysis and counselling? Is it possible that in order to move on in our lives, in order to operate in different realities, we need to 'talk out' old inappropriate selves before we are able to 'speak into being' newer, more appropriate selves?[5] This was another important issue for me at the time that I wrote *Cotton Everywhere*, because I was changing and developing an increasing commitment to feminism (though this was somewhat ambivalent at the time) and to a career. Thus, in the course of writing, the book became increasingly a reflection of my past: and the future that I believed I was heading towards.

CONCLUSION

In this chapter I have discussed the decision-making process that led me to create a 'popular' book, rather than an 'academic' text. The writing of this book enabled me to make a contribution to the wider community of Bolton; but in doing this, I relinquished any recognition that the research might otherwise have brought me from the academic community. I considered this sacrifice worthwhile however, because – as I have argued throughout this discussion – I do not believe that the outcome of research should always be presented in such a way that it operates solely for the benefit and interest of academics, while participants of research are excluded and left out in the cold.

Despite my commitment to remain true to the principles I refer to above, I found it much more difficult to address issues related to accountability, inclusion and empowerment than I had anticipated. Difficulties arose because of my lack of ability, at the time, to reconcile the still present (and very powerful) 'Christine' with the newly emerging 'I'. This 'I' was striving, on the one hand, to use her research to empower her participants, while, on the other hand, finding herself increasingly at odds with many of the principles that they held dear. This led to some feelings of alienation, and the academic community offered no asylum. When I reflect after some distance of time on my experience of writing *Cotton Everywhere*, I realise that I lived in a state of subjective exile: drifting on the margins of two subjective planes – my community of origin, and the academic community – unable to feel 'placed' with either of them!

I was also confronted by a host of other theoretical and practical problems that I had not considered in sufficient depth at the time that I set out my initial aims. For example, I became increasingly concerned that my very commitment to the notion of empowering my participants might be a little arrogant. Fourteen strong, capable and independent women took part in my study: who on earth did I think I was to imagine that they needed *me* to empower *them*! I remember when I considered this point, how frequently irritated I had been in the past by well-meaning professionals who had sought to empower me. Abstract principles such as 'empowerment', 'inclusion' and 'responsibility' are impossible to define, let alone implement in any universal or satisfactory way. I do not claim therefore that, in setting out to achieve some of the aims I formulated when I wrote *Cotton Everywhere*, I had confronted and resolved all of the problems. On the contrary, I actually created and opened up more questions and dilemmas than I resolved.

Cotton Everywhere became much more than a story of Northern women's experiences in the textile industry. The woman who 'Christine' was becoming/became, subjectively 'wrote out' the little girl – myself as child – who still lives and speaks in the history that I represented.

Notes

1. C. Kenny, *Cotton Everywhere: Recollections of Northern Women Mill Workers*, Bolton: Aurora Press, 1994.
2. In my experience this narrative style can sometimes be misinterpreted as evidence of a speaker's 'self centred' personality. However, when such stories are examined in greater depth, they suggest the presence of a fragmented self: a self that only has meaning in relation to its connection with other selves.
3. In some works, it may not be appropriate to make such an acknowl- edgement, though in such cases follow-up written work such as this chapter should be done. In the case of *Cotton Everywhere* I was a little concerned (perhaps wrongly I now think) that too much reference to academic writers might distract from the 'popular' focus of the book.
4. I occasionally ask myself, why was it so important for me to escape from this part of myself – I don't know!
5. I use the word 'appropriate' here to refer to all the selves a life has the potential to be, and the need to change one's outlook, perspective, and indeed often behaviour, so that these can be lived.

References

Berne, E. (1966) *Games People Play*, London: Quality Book Club

Bonet, J. (1994) 'Is Oral History Auto/biography?', *Lives and Works: Auto/biographic Occasions*, 3:1 and 3:2, pp. 17–30

Brown, P. A. (1992) 'What shall I tell my children who are Black?', *Update on Law Related Education*, vol. 16, no. 2, pp. 9–11

Brown, L. M. and Gilligan, C. (1992) *Meeting at the Cross-roads*, Cambridge Mass: Harvard University Press

British Psychological Society (1993) 'Ethical Principles for Conducting Research with Human Participants' *The Psychologist*, vol. 3, no. 7, pp. 33–5

Coakley, B. F. (1992) *Improving the Academic Achievement of Third and Fourth Grade Underachievers as a Result of Improved Self Esteem*, Washington DC: Heldref Publishing

Coles, R. (1989) *The Call of Stories*, London: Methuen

Finch, J. (1993) ' "It's great to have someone to talk to": the Ethics and Politics of Interviewing Women', in M. Hammersly, ed., *Social Research: Philosophy, Politics and Practice*, London: Sage, pp. 166–80

Frisby, C. L. and Tucker, C. M. (1993) 'Black Children's Perception of Self: Implications for Educators', *Educational Forum*, vol. 57, pp. 146–56

Frish, M. (1990) *Shared Authority: Essays on the Craft and Meaning of Oral and Public History*, Albany: SUNY Press

Hancock, E. (1990) *The Girl Within*, London: Pandora

Hutchinson, S. A., Wilson, M. E., Wilson, H. S. (1994) 'The Benefits of Participating in Research Interviews', *Journal of Nursing Scholarship*, vol. 26, no. 2, pp. 115–20

James, L. (1994) ' "This is Me!" Auto/biography and the Construction of Identities', *Lives and Works: Occasional Papers*, 3:1 and 3:2, pp. 71–82

Jenkins, R. (1971) *The Production of Knowledge in the IRR*, London Institute of Race Relations

Jorgenson, J. (1991) 'Co-constructing the Interviewer/Co-constructing Family', *Research and Reflexivity: Inquiries in Social Construction*, London: Sage, pp. 110–21

Kenny, C. (1994) *Cotton Everywhere: Recollections of Northern Women Mill Workers*, Bolton: Aurora Press

Kenny, C. and Wibberley, C. (1994) 'The Case for Interactive Interviewing', *Nurse Researcher*, 1:3

Mann, C. (1995) ' "How did I get to be here?" Educational Life Histories of Adolescent Girls Doing A Levels', *Lives and Works: Auto/biographical occasions*, 3:1 and 3:2, pp. 59–70

Miller, J. B. (1976) *Toward a New Psychology of Women*, London: Penguin

Miles, M. (1993) 'Towards a Methodology for Feminist Research', M. Hammersly, ed., *Social Research: Philosophy, Politics and Practice*, London: Sage, pp. 64–81

Norman, E. (1990) *Women at War: the Story of Fifty Military Nurses who Served in Vietnam*, Philadelphia: University of Pennsylvania Press

Oakley, A. (1991) 'Interviewing Women: a Contradiction in Terms', H. Roberts, ed., *Doing Feminist Research*, London: Routledge, pp. 30–6

Oliver, M. C. (1991) 'Changing the Social Relations of Research Production', *Disability, Handicap and Society*, 17:2, pp. 101–14

Parker, I. (1989) *The Crisis in Modern Social Psychology and How to End It*, London: Routledge

Reason, P. and Rowan, J. (1981) *Human Inquiry: a Source Book of New Paradigm Research*, Chichester: Wiley

Ribbins, J. (1989) 'Interviewing: a strange situation', *Women's Studies Forum* 6, pp. 579–92

Riley, D. (1980*) ' "Am I that name?" Feminism and the Category "Woman" in History*, London: Macmillan

Schon, D. (1993) *The Reflective Practitioner*, London: Temple Smith

Sieber, J. E. (1992) *Planning Ethically Responsible Research: a Guide for Students and International Review Boards*, London: Sage

Stanley, L. (1992) *The Auto/Biographical I*, Manchester: Manchester University Press

Temple, B. (1995) 'The Message and the Medium: Written and Oral Accounts of Lives', *Lives and Works: Auto/Biographical Occasions*, 3:1 and 3:2, pp. 31–46

Usherwood, B. (1992) 'Community Information', *Informing Communities* Margaret Kennell, ed., Community Services Group for the Library Association, Remploy Ltd.

Viney, L. and Benfield, L. (1991) 'Narrative Analysis: a method of psychosocial research for AIDS affected people', *Social Science and Medicine*, 32:1, pp. 737–65

Wilkinson, S. (1989) 'The Role of Reflexivity in Feminist Research', *Women's Studies Forum*, 11:5, pp. 493–502

4

Feminist Ethics and Issues in the Production and Use of Life History Research

LESLEY FORREST AND JUDY GILES

> An 'ethic' is a framework of thought concerned with morality and with moral choices between things and actions seen as good or bad. Our feminist fractured foundationalist epistemology specifies morally adequate means of knowing and understanding women's experiences, particularly through insisting that *feminist theory should at some level be consonant with experience*. (Stanley, 1993: 200; our emphasis)

Much of the literature on the subject of feminist research has focused on the search for appropriate research methods and the methodologies that underpin these. But it is only recently that feminists have begun to engage with the actual *experience* of doing research (Roberts, 1981; Maynard and Purvis, 1994). In this chapter, we would like to raise questions about what it means to see oneself as a feminist researcher. Ann Phoenix has argued that '"race" and "gender" positions, and hence the power positions they entail, enter into the interview situation but that they do not do so in any unitary or essential way' (Phoenix, 1994: 49); Diane Reay argues similarly for class positions (Reay, 1996). We, too, subscribe to the idea that the researcher and the researched bring diverse and shifting identities to the interviewing situation; but our discussion takes this a step further, and argues that the consequence of attempts by the researcher to maintain a coherent feminist identity might be to deny or invalidate the research subjects' understanding of their own experience. We both conducted our research in the 1980s as part of our wider auto/biographies: we were 'mature' students, anxious not only to acquire the necessary, as we perceived them at that time, academic qualifications, but also to authenticate our feminist identities within the new (to us) social worlds we had entered. In the mid-1980s, the concept of *feminisms* was still relatively undeveloped – there was FEMINISM, and we wanted to belong!

We were both engaged in research projects that involved our asking women to talk about experiences, attitudes, values and beliefs. The women Judy interviewed were in their 70s and 80s, a number had been fairly recently widowed, and for many of them the experience of being asked to remember not only specific moments, but also the values and beliefs they held as young women, was both painful and exciting. Recalling the past for these women was not simply a nostalgic trip down memory lane, but involved revisiting and perhaps defending, the identities they had 'chosen' as young women.

Lesley interviewed 14–15 year-old girls, and for these young women, still at school and on the threshold of adulthood, the experience of being interviewed was not only about reflecting on their present experience, but also about envisioning their dreams and aspirations for the future. Both groups of women were from working-class neighbourhoods, and none of the women had, nor were expected to achieve, high academic qualifications.

Judy's interviews were conducted on an individual basis in the respondents' own homes, while Lesley, whose concern was to explore friendship groups, talked to her interviewees in groups in a school setting. We return to the issue of location later, but our point now is that our understanding of what was at stake for our interviewees was something we learned only gradually over a number of years and a number of return-visits to the research material we had collected. Thus, any exploration of what might constitute feminist research using the life stories of both elderly and young women, equally and simultaneously, involves tracing our own research journeys, our own relationship with feminism, and our attempts to make sense of our own fluid and shifting subjectivities.

Feminist perspectives have offered radical, often revolutionary, frameworks for explaining and understanding women's lives; but, like any perspective, these alone cannot necessarily provide all the answers. The diversity of contemporary feminist approaches testifies to a willingness to encompass a range of methodologies and perspectives, and sustains a questioning and critical position with regard both to our own research practices and the material we thus generate. For this reason, we have tried to indicate when we are speaking in one voice and when we are in dialogue by the use of textual codes: **Judy** or **Lesley** in bold type signal points where our thinking diverges or we place the emphases differently. We hope this use of different voices will reinforce the arguments we are developing. To return to Liz Stanley's words which open this chapter, our aim is to raise questions about what it means to identify as a feminist researcher in the context of 'feminist theory [which] should at some level be consonant with experience': for us, this involves the experiences and subjectivities of both the respondent and the researcher herself.

FICTIONS AND FANTASIES OF 'THE SELF'

We approached our respondents with certain expectations about what we would find. On the one hand, Judy hoped to discover a group of strong, shrewd women whose struggle against insuperable poverty and hardship was worthy of feminist celebration. She wanted to unearth 'ordinary' heroines to set against the public figures of historical record and the victimisation of working-class women inherent in much historical myth-making. Lesley, on the other hand, expected to discover limited horizons and narrow lives heavily circumscribed by patriarchy.[1] We very quickly discovered that the women we talked to were neither victims nor heroines – their complexity was far greater than the two-dimensional narratives and stereotypes which constituted much of their 'official' history, and from which we had drawn our pre-research expectations. Moreover, although common patterns of response emerged, our respondents could not be perceived as homogenous groups. Both groups of women constructed versions of themselves, drawing on a range of fictions and fantasies: drawing for example, on the culturally significant myth that meeting 'Mr Right' will lead to a lifetime's happiness, or the equally powerful narrative that a mother's place is with her children. Conscious fantasies were tempered by an understanding of the parameters of social reality and operated within certain perceived constraints. The versions of self most frequently offered to the researcher matched prevailing and normative expectations (both at the time of telling and at the time remembered) of appropriate gender, class, and sexual behaviours.

Alongside the common patterns in the life narratives which emerged, each woman, in telling her story, 'chose' a mode in which to represent herself: for example as fighter, as stoic, as rebel, as excluded, as conformer. In doing so, the women drew upon the repertoire of myths and iconography available, choosing versions of identity which were both socially acceptable and *comfortable* to them. None of the women we interviewed, despite reading and enjoying romantic narratives such as the fictions in *Home Chat* and *Jackie* magazines, chose to represent themselves as romantic heroines; and all of them self-identified as 'respectable', although some may not have been thus defined by their peers. For example, Lizzie Smith, interviewed by Judy, had an illegitimate child, married and divorced a man who physically abused her, and lived as a single parent. When discussing sub-cultural styles like 'punks, skinheads and mods' the schoolgirls, interviewed by Lesley, constantly asserted:

Anne: We're none of these, we're just normal.
Angie: People think I'm a punk because of my hair but I'm not really.

It became clear that association with certain interpretations of adolescent femininity could be viewed by peers as not respectable and ruinous to the girls' reputations. To 'be normal' was paramount.

INTERVIEWS AS PUBLIC PERFORMANCE

The preferred versions of the self which were produced by the women interviewed also drew upon the immediate context in which they were being offered to us, the researchers. Our agenda for the interviews was to set up a private dialogue between the respondent and ourselves; one in which the exploitation and objectification of the research subject was obviated as far as possible by 'good' feminist research practices.[2] However, we came to see that for our respondents the research situation was understood, not as the private conversation we intended, but as a public performance with ourselves as 'first audience' (Stuart, 1993: 81). Social markers such as our professional position and the use of a tape recorder, suggested to the women interviewed the conventions of journalism and the media in which interviewees are asked 'to say a few words' (Giles, 1995: 27). Lesley's research diary for 1983 comments on the situation she attempted to negotiate when the girls were completing questionnaires:

> My role as one in a directive, ultimately powerful position was at odds with my desired presentation of self as an adult friend who could be trusted. Restrictions on level of noise, giving spellings and so on defined me, in their eyes, as 'teacher'. Their role was difficult also as I wanted them to act as an informal group and not look to me for approval and guidance; the setting (a classroom in official lesson time) and my perceived role combined to mitigate against this. (Extract from research diary; Forrest, 1983).

Although most women welcomed the opportunity to tell their stories, they were also uncomfortable about the possibility of exposure that public performance threatened. A number of the women interviewed by Judy sought reassurance about confidentiality and many were anxious in case their 'performance' was perceived as inadequate. 'Is this what you want?', 'My husband could tell you more interesting things' were common examples. Public performance through friendship-group interviews was a major feature of Lesley's research. Frequent teasing and censoring, alongside affirmation and approval, were in evidence throughout, which, we suggest, affected the viability and sustainability of the identities offered by individual girls from moment to moment in the group/public situation. It was important to record these exchanges. As Kitzinger points out, when discussing the focus-group method of research: 'Reading some such reports [of group interviews] it is hard to believe that there was ever more than one person in the room at the same time' (1994: 104).

Public performance was not welcomed by all schoolgirl participants, as the following exchange from the end of a session makes clear:

> Angie: I didn't say nothing with Tracey's mouth flapping all the time. I was right bored.
>
> LF: Perhaps you'd like to talk to me by yourself sometime?
>
> Jackie: You don't want that miss; *you'd end up getting her life story*!

So, the self which Lesley had been given of Angie thus far, was the self for public consumption: the identity presented for *and constructed by* her peers. Another version of the self, a more secret and private self, was a possibility. Angie's silence may have been a voluntary act of refusal to expose her preferred version of herself on this occasion. She was the one about whom the others were consistently most censorious.

The selves offered in such a situation by both groups of women interviewed were those appropriate for public consumption and, as such, emphasised those aspects of identity deemed most acceptable not only to us, the researchers, but to the women's sense of themselves as actors in specific social contexts. Their accounts of themselves were the versions they felt most comfortable with, and were neither necessarily nor simply produced to please us, the researchers. Indeed, the importance of sustaining the friendship group might take priority over pleasing the researcher for the schoolgirls.

Judy   At times I was frustrated by my respondents' refusal to acknowledge sexual yearning or the desire for emotional intimacy. The 'respectable' identity which the women adhered to had served them well materially, making it possible to escape the drudgery and poverty of their mothers' lives. The values of respectability had made sense to these women at a particular historical moment, and even if the accounts expressed, often via nostalgia for the 'good old days', a sense of loss, the internalisation of self-image, although never complete, was too comfortable to be dispensed with in old age. Equally, and this is important for the argument we are developing, although the women often wanted to please me and put on a 'good performance', there were occasions when this power relation was disturbed. As a woman in my early forties, brought up to 'respect my elders', I found myself, at times, deferring to their understandings and value systems.

The cultural norms of deference to the elderly meant my identity as 'adult friend' and feminist researcher in the interview situation was constantly challenged. My feminist belief that 'good' research ethics requires the giving back of knowledge to the researched was compromised by my concern not to negate or devalue the perceptions and beliefs that had underpinned the women's experience. Politeness, and a concern for their dignity, meant I was rarely able to interrogate, however mildly, their perceptions and I was often, frustratingly, at the mercy of their evasive strategies.

For example, Betty invited me to interview her: but when I arrived, she announced that George 'from over the road' would be coming round as 'he can tell you more than I can'. Betty was a tough, reserved woman, who had never married, but remained at home caring for her mother, and working in the offices of a local factory. It was not, I felt, that Betty needed a man to speak for her, but rather an act of collusion to exclude me.

Women like Betty, whose lives have been spent protecting themselves from the scrutiny and surveillance of professionals, have developed methods of evasion and resistance which may both challenge the researcher's feminist orthodoxies and undermine her sense of feminist identity. On a number of occasions, I found myself responding to the women as a deferential 'girl', accepting their views on personal and political issues even when these were directly at odds with my own convictions. The point I want to make is that a range of identities and aspects of myself might interact, and even conflict, during an interview, thus constantly disrupting my attempts to sustain my avowed identity as feminist researcher.

CONVERSATIONS, ROLES AND CONTEXTS

The situation in which I found myself, having to suspend my feminist identity on entering the research setting, was compounded by the location in which the research took place. I entered these women's homes as a visitor and a professional researcher, and as such was required to act out certain behaviours expected of this role. Many of the women reinforced their perception of me as 'privileged guest' by providing tea and biscuits on the best china, by quite obviously dressing for the occasion and by taking me into the 'best' room (never the kitchen).[3] In such a situation, even had I felt it ethical to do so, I would have transgressed the norms of hospitality had I probed their accounts of themselves. Hence, I can now see that my responses to the women's stories were as fluid and shifting as the positionalities (feminist, researcher, guest, girl) in which I placed or found myself. At the time I struggled to sustain a single position and identity (feminist researcher). This manifested itself as a concern for synthesis and over-interpretation and thus undoubtedly denied or suppressed aspects that did not comfortably fit the account I needed to produce (see Giles, 1995: 158).

Lesley Issues of generation and location impinged throughout my experiences with the schoolgirls, but whereas Judy struggled with the 'deferential girl' position, I tried (and failed) to cast off the role of 'teacher'. I was constructed as such by the girls – as indicated by their constant use of 'Miss' to address me – despite shifting the location from the classroom to the common room, the time from lesson time to lunch time, and my wearing of jeans from wearing a skirt.

The formal culture of the institution of the school – made manifest by bells indicating the end of lunchtime, the presence of timetables on walls, their wearing of uniform, albeit modified to express their adolescent style, and so on – invariably mitigated against the informal ambience I wanted to create. It was a clear example of identity being bestowed. This was overlaid in the second stage research – in the interpretation of data – where my feminist evangelical zeal came into play. Equally, I had to fight my identity as 'adult-who-knows-better' in their protestation that their lives would be different from their mothers. They created, in fantasy, a future for themselves wherein part-time jobs would neatly fit around the care of husband and children, and where childcare would be readily available after they gave up their careers as airline hostesses and models. Who was I to destroy their utopias? But the temptation was there and the subsequent analysis carries, I fear, a patronising tone.

Relations in the classroom which are officially given importance are those between teacher and pupil; that the pupils' relations with one another could be given primacy was novel to my interviewees. But in retrospect, I question the ethics of attempting to infiltrate their social world for my own gain: I set the agenda; I chose the topics for discussion; I selected which points to draw them on, and which to ignore, in order to fulfil the criteria of academic work which would subsequently award me the 'feminist identity' that I so much desired at that time.

The multiple identities of feminist, teacher, sociologist, adult friend and a woman who had lived what they were currently experiencing, jostled with one another to make sense of the interactions. The final account prioritises the feminist sociologist voice, and other voices are silenced to produce an orderly, scholarly account. But it is an account which lacks the warmth, humour and unspoken sharing of understanding that took place between myself and the schoolgirls *as women*.

THE FEMINIST RESEARCHER: A FRACTURED 'SELF'?

The above discussion, we believe, raises important questions about what it means to call oneself a 'feminist researcher'. Generational differences, and the varied locations where research is conducted, are two aspects of researching which suggest that a consistent feminist identity is neither possible nor perhaps even desirable. The fluidity of conflicting identities and positions in the research setting, manifests itself in a constant shifting and negotiation on the part of the researcher and the research subject, which requires recognition in research findings and in the written-up version of a research project. Feminist, nor indeed woman, is not the only identity we take into the research setting: identities of child, parent, teacher, young, middle-aged, may also be (re)activated simultaneously by the specific research interaction we encounter. Equally, as we have suggested, the formalised space/location in which interviewing is conducted invites both researcher and research subject to adopt specific identities: pupil/teacher, host/guest. Such identities have their own internal power dynamic which may cut across or undermine that of feminist researcher; or which make it difficult to sustain a feminist position.

As we argued at the outset, the act of researching – itself – may be a means of constructing a feminist identity at a specific auto/biographical moment, and requires accounting for by the researcher. It is only upon reflection that we are able to acknowledge and perceive this aspect of our own research practice, and the consequences it had (and has) for our thinking about the issues of interpretation and dissemination. So often it is the 'unspoken sharing of understandings', and the points at which these diverge, that remain unacknowledged in the final research product.

Theories of feminist research suggest that good practice feeds back to the researched, allowing them to reconceptualise themselves, if they wish, within the feminist frameworks offered. It seemed unacceptable to us to question or reinterpret the values and practices which had sustained these women in what they perceived as the public arena of the research interview. Nevertheless, in order to meet the criteria of the academic community, we were required to provide interpretation. Lesley's research diary suggests the dilemma before she was aware of poststructuralist theories that offered the possibilities of multiple readings rather than definitive interpretations:

> … feel like I'm trying to impose my meanings on what they say, should I interpret at all? … made me aware of danger of imputing motives, but if this is so how does one make sense of or record findings of research? Ultimately it would mean giving a descriptive account and asking the reader to make her own appraisal which surely will vary according to one's perspective (Extract from research diary; Forrest, 1983)

We do not feel that we have, as yet, fully resolved this dilemma and continue to engage in dialogue around these issues. In particular, to what extent does feminist academic interpretation and analysis produce privileged knowledge? Does this process work against the egalitarian relationship between researcher and researched that feminist methodology advocates?

Judy   I want to argue that, while I accept that interpretation can be a form of producing knowledge in order to control, simply to let women's accounts speak for themselves does not necessarily, of itself, contribute to a feminist politics: an argument predicated on the need to transform our understanding of gender and the power relations implicated in patriarchal ways of thinking and behaving. I believe that if we are to challenge normative ways of seeing the world, we have to avoid contributing to those processes that manufacture consent for patriarchal knowledges. Relinquishing the (feminist) responsibility to make sense of research findings could, by omission, allow the continued reproduction of normative (patriarchal) modes of understanding. I also believe that as a feminist researcher, I am accountable not only to the women interviewed but also to the wider feminist and academic community of which I am a part and which provides me with the income, skills, space and time to engage in research at all. Yet, I have to acknowledge that, within the context of the research situation, I do, whether I like it or not, have the last word, as well as a responsibility to enable the researched to portray themselves as agents of their own experience. How these responsibilities can be reconciled is an issue that continues to exercise me. To this end, I want to advocate the development of research practices in which both researcher and researched are enabled to offer their own readings of the experiences recorded in order to produce coexistent versions from which the individual reader can construct meanings.

Lesley I have some sympathy with Judy's view but tend towards a more relativist position by continuing to believe that women's stories should stand for themselves, as authentic in their own right. The dialogue between us continues, and seems to me to hinge on the problem of definitions of feminism or the variety of feminist positions with which we are confronted in the 1990s and which space prohibits us from exploring here. In brief, I am concerned to distance myself from a feminist standpoint position which struggles to (re)interpret the words of respondents in order to portray them as passive victims of patriarchal forces, rather than as agents of their own lives. To do so would be to invalidate the lived experiences of the elderly women and the aspirations of the schoolgirls as testified by them. Daydreams and fantasies about 'what might be', are modes of resistance which cannot be ignored. 'Telling it like it is' provides one means of accessing stories about the ways in which women and girls *resist* the day-to-day experiences of contemporary patriarchal society which *may* not be the same as the manufacture of consent to the patriarchal order.

We have so far identified three problems which seem to us worthy of further interrogation. First, how can any concept of 'feminist researcher' deal with the fractures of identity which occur in the lived experience of conducting research? Second, if, as we have suggested, the physical/geographical spaces in which research interviewing occurs are rarely feminist spaces, nor even neutral spaces which can be reconstructed as the feminist researcher desires, but are always, already, otherwise socially and culturally appropriated, where might the researcher locate herself in order to adopt the identity 'feminist researcher'? Finally, what does it mean to be a feminist researcher when, as our discussion of interpretation suggests, the epistemological and ethical frameworks upon which our practice is founded, can be disputed and fractured?

One possibility that we shall go on to explore might be that, rather than seeking an ideal location, a fixed identity, or an epistemological position which eschews control as a consequence of knowledge (if such a thing were possible), there could be potential in the metaphorical spaces offered via those forms of autobiography produced by personal retrospective ethnography. Carolyn Steedman (1993) has suggested that using autobiography in this way would place researchers in a position to theorise and extrapolate from their own experiences and thus avoid the inherent power dynamics discussed. In personal ethnography, the researcher becomes both subject and object of her own research: teller and subject of her own story.

THE FEMINIST RESEARCHER: A FICTIONAL 'SELF'?

Our own attempts to construct autobiographical accounts (see Giles, 1990; Forrest, 1993) suggest that such a methodology does not inevitably produce the deconstruction Steedman is advocating. For both of us, these autobiographical pieces were our first attempt at published writing, both appeared in an academic journal, *Gender and Education*, and have to be understood in both the context of our wider life narratives *and* the specific moment in those life narratives at which they were produced. When Lesley wrote 'as a white, heterosexual feminist originally from a lower middle-class background, I may offer a different perspective on college life from other women in my student peer group' (1993: 211), her concern was to define herself in certain ways for a certain audience/ readership. In so doing, the 'other women' of her account were constructed to fit the preferred version which Lesley required at that particular moment. Her account, she now recognises, played-up the rebellious student aspect of her self, and failed to acknowledge the equally powerful conformist self which operated simultaneously.

In order to foreground the specific identity required, aspects of the self which did not fit were denied, suppressed or trivialised. Equally, Judy's narrative is constructed according to the conventions of traditional autobiography following a linear trajectory that culminates in the present and 'explains' the narrator's current position or state of mind – 'and that's why I'm here today'. Writing such an account, she acknowledges, requires a high degree of selectivity: only those events which fit the explanation are chosen, and aspects of experience which conflict with or contradict this explanation are omitted. Yet, we recall how important it was to seek and construct a coherent and stable identity (Lesley's 'white, heterosexual feminist ...'), at a time in our lives when we felt unsure of our direction, our identities and 'our place'.[4]

Auto/biography is as much about making sense of experience as deconstructing and theorising from that experience. What we are able to do with our auto/biographies may vary according to our needs and desires at the specific moments when we choose to 'tell our stories' and the community to whom we wish to represent ourselves. Neither are we are able to occupy some neutral or 'pure' space from which we can 'tell it as it was': all telling is an act of making sense of the random nature of experience. Personal ethnography involves imputing meaning, and the attendant danger of imposing interpretation on historical selves. Hence, while we welcome the idea of personal retrospective ethnography, and the use of auto/biography as a potential way out of some of the dilemmas involved in trying to be a feminist researcher, we believe it is important to remain aware of the individual autobiographer's specific positioning *vis à vis* her own life story, the community to whom she offers that life and, attendant upon this, the greater or lesser need to produce an integrated identity.

CONCLUSION

In conclusion, we would suggest, first, that to be a feminist researcher means recognising and accounting for our own shifting identities, as well as accepting the fluidity of identity for our respondents during the research process. Second, it means acknowledging a range of positions from which to validate the diverse knowledges researchers and research subjects use to make sense of their own experience, the experience of others and the relation between the two. Finally, we need to remain aware of the dangers, as well as the benefits, of bringing the self into the research process. Self-reflexivity in such a context, while making visible the contradictions and fractures of that identity, can also function to reassert and reproduce a feminist identity in ways that avoid acknowledging or accounting for coexistent subjectivities, for example teacher, parent, young, old, among others.

The researcher's version of 'self' that is offered in the research account may be reconstructed within the academic community in ways which parallel the power relations between researcher and interviewee. In such circumstances, the researcher herself, like the women we interviewed, may offer the identity that is most comfortable for her in the public arena or community wherein her work is circulated. As Holland and Ramazanoglu have observed, 'interpretation is a political, contested and unstable process between the lives of the researcher and those of the researched' (1994: 127). Being a feminist researcher means interrogating not only what we do, but who we are, who we would like to be and who we think we ought to be, and with finding ways of integrating these questions into the research process. We want to advocate the development of research practices in which diverse versions/readings of the experience of both research subject and researcher are allowed to coexist as equally valid, while acknowledging that these were produced to meet different needs, for different purposes, and from different standpoints.

Notes

1.   Judy interviewed 21 working-class women who were born in the early years of this century and who had lived in council housing in the 1930s and 1940s in York and Birmingham. Lesley's friendship groups comprised 14–15 year-old young women of mixed class background who attended a secondary modern school located on a council estate on the outskirts of a Northern city. Women in both studies were of white, British origin. See Giles, 1989; and Forrest, 1985.
2.   See, among others, Graham, 1982; Oakley, 1982; and Roberts, 1982.
3.   The idea of a 'best room' is, of course, specific to working-class culture.
4.   We are not trying to suggest that we have now, some years later, achieved an integrated sense of identity. To do so would be to reproduce the teleological effect of the traditional autobiographical form.

References

Forrest, L. (1983) Unpublished research diary
——(1984) 'The impact of gender on the lives of adolescent schoolgirls: a case study', Unpublished MA dissertation, University of Bradford
——(1993) 'Femininities and Friendship in a College of Education' in *Gender and Education*, vol. 5, no. 2
Giles, J. (1989) ' "Something that bit better": working-class women, domesticity and respectability, 1919–39', Unpublished DPhil, University of York.

—— (1990) 'Second Chance, Second Self', *Gender and Education*, vol. 2, no. 3

—— (1995) *Women, Identity and Private Life in Britain 1900–50*, London: Macmillan

Graham, H. (1982) 'Do Her Answers Fit His Questions?' in Gamarnikov, E. *The Public and the Private*, London: Heinemann

Holland, J. and Ramazanoglu, C. (1994) 'Coming to Conclusions: Power and Interpretation in Researching Young Women's Sexuality', in Maynard, M. and Purvis, J., eds, *Researching Women's Lives from a Feminist Perspective*, London: Taylor & Francis

Kitzinger, J. (1994) 'The methodology of Focus Groups: the importance of interaction between research participants', *Sociology of Health and Illness*, vol. 16, no. 1: 102–21

Maynard, M. and Purvis, J., eds (1994) *Researching Women's Lives from a Feminist Perspective*, London: Taylor & Francis

Oakley, A. (1982) 'Interviewing Women: a Contradiction in Terms' in Roberts, H., *Doing Feminist Research*, London: Routledge & Kegan Paul

Phoenix, A. (1994) 'Practising Feminist Research: The Intersection of Gender and 'Race' in the Research Process' in M. Maynard and J. Purvis, eds, *Researching Women's Lives from a Feminist Perspective*, London: Taylor & Francis

Reay, D. (1996) 'Insider Perspectives or Stealing the Words out of Women's Mouths', *Feminist Review*, no. 53, Summer: 57–73

Roberts, H. (ed.) (1981) *Doing Feminist Research*, London: Routledge & Kegan Paul

Stanley, L. (1993) *Breaking Out Again*, London: Routledge

—— (ed.) (1990) *Feminist Praxis: Research, Theory and Epistemology in Feminist Sociology*, London: Routledge

—— (1983) *Breaking Out*, London, Routledge & Kegan Paul

Steedman, C. (1993) BSA. Autobiography Conference

Stuart, M. (1993) '"And how was it for you Mary?": self, identity and meaning for oral historians', *Oral History, Autumn*, 80–3

Walkerdine, V. (1986) 'Video Replay: Families, Films and Fantasies' in *Formations of Fantasy*, V. Burgin, J. Donald and C. Kaplan, eds, London: Methuen

Walkerdine, V. (1990) *Schoolgirl Fictions*, London: Verso

Part II
Practice

Recovering and Reading Women's Lives: Interpretive Issues

5

Recuperating the Love-Passions of Edith Simcox

PAULINE POLKEY

Historically, psychologically, intellectually – & it may be admitted from pure carnal curiosity too – I should like to know how many women there are who have honestly no story to tell, how many have some other story than the one which alone is supposed to count & how many of those who think it worth their while to dissect themselves are in a position to tell all they know of the result. (Edith Simcox, *Autobiography of a Shirt Maker*, 17 October 1887)

This chapter opens with a question for feminists working on recovery research, namely: what happens when the lives of women whom we 'recover' become entangled in a 'recuperative' purpose? In exploring 'what happens', I focus on the life and works of one particular woman – Edith Simcox (1844–1901) – who has been variously positioned, scrutinised and framed by feminists and non-feminists alike, with a single recovery aim in mind: to explain her relationship with, and passion for, George Eliot.

Interest in Edith Simcox arises principally from her handwritten journal, *Autobiography of a Shirt Maker*,[1] in which she records her life from 1876 to 1900. But the source to which most critics refer when commenting on Simcox's life and works is K. A. McKenzie's partial transcription of the *Autobiography*, published in his *Edith Simcox and George Eliot* ([1961] 1978), and which gave rise to three fundamental – and contiguous – modes of interpretation. Predominantly, there is the 'relational' mode, wherein Simcox's life is scrutinised merely for its relevance to Eliot; then there is the 'symptomatic' mode, wherein Simcox is diagnostically framed as a tragic, flawed and

61

rather tiresome admirer of Eliot; and finally, the 'revisionist' mode, intent upon tackling the homophobic treatment of Simcox (as espoused by Haight ([1961] 1978), and, in turn, with positioning Simcox as an unequivocal lesbian admirer of Eliot.

While each of these interpretive frameworks have played a crucial role throughout the past 30 years in 'recovering' Simcox's life, many of them contain a central flaw inasmuch as they refer to McKenzie's partial transcription of the *Autobiography* as a primary, rather than secondary, source. McKenzie's book is partial for two specific reasons: on the one hand, for omitting considerable sections of the *Autobiography*, and, on the other hand, for McKenzie's emphasis on Eliot. Admittedly, because Simcox's journal is held at the Bodleian Library, direct access to it is not straightforwardly convenient. Nevertheless, some considerable claims have been made about Simcox – and indeed about Eliot's relations with, and handling of Simcox – merely on the basis of reading McKenzie's transcription.

Amongst literary critics, certain versions of Simcox's life predominate and circulate, in perpetuity. 'She took Eliot for her muse and model', asserts Lillian Faderman (1985: 163); 'an undoubtedly emotional lesbian', Marghanita Laski explains (1973: 102). Or there is McKenzie's version: 'she belonged to the type which psychiatrists call leptosomatic … there is not enough evidence available for us to decide whether she reached the points of psychotic breakdown, but the extravagance of her passion and the depths of her moods of depression suggest that she was at times dangerously close to it' (McKenzie, 1978: 135). And then we have the inauspicious summary by Gordon Haight: 'In reading her private account of George Eliot we should … allow for the intermingling of fantasy with fact' (Haight, 1968: 496). Although there have been a number of perceptive and insightful analyses by feminists in more recent times (see Vince, 1995[2]), McKenzie's influence still pervades. 'Though McKenzie's book was written in a period of very different assumptions from the present,' advises Gillian Beer, 'his research into Simcox's later life is still invaluable' (Beer, 1995: 167, n. 2). But the time has now come for a thorough re-evaluation of Simcox's *Autobiography* – rather than the McKenzie–Haight version of it – and, in turn, to begin the inevitable process of unpicking (some) feminist and non-feminist accounts of Simcox's life and works.

WHO WAS EDITH SIMCOX? SOME SIGNIFICANT BUT LITTLE-KNOWN FACTS

Edith Jemima Simcox was born on 21 August 1844 and died on 15 September 1901. Her family background was secured by wealth derived from merchant banking, and the Simcoxes were renowned in London and Oxford for their intellectual, writerly and political connections.

Simcox's *Autobiography of a Shirt Maker* comprises the twenty-four-years' record of a woman whose involvement in progressive, radical politics was considerable and wide-ranging. Not only did she set up a women's co-operative shirtmaking firm in Soho,[3] she was also an avid campaigner for women's suffrage and women's trade union rights, and attended numerous Cooperative Congresses. In 1879 she was elected to the London School Board, from which she stood down in 1882. As the women's suffrage campaigner Helen Blackburn (1842–1903) triumphantly explains:

> [In the 1879 School Board elections] more women presented them-selves for election and in more divisions than on any previous occasion, and the result is emphatic; nine out of eleven [female] candidates have been returned. ... The City [of London], by elect-ing Miss R. Davenport Hill, Westminster, and Miss Edith Simcox, re-echoes the same demand for women on the Educational Parliament.[4]

Simcox was also active in the Lodger's League and Anti-Sweat Shop organisation (which, in turn, campaigned against exorbitant rates of rent for London's working class, and the severe working conditions imposed on those working in the manufacture of cheap clothing), the Industrial Remuneration Organization, and the Working Men's Club, for which she regularly campaigned and gave lectures. She played a crucial role in the 2nd International,[5] where she was delegate for the London Women's Trades Council, and attended many International congresses: Paris (1882, 1889, 1890), London (1888, 1892), Belgium (1890).

Fluent in German, French, Italian, Greek and Latin, Simcox pub-lished three substantial works. Her first book was *Natural Law: An Essay in Ethics* (1877), in which she states her belief in social progres-sion arising out of 'the attainment by the greatest possible number of [society's] members of the greatest possible amount of satisfaction of all their conscious desires and impulses' (1877: 282). In 1882, she published *Episodes in the Lives of Men, Women and Lovers*, a collection of 12 fictional and autobiographical 'Vignettes'. Her third book, *Primitive Civilizations, or Outlines of the History of Ownership in Archaic Communities* (2 vols, 1894–97), was a considerable work of historical scholarship, giving a socio-economic account of the ownership of wealth, and took her 12 years to complete. Her *Autobiography* not only reveals the considerable work that went into this book – working on manuscripts at the British Museum (and being there when electric lights were first installed!), discussing her ideas and lines of enquiry with Oxford scholars, and the numerous drafts and redrafts (eventually made easier when she bought a typewriter) that were produced – it also shows the desolation caused by countless rejections from publishers, until Swan & Sonnenschein finally agreed to bring the book out. Alongside these considerable publications, Simcox was also a regular contributor to such progressive journals and periodicals as the *Academy, Co-operative News, Englishwoman's Review, Fortnightly Review, Labour Tribune, Nineteenth Century* and *Women's Union Journal*. Numerous strands thus rub alongside one other – political, social, intellectual – and Simcox's published writings reveal a more complex and intelligent persona than Eliot's biographers and critics have acknowledged. But what of her 'private' writing, as ascribed in her *Autobiography*?

As is clear from the epigraph at the beginning of this chapter, Simcox's interest in life-writing was considerable, and she was all too aware of the problems besetting women who desired to 'put their lives into print'. Her own *Autobiography* is recounted in chronological fashion, with entry dates running from 10 May 1876 to 29 January 1900. But the journal also contains a palimpsest of autobiographical configurations: the letter, tucked into the final pages of the journal, from Simcox to Eliot, for example; and Simcox's transcriptions of letters exchanged between Barbara Bodichon and Eliot; alongside memoranda of daily tasks, accounts of expenditure on food and other goods. Moreover, although the entries are inserted in chronological sequence, some of them are retrospective: notably that of 26 December 1897, which recounts, in some considerable detail, her mother's long-term illness over a considerable period of time. Simcox utilises her *Autobiography* to offer both *vita contemplativa* ('life in review'), in which she offers a more self-reflective and retrospective record, and also *vita activa* ('life in flux/crisis'), wherein she records the day-to-day events, crises, situations, conversations, instanced by what she terms her 'struggle for existence' (1 October 1877). The *Autobiography* therefore contains a series of intersecting discourses and self-contained narratives, each contingent to the writer's sense of purpose. Moreover, running throughout the *Autobiography* are several organizing structures that cohere to 'make sense' of experience: epiphanies; day-to-day records of conversations with colleagues, political activists, family and friends; and the listing of tasks and jobs-in-hand that shape Simcox's daily routine.

The kinds of political and writerly activities as those listed earlier are frequently recorded as part of Simcox's daily routine in her *Autobiography*, as the following entry, dated 9 March 1880, illustrates:

> Stayed at home preparing a Lecture for the Democratic Club, & delivered same night, for the rest, School Board & Mortimer St.[6] – yesterday was not idle; had a cup of tea in bed, reached Mortimer St at 9, looked round, then to Hart St to see about Pupil & Assistant teacher, then to Vere St for drawing examination – surprised to find that the second step included geometry; then saw the visitor & received report of Street cases caught by other visitors, Managers Meeting, made Mrs Buxton's[7] acquaintance, then set off for the Rota, Works Committee & Educational Endowments, do. – home reading *Blackwood*[8] en route, wrote several letters & read beginning of Froude's Hist. of Henry VIII[9] for another Club Lecture.

More often than not, the matter-of-fact descriptions of daily and/or weekly schedules are characterised by a seemingly obsessional routine of work and sacrifice:

> I am just the least bit what people might call busy now – having Elma[10] to see as often as I can, & when I don't go, I make a conscience of writing, to amuse her a little – Mrs Lewes[11] to enquire after 3 or 4 times a week, the shop[12] always, today the father of a would-be partner to interview,[13] Saturday the adjourned meeting of Trade Unionists & Clergy & a paper to arrange for one of the latter to read, same evening a lecture to a club in Bermondsey which has to be invented & written, Sunday another lecture to read & for next Saturday another paper to write & now Mrs Charles Lewes[14] wants me to enlist for the Commons' preservation. However, I can't go far wrong in consenting to write or speak on the side of any useful movement when I have the distinct personal sense of the utility. (*Autobiography*, 5 March 1879)

What we glean from these extracts is evidence of a woman whose involvement with political and public spheres is manifest; the voice is matter-of-fact and industrious. Not only is there a distinct tone of 'professionalism' here – the work listed (most of which was unpaid) signifies businesslike efficiency: 'It wants doing, it has to be done, how can anybody do anything else?' (*Autobiography*, 29 January 1900) – the narrative also denotes a 'brisk' bodily presence – walking, talking, writing, reading – that is energy-packed. Various strands thus connect together once more: the *politics* (trades unionism, the shirtmaking 'shop' in Soho, the School Board) feeds into the *intellectual* endeavour (comprising of lectures given and books read); and then, of course, there is the *passion*: '– Mrs Lewes to enquire after 3 or 4 times a week' is 'slipped in' amongst the other tasks. And it is this passion that arguably forms the troubled centre of the journal: 'Last night ... I lay in bed strangled with sobs I could not stop & feared to have been overheard. It is painful to me to feel that my love for her [Eliot] is to bear no fruit' (6 January 1878). 'This is not the Autobiography of a Shirt maker' Simcox emphatically affirms, 'but a love'.

THE LOVE-PASSIONS OF EDITH SIMCOX

'All passion becomes strength' wrote Edith Simcox, 'when it has an outlet from the narrow limits of our personal lot' (*Autobiography*, 20 August 1881), and it is her journal's passionate landscape of selfhood that makes it so compelling. Some of her 'passions', like that for the women's shirtmaking firm in Soho, fragment and fall apart; or are short-lived, as with the School Board; others are exhibited in terms of steadfast, day-to-day commitment, as evinced by Simcox's full-time care for her semi-invalid mother during the 1890s. There is also, of course, Simcox's love-passion for Eliot: unrequited yet fulfilled, repressed yet excessive, agonised yet hugely gratifying. And then there is the curious passion that 'Miss Williams' felt for Simcox: 'Poor Miss Williams haunts me like an exaggeration of every foolishness with which I ever teased or wearied her [Eliot]' wrote Simcox, 'I hope I am not uncharitable in thinking she is more unreasonable and exigeante than I ever was' (*Autobiography*, 5 January 1882).

I shall now offer a reading of Simcox's relationship with Eliot that is at variance with those who construe Simcox as mad, sad and self-deceived. Here, my intention is to examine ways in which the

Autobiography reveals a more complex and beguiling story than the one that has hitherto been recognised. Following on from that, I disclose the identity of 'Miss Williams' – and the relevance of political networks that she and Simcox were so ineluctably a part – and ask why this woman has so far been ignored by George Eliot's critical 'canon'.

GEORGE ELIOT

As I explained above, Simcox utilises her *Autobiography* to 'make sense' of experience. One way in which she brings this about involves setting up a 'dialogue' between Eliot and herself, in which Eliot is construed as attempting to control Simcox – both morally and socially – fixated by the notion of marrying Simcox off. In her entry of 9 November 1877, for example, Simcox records the way in which both Eliot and Lewes present their views on relations between the sexes:

> He & she said as they have before, that among chance acquaintances men are more appreciative & courteous to her [Eliot] than women. I said that I had found women kinder than men, which she was "glad to hear", as showing that they could be kind to each other – & I didn't explain either that I had always taken their kindness as a sign that I was half a man – & they knew it; or that I thought it rather hard she should visit, as a fault, my constitutional want of charm for men.

Occasionally, Simcox's reaction to Eliot's endless reprimands about her unmarried status becomes one of frustrated anger, as the following extended extract reveals:

> It is rather humiliating to me to be told again & again that the association called up by my name is always that of a woman who might find a husband if she could take a little more pain with her dress & drawing room conversation – & this in the mind of someone that I love. I have digested so many worse rebukes that I could put up with a simple criticism of my manners or appearance if it was without *arrière pensée*, but I cannot feel I *ought* to allow weight to a suggestion that urges me to seek the meaning of my life in the solicited good will or good opinion of strangers. I don't think so meanly of the men I meet as to assume

they have nothing other to do than be persuaded to think me "charming." Without your encouragement, I should hardly think so meanly of myself as to say my life was worthless unless I could achieve that triumph. The charm that I revere & love is one that springs unconsciously & inevitably from a sweet nature & a noble life. ... It is not only I that feel humiliated, I am more pained by the shadow of something almost like insolence in you – "Let some one else love what I have despised.["] – And if you do not despise me, Darling, – God knows I am loth to think it – then spare me these words which makes me despise myself! – as if all that I am, all that I can wish or strive to be is nothing in your eyes, unless my outer shell can find favour in the eyes of men! ... I have no choice but to feel hurt or angry if I let myself feel your words at all. (13 June 1880; emphasis original)

The tone here is notably candid, and the direct address to Eliot – 'Without your encouragement', 'something almost like insolence in you' and 'if you do not despise me, Darling' – reveals an attempt on Simcox's part, even if only on paper, to express her feelings, to plead her case, and to justify her point of view with reason and argument. The keenly-felt passion is obvious, with little sense of passive submission. The voice of fawning devotee is nowhere to be heard.

The *Autobiography* is also redolent, both implicitly and explicitly, with narratological subtleties of irony and paradox: none more so, than in Eliot's duplicitous stance towards Simcox. Simcox's intellectual and rational self-control, as opposed to 'mad' abandonment, is thus in evidence. And despite all the discomfort that Eliot might have felt about Simcox's attraction towards her, the *Autobiography* tells of frequent requests made by Eliot for Simcox to visit her, and of their kissings and fondlings: often performed in front of Lewes. Indeed, there are numerous descriptions of Eliot's flirtatious gesturings, as instanced in the following entry, dated 12 January 1877:

She [Eliot] said marriages had seemed to be getting later & later, & she was – of course – rather wroth with me for expressing prejudice against late marriages ... she proceeded to affirm that I had never been so fit to marry as now – I answered "that wasn't saying much" – to which with a sweet laugh & a still sweeter gesticulation – that brought her hand within reach of my lips – that she didn't pretend her speeches amounted to much – it was enough if they came to little.

There is a degree of artful manipulation on Eliot's part, here. And yet, despite all of Eliot's reprimands, Simcox adamantly maintains her position of having no sexual interest in, nor desire for, men. Some seven years after Eliot's death, Simcox writes:

> To say that I never was in love with a mortal man is to say too little; I never wished to be nor contemplated the possibility of being – except in the abstract under the pressure of Mrs Lewes's real & supposed preferences, & that very reluctantly & against the grain. ... As it happened the woman I knew [Eliot] was sweeter & wiser, better & greater than any man of my acquaintance, but I did not fall in love with her person but with her qualities.* [in margin:]* nay this is not quite exact. I did fall in love with her person, so as to care infinitely more for her – qualities & all – than I should care for any human qualities otherwise embodied. (17 October 1887)

The wording of this self-reflexive entry is both precise and considered. There is no indication of an 'intermingling of fantasy with fact'. Simcox remains unshaken in her sexual convictions.

The seemingly boundless passion that Simcox felt for Eliot was as much of the mind, as it was of the body. In an entry of 16 April 1882, Simcox records:

> I shall be released [from Eliot] just 10 years after my first writing to Her little as the years have to show for themselves, they have really been less idle than all but the first of the ten years before. I have learnt to make
>
> nay 3 – whereof one unpublished –
>
> shirts & manage schools, have written two books ^ & lived through the love-passion of my life. Heaven knows I have felt idle enough as the time went by & now I begin to wonder how I shall find as much as that to fill the next decade. – For you see, *all* this came from Her influence. (emphasis original)

Eliot's capacity to affect Simcox's writing is conceived in deeply passionate terms: so much so, that she recalls how Eliot 'has never known how every word of hers enters into my flesh' (17 November 1877). Utilising metaphorical tropes of childbirth, wherein the 'mind' as an erogenous zone functions to create and 're'produce ideas and narrative formulations, she writes: 'She [Eliot] said – Love & feel ... & I wrote a book ... I thought how even my own poor offspring had been born & bred under a glad vision of her imagined approval' (28 November 1878). The exchange of letters and ideas between Simcox and Eliot thus provided a sexual-intellectual dynamic that functioned to recharge both women's desire and motivation to write.

However, it would be a reductive reading of the *Autobiography* to sum up, as Lillian Faderman does, that Simcox's intellectual and writerly 'efforts' were only 'possible because she took Eliot for her muse and model', or that Eliot provided Simcox with 'one of the few stimuli' that occasioned Simcox's 'achievement[s]' (Faderman, 1985: 163). From evidence given in her *Autobiography*, Simcox's network of friends, work colleagues and political comrades was both extensive and impressive. They included Bessie Belloc: co-founder and editor of the *English Woman's Journal*; Barbara Bodichon: co-founder and editor of *English Woman's Journal*, founder of Girton College, Cambridge; Emilia Dilke: women's trades union campaigner; Emily Faithful: co-founder of Victoria Press, a women's printing society; Elizabeth Garrett Anderson: physician and supporter of women's suffrage; Octavia Hill: socialist, philanthropist and secretary for women at the Working Men's Club, lived with Harriet Yorke for last 35 years of her life: they are buried together at Crockham Hill, Kent; Violet Paget (pseud. Vernon Lee): novelist, critic, reputably lesbian; Emma Paterson: leader of the Women's Protective and Provident League, co-founder of Victoria Press, and founder of the Women's Printing Society; Frances Power Cobbe: campaigner for women's rights and anti-vivisectionist; Emilia Dilke (prev. Pattison): women's suffrage campaigner, president of Women's Protective and Provident League, artist and critic, reputedly the source for Dorothea Brooke in Eliot's *Middlemarch*; Helen Taylor: women's suffrage campaigner and socialist.

The stimulation that must have arisen from these connections and networks should not be underestimated. As Liz Stanley points out in her critique of what she terms the 'spotlight approach' of orthodox/canonical auto/biography, we should avoid emphasising

> ... the uniqueness of a particular subject, seen in individualised terms rather than as a social self lodged within a network of others ... [since] it essentialises the self, rather than focusing on the role of social processes in producing – and changing – what a self consists of And it enshrines an entirely de-politicised notion of 'greatness', presenting this as a characteristic of individuals

rather than the product of political processes and constructions. (1992: 131–214)

Thus, while we might inevitably become drawn into the intimate facets and details of women's lives – both in terms of how we interpret and write auto/biographies – to overlook or omit the social and political frameworks of which lives are ineluctably bound-up, can only ever reveal a partial interpretation. Nowhere is this more pertinent, than in the story of 'Miss Williams'.

MISS WILLIAMS

I have discussed the process whereby I 'discovered' the identity of 'Miss Williams' elsewhere (see Polkey, 1995: 150–77). Both Simcox and Williams were part of political networks operating among women in London during the late 1870s and 1880s which campaigned for women's trades union rights and women's suffrage. They each knew Emma Paterson, and their names are listed on the 'provisional committee' of a 'Political Club for Women' in an article written by Williams for *Englishwoman's Review* (15 April 1879, vol. X). Among those registered on the Committee are 'Miss Hamilton' (Simcox's co-partner in the co-operative women's shirtmaking firm) and Emma Paterson. The aim of the Political Club was to 'secure the co-operation of all classes.... The only qualification of membership being interest in social and political questions' (570).

'Miss Williams' was, in fact, Caroline Williams, who gave her address in her *Englishwoman's Review* article, cited above, as '9, Porchester Square, London W'. She published widely on women's suffrage; women's history, organisations and networks; women's writing, newspapers, education and public speaking; as well as women in local government and school boards; and men's views on women's duties (see Polkey, 1995: 169). A 'Miss Williams' attended numerous meetings of the London Association of Schoolmistresses (see Emily Davies Papers, IX/LSM 2); and some of the LAS members were on the provisional committee of the Political Club for women.

The 'Political Club' meeting of 1879 was probably not the first time that Simcox and Williams had met, since in an entry dated 3 November 1878, Simcox writes:

This morning had Miss Orme[15] & Miss Williams to breakfast, who were both very happy in eager discourse. 'Twas not bad of its kind, but on the whole I am not sorry to have outgrown that appetite too, so that it will soon not be as a *pis-aller* but from complete choice that I live my hermit's life. Tomorrow or next day methinks I must wander round there[16] again – now the time is so near I cannot wait patiently to be summoned. – I was a fool not to ask their plans when I was there. – "There" it seems means only the place where she [Eliot] is. I am vexed with myself being so idle, but I doubt whether I physically can help it.

The tone of this entry is telling: signifying ennui, boredom and condescension; above all, there is a preoccupation with 'her': Eliot. And yet, as time passes, the narrative unfolds an altogether more intricate and troubling story.

There are two particular entries in the *Autobiography* which make explicit the extent of Williams's passion for Simcox. The first, written on 23 July 1881, states:

Just after I had come in Miss Williams called. My mother betrayed the fact we were just going to dinner & asked her to wait for me. We began conversation & were just started when she came again to fetch me. I was put out at the discourtesy & interference & bolted half a dinner, fidgetted for an interval & returned. I *hope* I was not to blame – of course I was in some way – the poor creature professed a feeling for me different from what she had ever had for any one, it might make her happiness if I could return it; & then she said – "Imagine what it is to have that feeling & to be obliged to go away from you." I did not feel any unkind dread – What would it be for her *not* to go away – but I thought of my like love & urged upon her that *I* did not deserve such love as I had given to Her [Eliot], it pained me like a blasphemy – I suppose I was wrong to say this – it hurt her & she had not the readiness to seize the confidence as a proof of kindness. She said I was very philosophical & a little cold … she went away a little hurt, though I rather wooed her at last. The only thing that checks my impulses of tenderness is the fear lest there is some flightiness & want of moral balance in her nature. (emphasis original)

Here, Williams's passionate intensity becomes fazed and confounded by despair, and parallels with the Simcox–Eliot relationship are apparent. Significantly though, there is evidence that Simcox was not at all isolated in her same-sex desire for Eliot, since Williams was clearly a woman with whom she talked about, and shared, the sexual nature of that passion. It also becomes apparent that Simcox positions herself as identifying with Williams, not only in terms of the intensity of same-sex erotic passion, but also the pattern of unrequited love: 'I thought of my like love & urged upon her that *I* did not deserve such love as I had given to Her [Eliot], it pained me like a blasphemy' (emphasis original). Moreover, there is the same flirtatious gesturing that Eliot often demonstrated towards Simcox in the lines: 'she went away a little hurt, though I rather wooed her at last'.

A sense of distrust – tension certainly – pervades the narrative, in terms of *how* Simcox perceives Williams: 'the fear lest there is some flightiness & want of moral balance in her nature' There is a possible class distinction to be made between the two women. Williams's disregard for social conventions, as instanced through her interrupting the family meal – which she was, significantly, not invited to join – makes Simcox feel 'put out at the discourtesy & interference & bolted half a dinner, fidgetted for an interval & returned'. Williams's breaking of social civilities is plainly regarded with reproof by Simcox.

In the second entry, made some nine months later, Simcox writes that 'Poor Miss Williams is not to be helped', and goes on to say:

> I do not know that it is my fault, when physical sanity is wanting, one cannot count on establishing a fundamentally wholesome relation, & it was not wholesome as we were. If I made any mistakes, I was not unpunished, for it is not pleasant to me to have quoted to any one those most sacred words of Her [Eliot] to me – still less to have made the sacrifice in vain. Poor thing! I am not very fortunate in my attempts to "play with souls"[17] & have "matter enough to save my own". (6 March 1882)

Simcox does not offer further details as to why she considers the relationship not to be 'wholesome', although her description of Williams lacking in 'physical sanity' suggests that Williams became, or in some way or other threatened to become, 'out' of control and unable to manage the 'sacrifice' expected of her.

But there is arguably an added dimension to the relationship, namely that the same cycle of behaviour appears to be repeating itself as previously shown between Simcox and Eliot. With

Williams, however, Simcox attempts to take the more dominant position, as revealed through her pity and condescension towards the other woman: 'Poor thing! I am not very fortunate in my efforts to "play with souls"'. The extent to which Simcox feels responsible for Williams's 'soul' is made clear in another entry, wherein she explains: 'Miss Williams's soul lays heavy on my conscience; have been glancing at St Ignatius's Life – I wish I had the power of constraining souls' (14 September 1881). Why Simcox should feel so repentant about her treatment of Williams raises some intriguing questions: Did she seduce Williams? Did she break her heart? Did she simply intend to 'play with her soul'?

Caroline Williams's presence in the *Autobiography* is short-lived – she eventually disappears after a couple of guilt-ridden apologies by Simcox about the way in which she behaved towards Williams. But her presence is intriguing, nevertheless. What we can gauge from the journal is that these women conversed about same-sex desire, and that their involvement was entrenched within the dynamics of political activism. The poignancy of unrequited love creates its own tragic spectacle: producing another yarn for critics and biographers to spin.

I return to my opening question: what happens when the lives of women whom we recover become entangled in a recuperative purpose? Having examined what such a project has done to the life of Edith Simcox, my reply falls within three time-frames: past, present and future.

Past tense: Simcox has been construed by some of Eliot's biographers as sad, mad and lonesome. Her 'interest value' is ranked high on the grounds that she knew George Eliot, G. H. Lewes, and many of those who were part of a particular cultural milieu at a particular time in British history. Her 'love-passion' for Eliot increases her value, inasmuch as she can provide a 'lens' through which Eliot can be 'seen'.

Present tense: this chapter scrutinises certain (past-tense) 'versions' of Simcox; it opens up debate and enquiry about how we 'recuperate' a life. The interpretation I offer is based on my own transcription of the *Autobiography*. Hence, new information is offered – principally concerning Caroline Williams – and a reading of Simcox's relationship with Eliot has been suggested that is at variance with the 'sad, mad and lonesome' canonical version. I suggest that, whilst Simcox was indubitably passionate about Eliot, their relationship was fraught with difficulty and challenge; it offers an unseamed story. Moreover, my interpretation takes issue with the 'spotlight' approach to biography (see Stanley, 1992), working, instead, within the paradigm that 'lives' are webbed together, and that individuals formulate networks that shape and impinge on their lives. The persona of 'Edith Simcox' is thus re-configured; it now takes a different shape.

Future tense: this concerns a version of Simcox that you, the reader, will construct on the basis of what you read here. A relationship will have developed, whereby you will piece together your own version of Simcox. It is hoped that some of you *will* want to dig further, and pursue the 'recuperative' project some more. And it is also hoped that someone *will* discover what happened to 'Miss Williams': who her lover(s), friends and colleagues were; the books she read; where she was born; who her parents were; where she is buried; and if she ever got over her love-passion for Edith Simcox. That would be 'recuperation', indeed.

Acknowledgements

My thanks to Julia Swindells and Liz Stanley: their plenary lectures for the 'Representing Lives: Women and Auto/Biography' conference (Nottingham Trent University, 23–25 July 1997) provided the stimulation for this chapter.

Notes

1. The *Autobiography of a Shirt Maker* (1876–1900) was donated to the Bodleian Library, Oxford, in 1958 (Bodleian ref MS, Eng. Misc. d. 494); it has survived the years in relatively good condition. Gerald Bullett (1893–1958), biographer and man-of-letters, was given the journal in 1951 by Mrs Annie L. C. Gill of Leeds, after hearing him discuss George Eliot on BBC's *Woman's Hour* in 1951. Mrs Gill's letters to Bullett are enclosed in the manuscript, in which she explains that 'The diary came into my possession after the death of my son while an undergraduate at Oxford. It was amongst his books and whether he picked it up secondhand, or had it lent I do not know' (7 April 1951, *Autobiography*, p. 179a). It should be noted that George Augustus Simcox, Edith Simcox's brother, was the last surviving member of the

Simcox family. In his will, he directed that 'gifts' be made to Queen's
College, Oxford, where he was a Fellow; the *Autobiography of a Shirt
Maker* was presumably one of those gifts, which explains how it then
came into the 'possession' of Mrs Gill's son. The *Autobiography* contains 189 leaves, and is bound in dark green morocco; the side-edges of
the paper are marbled in blue, red, green and yellow. Originally held
together by a substantial brass key clasp (now broken at the hinge), the
Autobiography is written almost entirely in purple ink. All references to
the *Autobiography* are from my transcriptions.

2.   Norma Vince's article 'The Fiddler, the Angel and the Defiance
     of Antigone: A Reading of Edith Simcox's "Autobiography of
     a Shirtmaker"' (*Women: A Cultural Review*, 6:2, Autumn 1995,
     pp. 43–165) is particularly insightful. But her transcription of Simcox's
     journal contains errors; she also replaces Simcox's use of ampersands
     ('&') with 'and'. Compare Vince's transcription of the 17 June 1880
     entry:

     > It is my hardest brief that the love I bear to you is fruit for your
     > good …

     with the original:

     > It is hardest grief that the love I bear to you is fruitless for your
     > good …

3.   For Simcox the firm was, crucially, a Co-operative enterprise, as out-
     lined in her article 'Eight Years of Co-operative Shirtmaking' in
     which she states her commitment to 'a co-operative workshop, where
     the shirtmakers should be their own employers, and divide among
     themselves the whole price paid by the hosier to the contractor'
     (*Nineteenth Century*, June 1884). See n. 6 below, for further details of
     the firm.

4.   Helen Blackburn, 'Women on the London School Board,
     Englishwoman's Review, 15 December 1879: 545–6.

5.   The International Working Men's Association. The 1st International
     (1864–81) was founded in London, under the organisation of Karl
     Marx. The movement split in 1876, as a result of power struggle
     between Marx and Bakunin. The 2nd International (1889–1914) was
     founded in Paris, and aimed for Socialist revolution through Parlia-
     mentary democracy, and had strong trades union links. It disbanded
     at outbreak of war in 1914. The 3rd International (1919–43) was formed
     by Lenin and founded in Moscow under the aegis of the Communist
     International and was disbanded in 1943 by Stalin.

6.   Mortimer Street, Cavendish Square, London: premises of 'Hamilton &
     Co.', the women's co-operative shirtmaking firm that Simcox ran with
     her co-partner, Mary Hamilton from 1875–84. Hamilton & Co. began
     at 68 Dean Street, Soho, London, and then moved to Mortimer Street
     in 1878. 68 Dean Street is currently under restoration by the English
     Heritage Society.

7.   Constance Mary (née Lubbock) Buxton, married to Sydney Buxton
     who served on the School Board from 1876 to 1882.

8. Blackwood's *Edinburgh Magazine*, first called *The Edinburgh Monthly Magazine*, ran from 1817 to 1905.
9. James Anthony Froude (1818–94), writer, historian, biographer. Simcox is referring to his *History of England* (12 vols), published 1856–70.
10. Elma Stuart (Evorilda Eliza Maria Fraser) (?1837–1903), a close friend of George Eliot and buried in the grave next to hers, 28 January 1903. Her tombstone is inscribed: 'One whom for eight and a half and a half blessed years George Eliot called by the sweet name of "Daughter"'. Stuart's son, Roland Stuart, edited her *Letters from G. E. to Elma Stuart 1872–1880*, published in 1909.
11. George Eliot: she lived, unmarried, as his 'wife', with George Henry Lewes from 1854 until his death in 1878.
12. Hamilton & Co. (see n. 6 above).
13. Mary Hamilton, Simcox's partner at Hamilton & Co., was leaving the firm; Simcox had to arrange for a replacement.
14. Gertrude (née Hill) Lewes, married to G. H. Lewes's eldest son, Charles Lewes; sister of the socialist and philanthropist, Octavia Hill.
15. Eliza Orme took a law degree but was not allowed to practice in the Courts. She was a member of the Women's National Liberal Association, and led a team of women Assistant Commissioners for the Royal Commission on Labour in 1892. Orme is listed as a member of Provisional Committee to set up a 'Political Club for Women' in which her address is listed as 38 Chancery Lane, London WC (see *Englishwoman's Review*, vol. ix, 1878: 569–70). She published a number of articles: 'How Poor Ladies Live' (*Nineteenth Century*, 1897), 'Our Female Criminals' (*Fortnightly Review*, 1898).
16. The Priory, 21 North Bank, Regents Park, London: the home of Eliot and Lewes, 1863–80.
17. A quotation from Robert Browning's 'A Light Woman'; see Polkey 1995, for a discussion of this connection.

References

Archives & Manuscripts

Blackburn Collection, Girton College Library, Cambridge
Emily Davies Papers, Girton College Library, Cambridge
Simcox, Edith Jemima (1876–1900) *Autobiography of a Shirt Maker*, Bodleian Library, Oxford (MS, Eng. Misc. d. 494)

Biographical

Allen, Walter (1965) *George Eliot*, London: Weidenfeld & Nicholson
Beer, Gillian (1986) *George Eliot*, Brighton: Harvester

—— (Autumn 1995) 'Passion, Politics, Philosophy: the Work of Edith Simcox', Women: *A Cultural Review*, 6:2, pp. 66–179

Cross, John W., ed. (1885) *George Eliot's Lift as Related in Her Letters and Journals*, Edinburgh and London: William Blackwood

Haight, Gordon ([1961] 1978) 'Introduction', McKenzie, K. A., *Edith Simcox and George Eliot*, Oxford: Oxford University Press

—— (1968) *George Eliot: A Biography*, Oxford: Oxford University Press

—— ed. (1968) *The George Eliot Letters*, Oxford: Oxford University Press

—— ed. (1985) *Selections from George Eliot's Letters*, New Haven and London: Yale University Press

Karl, Frederick (1996) *George Eliot. A Biography*, London: Flamingo

Laski, Marghanita (1973) *George Eliot and Her World*, London: Thames & Hudson

McKenzie, K. A. ([1961] 1978) *Edith Simcox and George Eliot*, Oxford: Oxford University Press

Redinger, Ruby V. (1975) *George Eliot: the Emergent Self*, London: Bodley Head

Stuart, Roland, ed. (1909) *Letters from George Eliot to Elma Stuart, 1872–1880*, London: Simpkin, Marshall, Hamilton and Kent

Taylor, Ina (1989) *George Eliot. Woman of Contradiction*, London: Weidenfeld & Nicolson

Uglow, Jenny (1987) *George Eliot*, London: Virago

General Reference

Clapinson, Mary and Rogers, T. D. (1991) *Summary Catalogue of Post-Medieval Western Manuscripts in the Bodleian Library, Oxford. Acquisitions 1916–1975*, vol. 1, Oxford: Clarendon Press

Dictionary of National Biography (1975) (complete text, compact edition), vols, 1–2, Oxford: Oxford University Press

Faderman, Lillian (1985) *Surpassing the Love of Men: Romantic Friendship and Love Between Women from the Renaissance to the Present*, London: Women's Press

Huff, Cynthia (1985) *British Women's Diaries: a Descriptive Bibliography of Selected Nineteenth-Century Women's Manuscript Diaries*, New York: AMS Press

Kanner, Barbara (1987) *Women in English Social History, 1800–1914: a Guide to Research*, vol. 3, New York: Garland

—— (1988) *Women in English Social History, 1800–1914: a Guide to Research*, vol. 2, New York: Garland

Polkey, Pauline (1996) 'Collaboration and Co-operation: a Contextured-Political Reading of Edith Simcox's Autobiography of a Shirt Maker', in Lucas, John, ed., *Writing and Radicalism*, Harlow: Addison Wesley Longman, pp. 129–50

Simcox, Edith Jemima (1877) *Natural Law: an Essay in Ethics*, London: Trubner

—— (November 1878) 'The Organisation of Unremunerative Industry', *Fraser's Magazine*, pp. 609–21

——(February 1879) 'The Industrial Employment of Women', *Fraser's Magazine*, pp. 246–55

——(May 1880) 'Ideals of Feminine Usefulness', *Fortnightly Review*, pp. 656–71

——(June 1884) 'Eight Years of Co-operative Shirtmaking', *Nineteenth Century*, pp. 1037–54

——(September 1887) 'The Capacity of Women', *Nineteenth Century*, pp. 391–402

——(1894) *Primitive Civilizations, or Outlines of the History of Ownership in Archaic Communities*, vol. 1, London: Swan Sonnenschein

——(1897) *Primitive Civilizations, or Outlines of the History of Ownership in Archaic Communities*, vol. 2, London: Swan Sonnenschein

Vince, Norma (Autumn 1995) 'The Fiddler, the Angel and Defiance of Antigone: A Reading of Edith Simcox's 'Autobiography of a Shirtmaker'', Women: a Cultural Review, 6:2, pp. 143–65

Webb, Beatrice (1980–5) *The Diary of Beatrice Webb*, N. and J. Mackenzie, eds, vols. i–iv, London: Virago (in association with LSE)

Williams, Caroline (1874) 'Shall a Women's Householder's League be Formed?', *Englishwoman's Review*, V, pp. 186–8

——(1875) 'Union Among Women', *Englishwoman's Review*, VI, pp. 55–7

——(1875) 'Suffrage', *Englishwoman's Review*, VI, pp. 79–81

——(1875) 'Women's Protective and Provident League', *Englishwoman's Review*, VI, pp. 84–5

——(April 1876) 'Suffrage', *Englishwoman's Review*, VII, pp. 165–6

——(15 April 1878) 'Three Decades of Progress', *Englishwoman's Review*, IX, pp. 337–44

——(14 September 1878) 'Suffrage', *Englishwoman's Review*, IX, pp. 413–14

——(15 October 1878) 'Women's Newspapers. A Sketch of the Periodical Literature Devoted to the Woman Question', *Englishwoman's Review*, IX, pp. 433–40

——(14 December 1878) 'Pegging Away', *Englishwoman's Review*, IX, pp. 529–37

——(14 December 1878) 'Political Club for Women', *Englishwoman's Review*, IX, pp. 569–70

——(15 February 1879) 'Duties and Rights of Women in Local Government', *Englishwoman's Review*, X, pp. 83–5

——(5 March 1879) 'The Issue of Two Debates', *Englishwoman's Review*, X, pp. 97–109

——(15 April 1879) 'Political Club for Women', *Englishwoman's Review*, vol. X, pp. 180–1

——(15 May 1879) 'Participation of Women in Local Government', *Englishwoman's Review*, X, pp. 206–12

——(15 October 1879) 'Men's Views on Women's Duties', *Englishwoman's Review*, X, pp. 448–50

——(14 December 1889) 'Literature of the Women's Suffrage Movement in Britain', *Englishwoman's Review*, XX, pp. 529–32

6

Travelling towards Selfhood: Victorian Religion and the Process of Female Identity

JOSS WEST-BURNHAM

In her essay on 'Culture, Cultural Studies and Historians', Carolyn Steedman reminds us that 'history is the most impermanent of written forms: it is only ever an account that will last for a while' (1992: 614). She refers then to the ways in which new excavations in the practice of historical research of different facts and further information work to challenge, change and question 'the historian's map of the past' (1992: 614). This act of what Steedman calls 'narrative destabilization' signifies that 'the written history is a story that can only be told by the implicit understanding that *things are not over*, that the story isn't finished, can never be finished, for some new item of information may alter the account that has been given' (1992: 614; emphasis original). This has particular resonance for feminist scholars, teachers and readers because, of course, the practices of feminist research and interpretation has consistently meant the retelling of stories or, as Adrienne Rich suggests (1980), at least the adoption of the processes of 're-vision' when working with narratives historical and or literary from the past.[1]

These processes of relocation and repositioning are additionally important for feminist scholars working across a number of perceived or recognised academic territories or disciplines: the latter term 'discipline', itself, invoking ideas about order, obeying certain rules and not contravening the dominant modes and methods of inquiry. In this way, feminist scholars, working across disciplines, can be seen by some as recalcitrant scholars: not fixed in one place, but perhaps travelling across various academic and intellectual boundaries; not wanting to provide arguments of closure, but rather asking questions which begin to open up the territories and 'free' us from received wisdom(s). In this essay, the disciplines of history, literature and religious studies are traversed and revisited in an attempt to re-envisage some of the issues with respect to selfhood and questions of female identity in the work of some nineteenth-century women writers.

In many respects, this transgression across boundaries as a mode of investigation can also be seen to be mimetic of the territories transgressed by the three women studied here: Grace Aguilar (1816–47), Harriet Martineau (1802–76), and George Eliot (1819–90). The reason for this selection is largely determined by the need to investigate women writers who were located in different religious denominations in order to ascertain similarities and differences with regard to issues of selfhood. In particular, I intend to look at how their religious placing worked to enable or disempower them with regard to issues of creativity and publication. Moveover, the choice is also determined by my desire to have a grouping which included both 'well-known' nineteenth century figures, as well as those which are more obscured by, or lost to, history. Grace Aguilar, for example, is now largely unknown and yet in her own time she was a best-selling popular novelist as well as a Jewish historian of some acclaim.

Research into these women's lives and their writings raises a number of important questions: not only about these women as individuals, but also the placing and perception of them and their ideas and influence for us today. The work of June O'Connor (1995) has been particularly thought-provoking in this regard, as she draws out the importance of feminists first establishing the origins and boundaries of our own knowledge(s) from which we begin (1995: 47). O'Connor suggests that 'The most powerful ideas are those *we think with*. They are the ideas that lie "behind" our eyes, enabling us: what we do see is shaped by them' (1995: 47; emphasis original). In order to demonstrate further what she means, O'Connor invokes a Chinese proverb: 'Two-thirds of what we see is behind our eyes', which means that 'much of what we see, we see because we have been trained, educated and socialised to see in certain ways' (1995: 47).

As an interdisciplinary scholar with some expertise in the Victorian period, I 'knew' that religion was an important phenomenon to all who lived in the nineteenth century. I also 'knew' that there had been major controversies within various religious denominations during this period, as the wider cultural debates and the realignment

of religion as its central place became challenged from many directions: by biblical and historical criticism, scientific discourse, as well
as political resurgence of socialism which provided a secular rather
than a spiritual home from which to voice dissent or agitate from.
What I didn't know – as a feminist cultural materialist – was (that
behind my eyes perhaps?) exactly how all these debates affected
particular individuals, their lives and their works. So, probably
typical of much research, from one small sentence this project
began.

This sentence: 'Women are by their nature more spiritual than
men, essentially more religious' (Obelkevich, 1978: 8), sent me on a
quest which is still only partly complete. The limitations of space
here prevent further detailed expositions regarding this larger project; but for now it is important to note how the focus of interdisciplinarity became a way in which issues of 'religion' could be fully
interrogated.[2] As with all projects, the selection process, the priori-
tization of materials and the consequent unearthing of findings not
envisaged, lead to much reshaping, rereading and change: a process
which, in itself, continues as part and parcel of feminist scholarship.[3] The model adopted by O'Connor remains, for me, a central
focus as a methodology. This is the three 'R's method of enquiry:
re-reading, re-conceiving and reconstructing works toward what
she calls 'reconstructing the past on the basis of new information
and, secondly, employing new paradigms for thinking, seeing,
understanding and valuing' (O'Connor, 1995: 102; 103; 104).

Ursula King notes how, in the study of religion and gender, two
fundamental problems arise for feminist scholars: 'one has to do
with the subject matter of the research, the other with the attitude
of the researcher' (King, 1995: 19). By this, she refers in particular
to the androcentric framework within which feminist scholars
have to work: 'The sources, concepts, models and theories of religious studies are male-driven and male-centred; they operate with
a generic masculine which implies that men have almost always
spoken for and about women' (1995: 19). She does, however, suggest a way in which this can be obviated asserting that 'women are
(were) not only readers of androcentric texts, they are also writers
and creators of such texts' (1995: 19). Drawing on King's approach,
this chapter focuses on religion via a gynocentric approach by
looking at 'women as *writers*: that is women who, as their own
agents, create their own structures of meaning' (King, 1995: 19;
emphasis original).

GRACE AGUILAR (1816–47)

To date, Grace Aguilar has received very little critical attention as a writer of popular novels in the early nineteenth century. She, along with another woman writer in this study, Harriet Martineau, falls into that 'gap' in the mapping of 'English' literature that runs from 'Jane Austen and the sudden eruption in 1847 of the Brontë sisters in the literary scene' (Figes, 1982: 113). Grace Aguilar was born in Hackney, England, the only daughter of Jewish parents of Spanish descent.[4] Whilst educated at home by her parents, Grace Aguilar's acquisition of knowledge cannot be viewed as limited or limiting since the curriculum included the classics, history and languages. Both her learning schedule and her early foray into writing and producing plays and poetry was also 'aided' by ill-health. This pattern is also a feature in Harriet Martineau's childhood.

However, it was to be as a consequence of her father's death when she was 19 years old that Grace felt the need to write: principally in order to provide a subsistence allowance for herself and her mother. In this respect, there emerges yet another analogy with Harriet Martineau who also had to earn her living (and keep her mother) by a mixture of sewing and writing following the collapse of the family business and her father's death. Thus, this tragic family occurrence became a main impetus for writing: not just for pleasure, but for profit. Grace's faith in Judaism also provided her with a strong basis from which to write, and her Jewish 'history', combined with her conviction that Judaism had as much to offer as Christian religions with regard to providing moral codes and guidance on social responsibilities. In fact, Grace Aguilar's early published works can be read alongside many Christian etiquette books which are primarily aimed at the woman reader, outlining their duties and responsibilities in the world as well as in the home.[5] Close examination of Aguilar's books also reveals an incisive critique of Christian philosophy and morality within the prevailing ideologies of femininity during the early nineteenth century, as seen in her remark that 'Christian writers have unjustly identified feminine virtue with Christian virtue' (1847, Preface). She maintains in her first published works, *The Spirit of Judaism, The Women of Israel*, and elsewhere, that Jewish women have a station to uphold, and a 'mission' to perform not merely as daughters, wives and mothers, but also as witnesses of that faith which first raised, cherished and defended them (see Todd, 1989: 5).

From these more factual 'histories' or 'narratives of the past', Grace Aguilar later turned to the production of popular fiction. But it is here that her Jewish faith can be seen as becoming problematic for two reasons. First, she wants her work to be successful and taken seriously, and second, she does not want to offend a largely Christian audience. Thus, in the Preface to her novel *Home Influence, A Tale for Mother's and Daughters* (1847), interestingly written in the third person, she is at pains to assure her readers that:

> Having been brought before the public principally as the author of Jewish works, and as an explainer of the Hebrew Faith, some Christian mothers might fear that the present work has the same tendency, and hesitate to place it in the hands of their children. She, therefore, begs to assure them, that as a simple domestic story, the characters in which are all Christians, believing in and practising that religion, all *doctrinal* points have been most carefully avoided, the author seeking only to illustrate the spirit of their piety, and the virtues always designated as the Christian virtues hence proceeding. (1847, Preface; emphasis original)

Grace Aguilar states that her sole aim 'with regard to Religion has been to incite a train of serious and loving thoughts towards God and man, especially towards those with whom He has linked us in the precious ties of parent and child, brother and sister, master and pupil' (1847, Preface). Within the domestic environment, the familiar provides the setting for this particular fiction and the focus on the moral education of children is the central argument throughout. The maxim provided in her Preface that '**Sentiment** is the vehicle of **Thought** and **Thought** the origin of **Action**' makes very clear the trajectory of association and connection.

Grace Aguilar's output in relation to her relatively short life span was quite prolific; and indeed all of her work received favourable reviews. An example of the reception of her work can be demonstrated from this extract from Mrs Hall's *Pilgrimages to English Shrines* (1872), who records that:

> Grace Aguilar wrote and spoke as one inspired; she condensed and spiritualised, and all her thoughts and feelings were steeped in the essence of celestial love and truth. To those who really knew Grace Aguilar, all eulogium falls short of her desserts, and

she has left a blank in her particular walk of literature, which we never expect to see filled up. (1872: 80)

This 'blank' can also be seen to apply to any critical reception to Grace Aguilar in the twentieth century.

HARRIET MARTINEAU (1802–76)

A similar fate was to befall the writings of Harriet Martineau, for, until the republication by Virago Press of her novel *Deerbrook* (1839; 1983), and her two-volumed *Autobiography* (1877; 1983), her work was largely unknown and unobtainable for contemporary readers despite an extremely prolific publication during her own lifetime.[6] Harriet Martineau also shares with Grace Aguilar an ancestry that can be traced as one of a persecuted minority. She provides evidence of this in the first volume of her *Autobiography*:

> On the occasion of the Revocation of the Edict of Nantes, in 1688, a surgeon of the name Martineau, and a family of the name of Pierre, crossed the channel, and settled with other Huguenot refugees, in England. My ancestor married a young lady of the Pierre family, and settled in Norwich, where his descendants afforded a succession of surgeons up to my own day. (1877; 1983: 7–8)

The presentation of her personal context is highly significant in relation to the focus and importance Harriet Martineau gives to the particular cultural formation of her 'inherited' Dissent. Martineau thus establishes herself in a nineteenth century Unitarian context founded in the tradition of Old Dissent. There is also an implicit acknowledgement of legislation concerning the Act of Toleration of 1813, since, prior to this, Unitarians had been excluded from power and prestige in public office. As a sect, the Unitarians had in fact made a virtue of exclusion, culminating in a strong tendency to political radicalism.

The Unitarian church and community was also to provide great solace to Harriet Martineau as a child. She records in her *Autobiography* how the attendance at services of the Octagon Chapel in Norwich made 'Sundays … marked days, and pleasantly marked, on the whole' (1877; 1983: 11, vol.1). She also reflects that, as an adult looking back on her life, it is solely religion that provided her with support and personal pleasure. Just as Grace Aguilar is instructed by her mother from an early age to pursue daily readings from the Christian Bible, so too with Harriet Martineau, who, at the age of seven years, records a resolution to 'become practically religious with all my strength' (1877; 1983: 28, vol.1). Thus, religion for Harriet Martineau, as for Grace Aguilar, provides both a resource and a comfort.

Harriet Martineau's family faith and her studies in religion inspired her to put her ideas into print in a very similar way to that of Grace Aguilar. Martineau constructs three essays (which all received prizes from the Central Unitarian Association), in which ideas were put forward which could be used to convert the Catholics, the Jews and the Mohammedans to the Unitarian faith. While the essays, in themselves, may not have actually converted anyone, they did supply Harriet with a taste for receiving financial reward for her writing; in addition to which she was able to extend her own ideas about religion and the nature of belief itself. Other publications were to follow, and Harriet's next publication, 'Female Writers on Practical Divinity' (1822), was placed in the Unitarian journal *the Monthly Repository*. There is some dispute over the signatory name used by Harriet Martineau in these early publications, but for this particular one there is evidence that she used the name Discipulus.[7]

The taking of this pseudonym is extremely poignant, for Discipulus is the masculine form of the Latin for learner or apprentice. A particularly fitting title then, for a young new writer beginning the craft of writing; but also – for contemporary readers perhaps – problematic with its masculine connotations and associations. The taking of the masculine pseudonym has further significance in the context of its day, for to take on or adopt the masculine was also to assume that what one wrote, would obtain a fairer hearing and less partial judgements. As one contemporary commentator observed:

> Surely, as our Discipulus takes her place in this list with George Eliot, George Sand and Currer, Ellis and Acton Bell, a great deal is disclosed to us about how women in the past have had to make their way to recognition against the tide of public opinion. (Fenwick Miller, 1884: 39)

There may be even further conjectures to be made in this case however, because Harriet Martineau's 'Female Writers on Practical

Divinity' was intended for a Unitarian journal; and the areas of religious and theological debate were (or have been constructed as) the province of the masculine. Women, particularly middle-class women, were 'protected' from the public realm and hence thought unfit or ill-equipped to comment upon these worldly issues. Therefore some discussion of this first publication by Harriet Martineau is both important and useful in terms of the way in which the contents of this early work can be seen, with hindsight, to be a prolepsis for what is to come later in her career and intellectual development.

The opening words of 'Female Writers on Practical Divinity' are noteworthy with regard to the subject matter (women) and the light it shed on Harriet Martineau's own position regarding the placement of female intellectuals and the concerns of theology. She writes:

> I do not know whether it has been remarked by others as well as myself, that some of the finest and most useful English works on the subject of Practical divinity are by female authors. I suppose it is owing to the peculiar susceptibility of the female mind, and its consequent warmth of feeling, that its productions, when they are really valuable, find a more ready way to the heart than those of the other sex; and it gives me great pleasure to see women gifted with superior talents applying those talents to promote the course of religion and virtue. (Martineau, 1884: 40)

One is conscious here of the irony of masquerade at work as Harriet Martineau (writing as the male apprentice) also takes on the mantle of masculine authority and judgement to pour praise on the women and, of course, on her hidden 'self'. This vein continues throughout. The article ends:

> I cannot better conclude than with the hope that these examples of what may be done may excite a noble emulation in their own sex and in ours such a conviction of the value of the female mind, as shall overcome our long cherished prejudices, and induce us to give our earnest endeavours to the promotion of womens' best interests. (Martineau, 1884: 42)

In some ways then, this can be read as a clarion call for other women to take up the pen and write on religious and theological matters. But, perhaps more importantly in the context of nineteenth century attitudes, it also points up issues of propriety and gender, as instanced by her writing a note to 'other' male readers to rethink their hitherto prejudicial stances to the female intellect.

The tension between this resounding prose and Martineau's need to keep her authorial identity a secret is remarked upon within the *Autobiography*, where she records her own awareness of the impediment of propriety and femininity with regard to writing and public credibility.

> It was not thought proper for young ladies to study very conspicuously; and especially with pen in hand. Young ladies (at least in Provincial towns), were expected to sit down in the parlor and sew – doing reading aloud was permitted, or to practice their music, but so as to fit to receive callers without any signs of blue-stockingism which could be reported abroad. (Martineau, 1877; 1983: 100, vol.1)

Despite these obstacles, Harriet Martineau continued her writing endeavours; a year later she anonymously published *Devotional Exercises: Consisting of Reflections and Prayers for the Use of Young Persons, to which is added a Treatise on the Lord's Supper* (1823). This text is constructed, in part, as a devotional exercise to evaluate the Scriptures; but it is also a text which the individual reader can use to reflect upon their own behaviours and psychological predispositions and habits. *Devotional Exercises* can also be read in connection to the social etiquette texts of the period with its highly didactic tone and its implicit assumptions about dominant femininity and Christianity. It has a number of exercises and affirmations, for example, in the section called 'Duties on the Sabbath':

> Great as are the delights of devotion in times of prosperity, in affliction their value will be infinitely increased. From the portion of sorrow which has been my lot, I am aware of the insufficiency of worldly comfort. The consolations of religion alone are able to relive the wounded heart. (1823: 3)

The clear emphasis here on the personal resource of religion to individuals draws on Harriet Martineau's own experience. This connects to the self-reflexive representation of her own childhood as deeply unhappy; one where, through a series of episodes of ill-health and parental neglect, Harriet Martineau had herself sought refuge and relief in religion.

Both Martineau and Aguilar maintain a stance of social action and guidance throughout their literary output, and their work had considerable effect on other women. While both women moved on to writing fiction, they still retained a particular religious dimension in the execution of their plots and narratives. In a letter to Harriet Martineau about her novel *Deerbrook*, Charlotte Brontë (writing as Currer Bell) notes how this novel has 'really done him [*sic*] good, added to his stock of ideas, and rectified his views of life' (Martineau, 1877; 1983: 322, vol.1). Here, the 'doubleness' of association with both women writers masquerading as male, and yet recognising and identifying with each others work and ideas as women, is significant in terms of the way in which issues of female identity and intellectual networks existed during this period.

GEORGE ELIOT (1819–90)

George Eliot's personal life of change and transition from faith to unbelief is regarded by some critics as symbolic or indicative of the period in matters religious. One of these, Basil Willey, asserts,

> ... needs to occupy a central place when discussing the main currents of thought and belief in Nineteenth century England for [Eliot's] life, her intellectual biography becomes a graph of its most decided trend starting from Evangelical Christianity to doubt to reinterpreted Christ and religion to humanity – beginning with God it ends with Duty. (Willey, 1964: 215)

However, there are limitations to this model, since it works to suggest that the image of her individual journey from belief, to doubt, and eventually to unbelief operates as a simple, uncomplex, linear paradigm. Such a trajectory works to deny the complexity of these issues, and denies an all-consuming interest in religion and knowledge about religious matters that propelled and preoccupied George Eliot throughout her life and her writings. Such a position can be substantiated through reading her Letters and her Writers Notebook.[8] One illustration from her Letters finds her giving advice to Emmanuel Deutsch (a Jewish scholar and expert on the Near East) to 'return often to that note to reproach for unashamed ignorance, and insist that the conscientious effort to *know* is part of religion' (cited in Haight, 1985: 334; my emphasis). For Eliot then, the epistemological significance of religion should not be overlooked.

George Eliot's loss of faith is often located to 1842, when she refused to attend church with her father: a period of her life which she describes as 'Holy War'. However, on closer examination of her letters, there is much evidence to suggest that Eliot's concern with religion (as both knowledge system and practical intervention to do good) remain with her. In a letter written to Harriet Beecher Stowe on 8 May 1869, for example, Eliot proclaims:

> I believe that religion too has to be modified – "developed", according to the dominant phrase and that a religion more perfect than any yet prevalent, must express less care for personal consolation, a more deeply-awing sense of responsibility to man, springing from sympathy with that which all things is most certainly known to us, the difficulty of the human lot. I do not find my temple in Pantheism, which, whatever might be its value speculatively, could not yield a practical religion, since it is an attempt to look at the universe from the outside of our relations to it (that Universe) as human beings. As healthy, sane human beings we must love and hate – love what is good for mankind, hate what is evil for mankind. For years, of my youth, I dwelt in dreams of a pantheistic sort, falsely supposing that I was enlarging my sympathy. But I have *travelled far away* from that time. (cited in Haight, 1985: 360; my emphasis)

One can see here the influence, on the now mature and successful writer, of the ideas from Strauss and Feuerbach;[9] but one is also reminded of an earlier influence on George Eliot, namely: her friend and tutor Maria Lewis, whose 'serious evangelicalism rested on the diligent study of the Scriptures' (Haight, 1985: 9). Indeed, it was Lewis who fostered in her devoted pupil a belief that religious practices in everyday life included not only close reading of the Bible, but also visits to the sick and the needy.

Like Grace Aguilar and Harriet Martineau, George Eliot's first entry into print is empowered by her religious interests, for in 1840, at the age of 21, she published 'On Being a Saint' in *the Christian Observer*. The form of the work is also important, because it is a poem which records an individual saying goodbye to all earthly things apart from the Bible (Haight, 1985: 25–6). This poem has received little attention, but its significance should not be over-looked since George Eliot returns to the poetic form again to explore other religious issues in 1868, when she published her poetic drama, *The Spanish Gypsy*.

The statement from Eliot of 'travelling far away', in her letter to Harriet Beecher Stowe, quoted previously, continues to work well as a metaphor for the three women discussed here, in terms of their journeys towards selfhood and identity through the processes of creativity. Ideas about travelling become very important in a number of ways. Fundamentally, to travel or move from a to b (literally/intellectually) denotes an aspect of personal transformation; but it also provides a plot that makes the story of a life worth telling.[10] This is perhaps most obvious in the literary texts later produced by the women under discussion here: Grace Aguilar's novels – represented here by the example of *Home Influence* (1847), Harriet Martineau's *Deerbrook* (1839) and George Eliot's lesser-known epic poetic drama *The Spanish Gypsy* (1868). These ideas are also encoded within fictional adventures, in which female heroines have a 'larger-than-life' role to surmount: not only with regard to their personal problems, but also to provide support and knowledge for others. A key element in these plots is the desire to reach some spiritual resolution and understanding of the individual and her place/role within the wider social and cultural context. In some cases, this spiritual resolution leads to religious conversion or confirmation within a wider exploration of religiousity via practical acts of human sympathy and goodness. These sometimes read, in the case of Eliot's fictional heroines for instance, like extreme acts of sacrifice and personal renunciation for the sake of others.

It is impossible to read these fictional representations without encountering the array of religious iconography which appears to have been employed deliberately to articulate questions of selfhood and destiny. It is also pertinent here to note that issues of gender differentiation become manifest when the landscape depicted in their writings moves beyond the enclosed domestic sphere central to the dominant myths and stereotypes of femininity that we have of nineteenth-century 'English' woman. Indeed, it is possible to assert that one of the reasons why George Eliot's *The Spanish Gypsy* changes location – from the familiar 'English' domestic terrain of many of her novels, to fifteenth-century Spain – is in order to allow her the possibility of asking questions with respect to gender, class, race and religion. By placing her narrative plot in a different country and a different cultural context, the past provides a different, and perhaps 'safer', discursive space for her as a woman writer to raise issues and yet still retain propriety. Such a strategy enables her to present a new perspective or critique on issues of gender and 'home', and work against ideas about woman enclosed within the domestic space. This allows, for example, the heroine of *The Spanish Gypsy* – Fedalma – to abandon a 'traditional' pathway of marriage and security under patriarchy, in favour of her taking on 'social, public duty' as leader of the homeless gypsy tribe, and to lead them on another journey from Spain (where they suffer deprivation and persecution) to their 'spiritual' homeland of Africa.

In the abandonment of the personal life, George Eliot depicts a heroine who foregoes a life of personal happiness and love in favour of 'mothering' her tribe and working for the greater good of others.[11] Eliot thus begins to ascribe to many of the social and political challenges taking place in the nineteenth century, using religion as one of the key areas of growth, development and 'home' for women's self-identification. Indeed, Eliot is using religion as a discursive framework: its legitimate status is primary, but she is also subversively deploying it in relation to women's autonomy and their public role.[12]

Through the employment of strategies of investigation raised at the beginning of this chapter, there are 'still stories to be told' about the impact of religion on issues of female identity. The writings of Aguilar, Martineau and Eliot can be seen as the beginnings of a wider field of research that embraces the continued need for cross-disciplinary scholarship. Here, through the adoption of the motif of the 'traveller' – through culture, history (time), places (space) – these writers can be seen to have adopted a model/form of representation which both transgresses and challenges the 'perceived' or 'received' versions of them, their lives and their works. This trope of new territories – of crossing borders – thus becomes a point of intersection, a participatory hermeneutic.[13]

Notes

1.   Adrienne Rich, 'When We Dead Awaken: Writing as Re-Vision' in A. Rich, *On Lies, Secrets & Silence: Selected Prose, 1966–1978*, London: Virago Press (1980: 35). In this essay Rich states: 'Re-vision – the act of looking back, of seeing with fresh eyes, of entering an old text from a new

critical direction – is for women more than a chapter in cultural history: it is an act of survival.'

2. The work of June O'Connor has been very instructive and influential, see her essay 'The Epistemological Significance of Feminist Research in Religion', in U. King, ed., *Religion & Gender*, Oxford: Basil Blackwell (1995: 45–65).

3. In the essay referred to in note 2, above, O'Connor notes how 'feminist work is investigatory. It is also much more than investigatory. It is transformative in character.... The investigative arm of feminist inquiry leads to the transformative function of feminist inquiry' (King, 1995: 48).

4. An interesting cross-over of relationships is beginning to emerge between the 'actual' real-life record of Grace Aguilar and the fictional encodement of issues to do with Spanish Jewry in George Eliot's poetic drama *The Spanish Gypsy*, which is also an element of this research. Grace Aguilar also composed a novel about events in fifteenth century Spain and the key concern of the narrative of *The Vale of Cedars or The Martyr: A Story of Spain in the Fifteenth Century*, London: Groombridge (1876), is the depiction of a Jewish utopian society at that time.

5. The most well-known of these being Sarah Stickney Ellis's *The Women of England: Their Social Duties and Domestic Habits* (1839); *The Mothers of England* (1843); *The Wives of England* (1843); and *The Daughters of England* (1845). Further useful references to texts of this kind can be found in Martha Vicinus, ed., *Suffer and Be Still: Women in the Victorian Age*, London: Methuen (1980: 178–81).

6. These Virago editions are used throughout this chapter for citation purposes.

7. Harriet Martineau claims in her *Autobiography* that she signed her early writings 'V' from Norwich, whereas Mrs Fenwick Miller in her early biography of Harriet Martineau (*Harriet Martineau*, London: W.H. Allen (1884)) presents convincing evidence from facsimiles that the early signature was used more commonly that of Discipulus.

8. This is not always a straightforward task because of the way in which they were first edited by George Eliot's husband, John Cross (*George Eliot's Life, as related in her Letters and Journals*, London: William Blackwood (1885)) who was concerned to delete some sections he considered ill-advised to have published. Later publications by Gordon Haight – *George Eliot, A Biography*, Harmondsworth: Penguin (1985) and *Selections from George Eliot's Letters*, New Haven: Yale University Press (1985) – while receiving accolades as 'definitive' and 'true', can also be seen to adopt an unquestioning stance to Cross's approach. In much of my research, these matters have been interrogated with the aid of the publication by Joseph Wiesenfarth, ed., *George Eliot: A Writer's Notebook 1854–79, and Uncollected Writings*, Charlottesville: University Press of Virginia (1981).

9. George Eliot translates their works – Strauss's *Life of Jesus* (1848) and Feuerbach's *Essence of Christianity* (1854) – before she embarks upon her career as a novelist, marked by publication of *Scenes from Clerical Life* in 1856.

94 Joss West-Burnham

10. I am indebted to Karen Lawrence and her arguments *in Penelope Voyages*, Cornell University Press (1994) for this line of thought and perception.
11. I expand on these issues in more detail in 'Fedalma: "The Angel of a Homeless Tribe"': Issues of Religion, Race and Gender in George Eliot's Poetic Drama *The Spanish Gypsy*', in Anne Hogan, Andrew Bradstock, Mary Read, eds, *Women of Faith in Victorian Culture: Reassessing the Angel in the House*, London: Macmillan (1997).
12. I am grateful to the editor, Pauline Polkey, for making these connections overt.
13. Ursula King uses this term to describe the reflective nature of the feminist researcher to the cultural context of her research and her own position in it. I think it is also possible to see this practice in operation in the work and lives of the women under investigation here.

References

Aguilar, G. (1847), *Home Influence, A Tale for Mothers Daughters*, London: Routledge
Aguilar, G. (1876) *The Vale of Cedars or The Martyr: A Story of Spain in the Fifteenth Century*, London: Groombridge
Cross, J. (1885) *George Eliot's Life, as related in her Letters & Journals*, London: William Blackwood
Eliot, G. ([1858] 1973) *Scenes of Clerical Life*, Harmondsworth: Penguin Books
Eliot, G. (1868) *The Spanish Gypsy*, London: William Blackwood
Eliot, G. ([1871–2] 1865) *Middlemarch*, Harmondsworth: Penguin Books
Eliot, G. ([1876] 1967) *Daniel Deronda*, Harmondsworth: Penguin Books
Eliot, G. (1884) *Essays & Leaves from a Notebook*, London: William Blackwood
Figes, E. (1982) *Sex & Subterfuge*, London: Macmillan
Fenwick Miller, F. (1884) *Harriet Martineau*, London: W.H. Allen
Grossberg, L., Nelson, C., Treicher, P. (1992) *Cultural Studies*, London: Routledge
Haight, G. (1985) *George Eliot, A Biography*, New York and London: Yale University Press
Haight, G., ed. (1985) *Selections from George Eliot's Letters*, New York and London: Yale University Press
Hall, Mrs (1987) *Pilgrimages to English Shrines*, London: Goombridge & Sons
King, U., ed. (1995) *Religion & Gender*, Basil Blackwell, Oxford
Lawrence, K. R. (1994) *Penelope Voyages, Women & Travel in the British Literary Tradition*, Ithaca and London: Cornell University Press
Martineau, H. (1823) *Devotional Exercises Consisting of Reflections and Prayers for the use of Young Persons to which is Added a Treatise on the Lord's Supper*, London: Rowland Hunter
Martineau, H. ([1839] 1983) *Deerbrook*, London: Virago Press
Martineau, H. ([1877] 1983) *Autobiography*, 2 vols, London: Virago Press

Obelkevich, J., Roper, L., Samuel, R., eds (1978) *Disciplines of Faith: Studies in Religion, Politics & Patriarchy*, London: Routledge

O'Connor, J. (1995) 'The Epistemological Significance of Feminist Research in Religion', in King, U., ed., *Religion and Gender*, Oxford: Basil Blackwell

Pinney, T., ed. (1963) *Essays of George Eliot*, London: Routledge & Kegan Paul

Rich, A. (1980) *On Lies, Secrets & Silence: Selected Prose, 1966–1978*, London: Virago Press

Steedman, C. (1992) 'Culture, Cultural Studies and the Historians', L. Grossberg, C. Nelso and P. Treichler (eds) *Cultural Studies*, London: Routledge

Todd. J., ed. (1989) *Dictionary of British Women Writers*, London: Routledge

Vicinus, M., ed. (1980) *Suffer & Be Still: Women in the Victorian Age*, London: Methuen

Wheatley, V. (1957) *The Life & Work of Harriet Martineau*, London: Secker & Warberg

Willey, B. (1964) *Nineteenth Century Studies: Coleridge to Matthew Arnold*, Harmondsworth: Penguin Books

Wisenfarth, J., ed. (1981) *George Eliot: A Writer's Notebook 1854–1887, & Uncollected Writings*, Charlottesville: University Press of Virginia

7

Other People's Truths?
Scientific Subjects in the
Personal Recollections,
From Early Life to Old Age,
of Mary Somerville

JULIA SWINDELLS

In her eighty-ninth year and as what turned out to be her final piece of writing, Mary Somerville set out to produce an account of her life. After her mother's death in 1872, Martha Somerville was persuaded to publish the resulting text, despite some hesitation on her part, knowing that her mother had been 'strongly averse to gossip, and to revelations of private life' (1873: 1–6). Martha Somerville can hardly be blamed for sharing what is a commonly held view about autobiography, that its impetus comes from giving readers insight into private lives, but the process of writing and publication of Mary Somerville's *Recollections* sets up some significant tensions around that idea. For, what is of primary interest about the *Recollections*, is the *public* 'revelations'. This is the story of a girl growing up in late eighteenth-century Britain, getting access to education and eventually a reputation as a leading scientist, after having been, according to her own account, practically illiterate until the age of nine. This is the story of an individual, but it is also the story of a professional community: the life of a scientist, and the life of science; the story of the human subject, and of an epistemological one.

In agreeing to edit her mother's memoir, Martha Somerville is more than ready to attempt to do justice to, and further, her mother's reputation as a scientist, encouraged to do so by 'valued friends'. However, there is a problem here, in that the whole issue of private life cannot, and will not, be left out of the equation, but

rather constantly shadows editorial attempts to support the construction of a professional and public identity. Martha Somerville
comments in her introduction that Mary Somerville was 'a woman
entirely devoted to her family duties and to scientific pursuits'
(1873: 1–6), as if to say that the two contexts – the domestic and the
professional – explain everything about her. However, it is also as if
the two categories threaten to cancel each other out, and render
the entire project of publishing the memoirs unsustainable, for,
out of such a life, there is, as Martha Somerville puts it, almost
seeming to lose her nerve, 'little scope for a biography' (1873: 1–6).
Alternatively, to separate off the passages about science, appears to
prompt questions about whether to include them at all. Elizabeth
Chambers Patterson notes that Frances Power Cobbe, a close friend
of Mary Somerville, advised Martha Somerville to edit out many
sections involving the representation of science (1983: 193–5). As in
all cases where the knowledge of editorial excisions has been
brought to the reader's attention, there is something of a sense of
frustration and inhibition about what might have gone missing. We
cannot know, for instance, whether or not the inclusion of those
removed passages about science would have produced a different
reading of Mary Somerville's life, particularly of the relationship
between professional and domestic identity.

In relation both to the domestic sphere itself and to Victorian
questions of 'femininity', Martha Somerville's editorial comments
and insertions do rather threaten to leave us a stereotype of an
'angel in the house' genus. There is a certain repetitive insistence on
Mary Somerville's 'remarkable and beautiful character', her 'rare
and delicate beauty, both of face and figure' and her 'simple and
loving disposition'. It seems important to Martha Somerville to construe her mother's working environment and persona in terms of
an extension of these and other 'feminine virtues':

> My mother was at all times both neatly and becomingly dressed.
> She never was careless; and her room, her papers, and all that
> belonged to her were invariably in the most beautiful order.
> (1873: 61–2)

The subject herself might have been somewhat averse to the
'Victorian touches' (Patterson, 1983: 193–5) which colour Martha
Somerville's editing. Nevertheless, one area in which editorial com-
ment is uncompromising, and from which it might be possible to

detect a shift in climate of opinion between Mary Somerville's girlhood and her daughter's adulthood, is in relation to the education of
women. Martha Somerville is not shy of putting the case forcefully:

> Few thoughtful minds will read without emotion my mother's
> own account of the wonderful energy and indomitable persever-
> ance by which, in her ardent thirst for knowledge, she overcame
> obstacles apparently insurmountable, at a time when women
> were well-nigh totally debarred from education; and the almost
> intuitive way in which she entered upon studies of which she
> had scarcely heard the names, living, as she did, among persons
> to whom they were utterly known, and who disapproved of her
> devotion to pursuits so different from those of ordinary young
> girls at the end of the last century. (1873: 2)

Nor does she demur in castigating those who oppose her mother's
scientific interests, appearing to demonstrate that she is far from
upholding Victorian domestic and marital ideologies as against the
pursuit of intellectual endeavour. The daughter agrees readily with
her mother that, 'It was not only in her childhood and youth that my
mother's studies encountered disapproval' (1873: 1–6), and manifests no inclination to excise Mary Somerville's own frank remarks
on some of her first husband's attitudes to women studying:

> I was alone the whole of the day, so I continued my mathematical
> and other pursuits, but under great disadvantages; for although
> my husband did not prevent me from studying, I met with no
> sympathy whatever from him, as he had a very low opinion of
> the capacity of my sex, and had neither knowledge of nor interest
> in science of any kind. (1873: 75)

And the daughter appears to affirm her mother's interest in gener-
alising the case of prejudice beyond her own direct experience,
apparently leaving Mary Somerville's strong ethical and political
statements as they stand – 'I thought it unjust that women should
have been given a desire for knowledge if it were wrong to acquire
it … I resented the injustice of the world in denying all those privileges of education to my sex which were so lavishly bestowed on
men' (1873: 28; 45–6).[1] Clearly then, Martha Somerville is not
averse to defending her mother's radical opinions or her personal
struggle for equality. It is more that she cannot avoid that shadow
cast by the private life, however exemplary, over the professional

one; as if her mother's alleged conformity to appropriate feminine and domestic behaviour confers moral and social authority on her, and protects her public and professional reputation against censure.

It is possible to speculate that what motivated Mary Somerville most highly in starting on her autobiography at the age of eighty-nine was not necessarily a simple question of age, or even that classic catalyst for much autobiographical writing, the combination of age and eminence. It is rather that there were reasons why, at that stage, autobiography could share in this same project which is later to cause trouble for Martha Somerville – explaining and accounting for the life of a woman scientist lived in the domestic context. In the *Recollections*, she writes of the pride she takes in sustaining her intellectual activities in old age. In particular, she speaks of her continuing passion for mathematics, and an adeptness by no means diminished by her advanced age.

> I am now in my 92nd year (1872), still able to drive out for several hours; I am extremely deaf, and my memory of ordinary events, and especially of the names of people, is failing, but not for mathematical and scientific subjects. I am still able to read books on the higher algebra for four or five hours in the morning, and even to solve the problems. Sometimes I find them difficult, but my old obstinacy remains, for if I do not succeed today, I attack them again on the morrow. I also enjoy reading about all the new discoveries and theories in the scientific world, and on all branches of science. (1873: 364)

The memoir captures the distinction between 'ordinary events' and a specialised interest in mathematical and scientific pursuits, for which the 'old obstinacy' remains. Prior to setting out on the project of the *Recollections*, Mary Somerville had discussed the question of her writing with her daughters. They had dissuaded her from reworking some of her former writing about the physical sciences, advocating that she write a new book. She had decided to take their advice, despite believing that this was 'a formidable undertaking at my age, considering that the general character of science had greatly changed' (1873: 330).[2] Later, she regrets writing the new book, *Molecular and Microscopic Science*, in the following terms:

> In writing this book I made a great mistake, and repent it. Mathematics are the natural bent of my mind. If I had devoted

myself exclusively to that study, I might probably have written something useful, as a new era had begun in that science.
(1873: 338)

At the same time, she believes that her daughters were right to
influence her against rewriting previous work. Critically distancing
herself from both the new work and the idea of reworking the old,
she appears to turn to autobiography to supply her, in a way that
other versions of writing cannot, with an answer not only to the
question of what direction her writing should take, but also to that
of what the entire experience has been about – the life of a woman
scientist. The result is an autobiography which negotiates (abetted
by editorial processes) its subject, its first-person, and its narrative
around the relationship between science and domesticity.

> On one occasion I had put green gooseberries into bottles and
> sent them to the kitchen with orders to the cook to boil the bottles
> uncorked, and, when the fruit was sufficiently cooked, to cork
> and tie up the bottles. After a time all the house was alarmed by
> loud explosions and violent screaming in the kitchen; the cook
> had corked the bottles before she boiled them, and of course they
> exploded. For greater preservation, the bottles were always
> buried in the ground; a number were once found in our garden
> with the fruit in high preservation which had been buried no one
> knew when. Thus experience is sometimes the antecedent of sci-
> ence, for it was little suspected at that time that by shutting out
> the air the invisible organic world was excluded – the cause of all
> fermentation and decay. (1873: 17–18)

Until that final sentence, the passage can be read simply in terms of
the everyday detail of domestic life, using the familiar autobiographical trope of hindsight on childhood with the child as an
ingenue figure, evincing 'innocent' curiosity. But the intrusion of
'science' and its discourses draws the reader into scientific knowledge – causation, the processes of the 'invisible organic world', little
understood in the former time – and reworks childhood curiosity in
the direction of experiment and discovery. The reader witnesses the
biography of the scientist of a particular kind, one for whom 'experience' is often 'the antecedent of science', one for whom everyday life
in the domestic context provides grounds for the scientific enquiry
and deduction. Thus, the autobiographical narrative, as well as the

human subject, is constructed out of the life of a scientist and out of the epistemology of science. This type of writing is not unusual in the *Recollections*, and is not confined to the representation of childhood. Much later in life, Mary Somerville witnesses the eruption of Vesuvius, and the account of the event draws on a similar method.

> Behind the cone rose an immense column of dense black smoke to more than four times the height of the mountain, and spread out at the summit horizontally, like a pine tree, above the silvery stream which poured forth in volumes. There were constant bursts of fiery projectiles, shooting to an immense height into the black column of smoke, and tinging it with a lurid red colour. The fearful roaring and thundering never ceased for one moment, and the house shook with the concussion of the air ... One of the peculiarities of this eruption was the great fluidity of the lava; another was the never-ceasing thundering of the mountain. (1873: 367–71)

After this passage, further deliberations follow over a few pages on the 'peculiarities' of the eruption, and on its possible social and ecological consequences. As with the episode of the exploding bottles, the initial representation relies on the vocabulary and metaphor of the commonplace – the column of smoke like a tree, the lurid red – but this becomes the basis from which to move to a more analytical language transforming 'experience' into observed 'phenomena' – the fluidity of the lava, the never-ceasing thundering – from which to speculate about causation, from which to produce the scientific hypothesis. The account of the eruption of Vesuvius is perhaps left unedited by Martha Somerville because there can be little doubt of its interest to the reader as a spectacle and a drama (the bottle-exploding episode has the same qualities in its own way); Mary Somerville is quite ready to exploit the dramatic potential of an incident, but she has a larger purpose – that of drawing the reader into scientific speculation on the meaning of the incident, transforming it from a drama to a set of phenomena, or a discovery, or an experiment.

THE CONTEXT OF SCIENTIFIC ENQUIRY

From her own account, corroborated by that of her daughter, Mary Somerville's relationship to her scientific pursuits changed dramatically after her marriage to William Somerville. Her second husband, apparently prioritising her career over his own, was as encouraging as her first husband had been disparaging. In contrasting her first marriage with her second, Mary Somerville comments: 'In those early days I had every difficulty to contend with; now, through the kindness and liberal opinions of my husband, I had every encouragement' (1873: 95). It was not only in the context of family life that her fortunes changed in favour of scientific enquiry. She comments in relation to the community of scientists that, 'I have uniformly met with the greatest kindness from scientific men at home and abroad' (1873: 158). The *Recollections* are replete with evidence of support and interest from the leading scientific men who were her contemporaries – John Herschel, Charles Babbage, Michael Faraday, and others. Perhaps it was no accident that the change of Mary Somerville's domestic fortunes coincided with the emergence of a liberalising movement in science. Certainly, the behaviour towards her of contemporary male scientists mirrors that of her second husband in terms of support and encouragement.

Mary Somerville's work was produced at a time when the epistemological basis of science was in an open state of change and germination, characterised by the emergence of shifting taxonomies and 'new groupings' (Patterson, 1983: 123). In the early 1830s, her work was in the forefront of scientific enquiry, presaging the development of new areas of specialisation and the professionalisation of science, not least in her exclusion of chemistry and biology from her working definition of the physical sciences. Her mode of working was also compatible with science at this moment of empiricism prior to rigorous institutionalisation, when new fields of study such as minerology, geology and astronomy were emerging out of passionately pursued, individual leisure interests as much as in the laboratory. All the same, the ease with which Mary Somerville was welcomed into the scientific community, and the equality of the terms on which that invitation occurred, can be overstated. Lord Henry Brougham's 'support' for Mary Somerville's work gives some insight.

Martha Somerville's edition of the *Recollections* includes a number of letters, including one from Henry Brougham to William Somerville, which, she comments, 'very importantly influenced the further course of my mother's life' (Somerville, 1873: 161–2). In the letter, Brougham explains that he wishes to commission some scientific writing to publish through the Society for Diffusing Useful

Knowledge, on behalf of which he is an advocate. He appeals to William Somerville to act as an intermediary between himself and Mary Somerville, professing to believe that she is the only conceivable person who can provide an accessible account of the Marquis de Laplace's *Mécanique Céleste* – 'none else can' perform this task but she, and without her, 'it must be left undone'. Mary Somerville's own account registers that the letter surprised her, 'beyond expression', her initial reaction being one of acute self-doubt:

> My self-acquired knowledge was so far inferior to that of the men who had been educated in our universities that it would be the height of presumption to attempt to write on such a subject, or indeed any other. (1873: 162–3)

Nevertheless, it is this invitation which appears to be instrumental in launching her as a scientific writer, in her own words changing, 'the whole character and course of my future life'. In this sense, Henry Brougham can take the credit for being a prime mover in setting Mary Somerville on her path to fame. However, the terms in which the invitation are couched require further scrutiny. It should not escape notice, for instance, that the letter of invitation is addressed not to Mary Somerville herself, but to her husband. When Brougham appeals to William Somerville to be intermediary, representing himself as being 'very daring' in hoping that the latter will act as advocate in his cause, he is surely playing a gentlemanly game rather than harbouring a real fear of approaching Mary Somerville with the offer. No doubt Henry Brougham knew William Somerville's reputation well enough to be able to rely on a favourable response, but nevertheless he had put the husband, if he had so chosen, in a position to block the wife's involvement in the project and even her knowledge of it. The gesture meets the letter of Victorian property law prior to 1870, in which the husband chooses on behalf of his wife, as she is his commodity, subject to his will. Brougham's courtesy to William Somerville and the latter's gallantry in agreeing to act as intermediary are social forms which only serve to emphasise that set of relations.

Equally significant are the terms of the project itself, as Brougham describes them. His choice of Mary Somerville for the task in his belief that 'none else than' she can undertake it, is arguably as informed by gender preconceptions as it is by an informed judgement of her scientific abilities. What he particularly requires of the Laplace text is a work of explication for 'the unlearned' and 'ignorant'. In other words, his mission on behalf of the Society agrees well with one construction of the Victorian middle-class woman, socialised into mediating male discourse to 'the masses', through voluntary educational and philanthropic channels. Appropriately, Brougham is more than ready to acknowledge that Mary Somerville is a specialist *reader* of science, knowing and understanding Laplace when there are 'not twenty people' in England who do, but this appreciation of her arises precisely because she is 'inexpert' as a practitioner, is not a university-educated scientist, not a professional; in these negatives lie her usefulness. She is rather a brilliant mediator of 'wonderful truths', other people's truths.

What Brougham asks of Mary Somerville is that very relationship which had preoccupied both the scientist herself in writing her memoirs and her daughter in editing them, that is, a version of science and scientific identity in which the two sets of ideologies – the domestic and the professional – can be reconciled in the woman scientist and her work. That the profession should constitute itself around gender-specificity in this way, is a question which dogged the Victorian period, showing itself rather vocally, indeed vociferously in a debate about the relative qualities of female and male scientific intelligence. In 1887, Edith Simcox contributed to that debate, specifically instancing Mary Somerville as someone whose relatively comfortable class position did not necessarily compensate for how being a woman acted as a disqualification from gaining access to the institutional and material resources of the developing profession.[3]

> She was over thirty before she obtained possession of such a mathematical library as an undergraduate begins his college course with. When she was over forty she taught herself to stop in the middle of a calculation to receive morning callers, and to take it up where she had left off when they were gone. Can we wonder that no original work was done in a vocation thus cavalierly treated? (1887: 391–402)[4]

Mary Somerville is also singled out, this time for special censure on grounds of her sex, in a speech by the Reverend William Cockburn denouncing the new geologists from the pulpit of York Minster. Women scientists may have been treated to a smooth reception by members of the scientific community, but this was clearly not a courtesy extended to them automatically elsewhere. Mary Somerville does not necessarily help her own cause, as she tends to privilege a particular model of scientific intelligence, deriving primarily from the university context. This is to accept evaluations which diminish the significance of contributions to the developing profession from women, including her own.

> Although I had recorded in a clear point of view some of the most refined and difficult analytical processes and astronomical discoveries, I was conscious that I had made no discovery myself, that I had no originality. I have perseverance and intelligence but no genius, that spark from heaven is not granted to the sex. (Somerville, cited in Patterson, 1983: 89)

This line of argument clearly runs the risk of privileging the university (and later specifically the laboratory) and the act of discovery, which is seen as separable from and inherently superior to the process of recording scientific analysis. However, such debates, whilst crucially highlighting the significance of conditions of material production in constructing women and men scientists in different ways, tend to underestimate both issues of epistemology and discourse themselves, and the value of the actual contribution made by women scientists in shaping the progress and development of the profession. Mary Somerville's contribution as a scientist occurs in an era when the scientific community, concerned by its own insularity, is opening up the boundaries of the discipline beyond the profession itself, and in the direction of public accountability. Part of this process involves exposing what constitutes received wisdom about scientific intelligence to critical enquiry and reform. It also involves extending the physical boundaries of the discipline beyond the context of formal education and the university to extensive fieldwork and empiricism. Women cannot be physically excluded (as they can by the closed doors of the university), and can engage with the scientific project in the domestic context. To accept Mary Somerville's own judgement of her contribution on her own terms is to underestimate the significance of that broadening movement within the scientific community, in the directions of fieldwork, interdisciplinary study and public accountability to the wider community.

The narrative method of the *Recollections*, together with the editorial approach to the text, demonstrates the pressure to reconcile the professional work and the domestic context in the autobiographical subject and the narrative. It is that intriguing sense that the private life of the woman subject must be invoked as some kind of alibi for her public and professional achievement, which both vouches for the continuing constraint on women of domestic life and locates women scientists as the philanthropists of the profession, of whom a different public and professional identity is required from that of their male contemporaries and supposed counterparts. To show the evaluative scientific mind at work in the 'domestic' context is to aid and service the project of the mid-Victorian scientific community, germinating ideas, open to a spirit of enquiry and eager to communicate, mediate and celebrate its discoveries with a wider readership and community; *but* it is also to demonstrate the requirement that women continue to be defined primarily in terms of domesticity. Women scientists can sustain marital and familial duties without putting them in jeopardy, and benefits to the scientific community can accrue in an extension of those duties into the public sphere – the helpmate to scientific men serving the public. Henry Brougham's treatment of Mary Somerville – on the one hand, soliciting her involvement in scientific projects, on the other, appearing to register or even demarcate her limitations – both exploits and bears witness to this dual aspect.

If male scientists were 'cordial' in their welcome to Mary Somerville and one or two other women scientists, it may not only have been because they were helpfully unconscious of gender-difference, or that these women did not exist in sufficient numbers to represent a threat to male domination of the profession, or that the profession was not yet sufficiently organised and established to exclude women systematically (although all may have been factors).[5] Just as Henry Brougham,[6] however cavalier he was later to prove in his support, had found Mary Somerville's contribution crucial at a particular moment, believing that without her the work might well have been 'left undone', so it is possible to argue that her work, and what it represents, was of more than passing importance to a scientific community who had, only a generation before, been bewailing the state of British science, describing it as barren of ideas and archaic in its epistemological apparatus. Brougham, along with Herschel, Babbage, Faraday and others, had perhaps recognised that, in giving their support to Mary Somerville, their own work was dependent on the revitalising and generative capacities of a research community without which 'that spark from heaven' which would produce the critical 'discovery' might fail to take fire. A more cynical interpretation, though, is that the scientific community was finessing its ability to absorb and exploit women, in the understanding that other ideologies, above all that of domesticity itself, would neutralise any latent threat from women to professional interests, at the same time as ensuring that through those very ideologies, women's services could be harnessed to the donkeywork of disseminating and popularising scientific ideas, freeing the men to engage, unencumbered, with those elusive sparks from heaven, apparently available to illuminate members of the male sex, only.

Notes

1. There is plenty of evidence of Mary Somerville's strong political affiliations. She was the first signatory on J. S. Mill's petition for women's suffrage, and maintained a staunch liberalism, despite being surrounded, at least until the time of her second marriage, by Tory family members and friends. The *Recollections* capture her interest, from an early age, in ecological preservation, her childhood sympathies with birds and animals, particularly in relation to any threatened destruction of their habitation or of the Burntisland environment in which she lived, and her commitment to the campaign against slavery, which she maintained throughout her life, professing in her nineties, 'I regret most of all that I shall not see the suppression of the most atrocious system of slavery that ever disgraced humanity – that made known to the world by Dr Livingstone and Mr Stanley.' (1873: 373) Ever after she had heard about the conditions on the sugar plantations, she had not been able to stomach sugar in her tea.

2. I note in passing that Mary Somerville's daughters have no hesitation in encouraging their mother in her professional career about which they appear rather well informed. An explanatory factor in relation to the gloriously unashamed enthusiasm with which they do this is the intervention, between the respective generations, of the suffrage movement, endorsing not only women's entry into professional work, but also women's support of other women.

3. I write 'comfortable class position', although both Patterson and Mary Somerville herself comment on the economic vicissitudes which beset the Somerville family from time to time. Mary Somerville, in the *Recollections*, comments that, 'we lost almost the whole of our fortune, through the dishonesty of a person in whom we had the greatest confidence' (1873: 152–4) Patterson gives a fuller account of this, but it is possible that neither Mary Somerville nor Martha Somerville wanted to be explicit about it.

4. Many thanks to Pauline Polkey, editor, for referring me to the Edith Simcox piece.
5. See Patterson (1983: ix–xiii) for more on this issue of the cordiality of the welcome.
6. Brougham did not sustain his committed interest in Mary Somerville's work.

References

Mary Somerville (1873) *Personal Recollections, From early life to old age, of Mary Somerville, with selections from her correspondence by her daughter, Martha Somerville*, London: John Murray
Elizabeth Chambers Patterson (1983) *Mary Somerville and the Cultivation of Science, 1815–1840*, The Hague: Martinus Nijhoff
Edith Simcox (1887) 'The Capacity of Women', in *The Nineteenth Century*, September edition
Simon Schaffer (1994) *From Physics to Anthropology – and back again*, Cambridge: Prickly Pear Press

Further Reading

Clarissa Campbell Orr (1995) 'Albertine Necker de Saussure, the Mature Woman Author, and the Scientific Education of Women', in *Women's Writing*, Volume 2, number 2. Also, thanks to Clarissa Campbell Orr for a recent exchange about the problems of twentieth-century historians visiting our own preconceptions about civil society, its institutions and demarcations, on Victorian Britain, when the relationship between the public and the private, and the whole construction of the public was very different, particularly in the fluidity of the early Victorian period
Margaret Alic (1986) *Hypatia's Heritage, A history of women in science from antiquity to the late nineteenth century*, London: Women's Press
Laura Marcus (1994) *Auto/biographical Discourses*, Manchester and New York: Manchester University Press

And Further Possibilities

Anne Shteir, *Cultivating Women, Cultivating Science: Flora's Daughters and Botany in England, 1760–1860*
Mary Somerville's scientific library was donated to Girton College, Cambridge, and reviews of her *Connexion of the Physical Sciences* appeared in the *Edinburgh Review* in April 1834

8

Alice Havergal Skillicorn, Principal of Homerton College, Cambridge, 1935–60: Gender and Power

ELIZABETH EDWARDS

Alice Havergal Skillicorn ruled Homerton Teacher's Training College for 25 years from 1935 to 1960. In this chapter I show how she constructed a subjectivity which was dual gendered. In her public life as principal, she adopted a masculine discourse of power which subordinated feminine discourse into the private sphere. But this marginalisation of feminine discourse in her public life made her unable, except in the intimacy of homoerotic friendship, to enact an appropriate femininity in her private life. She negated this femininity through her body by failing to adopt feminine standards of attractiveness in her appearance and clothes. In the public sphere, however, she successfully wielded autocratic power with a masculine discourse of political skill, financial acumen and an approach to her staff and students that was entirely instrumental.

I

Skillicorn was born in 1894 in Romsey, Isle of Man: the eldest daughter of Edward Skillicorn, a master shoemaker, and his wife Alice who ran a baker's business from the family home. This business was later taken over by Alice's second daughter Muriel. Skillicorn was thus born into the heart of the lower-middle class shopocracy, and her early subjectivity was constructed within a close-knit family whose hard work and business acumen earned them a prominent and respected place in the local community. She also, importantly, learned from her early family life that femininity

109

did not preclude a public role for women. She remained attached to her family throughout her life and frequently visited them at home in the Isle of Man. Her desire to 'keep quiet' about her lower-middle-class origins was entirely understandable in the context of the social and academic values of her public role at Homerton. Moreover, her own early experience gave an added impetus to the importance she attached to academic success.

After leaving a private school, Skillicorn served as a pupil teacher before going to Hereford Teacher Training College – a fact which, interestingly, she suppressed in her *Who's Who* entry. She obtained a BSc at the London School of Economics in 1923 when she was nearly 30, and subsequently became a lecturer at St Hild's Training College in Durham. Four years later, she obtained a higher degree before returning to London to become an HMI. The experience of coming up 'the hard way' academically was deeply embedded in Skillicorn's subjectivity. She was surprised when she was appointed principal of Homerton in 1935, and the contacts she made during her principalship with distinguished academics at Cambridge University gave her deep personal satisfaction, as well as being entirely consonant with her public policy for the college (Homerton College Archive (HCA), Acc. nos. 237; 1404, nos. 3 and 39; 1405: 1533).

II

My use of existing sources in the Homerton college archive, and my 'creation' of additional material, has been informed throughout by a distinctively 'auto/biographical' approach. In such an approach 'our understandings of our own lives will impact upon how we interpret other lives' (Stanley, 1994: i). As a member of staff at Homerton, I was arguably better positioned to engage reflexively with my subject, as reflected through my sources, because we had shared the same institutional culture. Further details of my auto/biographical approach can be read elsewhere (Edwards, forthcoming). My 'created' material included face-to-face interviews with former members of Skillicorn's staff, and completed questionnaires received from over eighty of her former students.

I begin my study of Skillicorn's gendered subjectivity by examining how she projected her gender through her body, appearance and clothes. She was a very ugly woman, which in itself contradicted the ideal of beauty that lay at the heart of early twentieth century femininity. But it was her failure either to take steps to remedy this ugliness by cosmetic action, or to conceal it with becoming clothes, that was so deeply transgressive. Her careless unconcern with her appearance directly contradicted the mandatory requirement of the period that every woman, whatever her class, status or age, should constantly strive to make herself as physically attractive as possible (Beddoe, 1989: 67–8; Betterton, 1987). Her lack of physical attractiveness resonates through the recollections of her former students, as does their feminine disapproval of her failure to alleviate the defects of her body by remedial action:

> Quite unforgettable, alas. She was small, dumpy, dowdy … with piercing eyes and protruding teeth. She made little effort to be attractive in any way. (HCA, Acc. no. 1404, no. 10)

> Not a pretty woman. Her teeth protruded. She wore her hair drawn back in a severe way. She wore very plain tweedy clothes which were in no way stylish. (HCA, Acc. no. 1403, no. 8)

The iconographic power of these images was memorably fixed in Henry Lamb's portrait of Skillicorn, exhibited at the Royal Academy Summer Exhibition in 1954 and subsequently hung in the college. Lamb wrote to the college that he considered the portrait to be 'the best of my commissioned portraits so far completed'. He also reported that he had received 'several valued appreciations from fellow Academicians.' 'The work gave me the greatest possible pleasure,' he continued, 'in addition to that I had of becoming so well acquainted with Miss Skillicorn and her several friends who came to the sittings' (HCA, Acc. no. 1892). This comment is interesting, for, as I shall show, Skillicorn was not only totally unconcerned with her appearance, she was also not at all easy socially. Clearly for her, having her portrait painted was part of her professional life, in which she was so competent and took such pride, rather than a revelation of her physical shortcomings.

Skillicorn's neglect of her appearance also excited adverse comment because it was perceived as incongruous with her status as principal:

> She dressed as though her appearance was a matter of indifference. Unremarkable and unmemorable. (HCA, Acc. no. 1404, no. 27)

> My mother thought she was one of the cleaners. (HCA, Acc. no. 1404, no. 45)

Alice Havergal Skillicorn. Portrait by Henry Lamb, 1953

The unvarying nature of her appearance over the years was a further indication of her negation of the feminine dictates of fashion.
The 'fair gingery hair' of the mid-1930s, had turned grey by the late
1940s, but when she retired in 1960, it was still scraped back into
the same bun which she had worn at the start of her principalship
25 years earlier (HCA, Acc. no. 1403, nos. 28 and 40). Similarly she

wore the same unvarying style of brown suit throughout the period. (HCA, Acc. nos. 1403, no. 2 1404, no. 41)

Skillicorn's lack of physical attractiveness was accentuated by the awkwardness and lack of grace of her posture and movements: 'She seemed, to carry one shoulder somewhat higher than the other' looking 'like a crouching monkey' or 'a hunched up bird' (HCA, Acc. nos. 1403, no. 4, 1404, nos. 37 and 35). She was also reported as having 'a lop-sided way of walking … with a limp as if she suffered from an arthritic hip' (HCA, Acc. no. 1404, nos. 27 and 37). (There is no evidence that she suffered from any physical deformity.) One member of staff memorably recalled Skillicorn 'kicking her feet together and rubbing her tummy at times of emotion' (HCA, Acc. no. 1405).

There was only one item of clothing to which Skillicorn attached any importance – and that was her academic gown: 'When wearing her gown, she often stood holding the lapels and walking about holding one lapel' (HCA, Acc. no. 1403, no. 4). I read this posture, which Lamb enshrined in his portrait, as Skillicorn's desire to cling onto and wrap herself round in her academic status. Her gown was less an item of clothing to her than the emblem of the academic/masculine authority with which she directed the affairs of the college. Indeed, however much her appearance, dress and general handling of her body fell short of both the ideals of femininity and her status as principal, she had no difficulty in projecting this status and her masculine authority as head of the college through this transgressive body:

> Small, unprepossessing, I remember her most with shoulders slightly forward in her black gown walking into Hall – when she was there, one never looked at anyone else. (HCA, Acc. no. 1403, no. 19)

III

Skillicorn inherited and improved on the political strategy of her predecessor, Mary Allan (1903–35), to make Homerton the best institution for the training of women teachers in Great Britain; and her single-minded devotion to furthering the best interest of the college at all times was universally acknowledged, as was her power:

> Miss Skillicorn's career as principal of Homerton College was driven by an overriding purpose: that the college should be the

outstanding women's college in its field. She was of that last generation of college principals who exercised autocratic power. (HCA, Acc. no. 1214)

Skillicorn had other formidable masculine qualities which enhanced her ability to perform her public role. She possessed unusual financial acumen, and on her appointment she immediately saw the necessity to improve the college's financial position by the better investment of its capital, then largely on deposit in the bank. Early in 1936 she persuaded the college trustees to purchase government stock, and four years later, at the beginning of the Second World War, she seized the opportunity to invest a substantial sum in defence bonds and war stock (HCA, Acc. no. ACa 61). One of her canniest investments was the purchase in 1946 of a large hostel in North London for only £5500. Millbrook House not only provided the opportunity for Homerton students to gain teaching experience in inner city schools, it also saved the college some £1000 a year in teaching practice travelling costs (Simms, 1979: 65).

This ability to combine a masculine strategic perception of new educational potential for the college, with a feminine tactical/practical skill in turning such potential into actual opportunity, was one of Skillicorn's most formidable attributes. Her campaign to build a nursery school at Homerton brought out all her strengths.

Skillicorn's decision in the autumn of 1938 to 'float' the idea of a nursery school to the college's trustees was prompted by two factors. The first was the decision by Cambridge University to discontinue the one-year Geography Diploma, which for the past 20 years had afforded some Homerton students the opportunity for a third post-certificate year of advanced work in a university setting. Secondly, the loss of 'this most cherished branch of our work' coincided with the college's first experience of evacuees. In the wake of the Munich crisis in September 1938, a year before the outbreak of the Second World War, 46 infants from a London Child Welfare Clinic were temporarily billeted at Homerton. Skillicorn' proposal was carefully worded:

It might be well during the present session to review the educational policy of the college, and to consider the wisdom of developing the non-academic and professional side of the work, particularly that which is concerned with training for teaching in nursery, infant and junior schools. Such a policy, if adopted, would involve the provision of a nursery school on the college premises. (HCA, Acc. no. ACa 1320)

By March 1939 the college had obtained the co-operation of the Cambridge Borough Council, who agreed to pay one-quarter of the maintenance cost of the nursery, which would provide the Borough with a valuable facility for its less advantaged children. When the necessary approval from the Board of Education was slow in coming, Skillicorn was able to employ her tactical skill and take advantage of her female network to expedite matters. She persuaded the Board's female medical adviser to visit Homerton with the result that she gave her endorsement to the scheme. A well-known architect, Maxwell Fry, was retained and tenders for the building work invited. However, by the time the Board of Education gave its approval to the plans in October 1939, war had broken out. The Board consequently advised that because of the shortage of building materials, the nursery scheme should be put in abeyance. Skillicorn immediately saw that the wartime situation, far from signalling the defeat of her plan, in fact provided an enhanced opportunity for achieving her purpose. She urged the board to reconsider its advice 'as some anxiety had been recently expressed as to the educational provision for smaller children who had been evacuated'. Work on the building was started in the summer of 1940, and by January the following year the school was ready to receive its first pupils. It was then that Skillicorn crowned her achievement with a final tactical manoeuvre. Having already indicated that some of the nursery pupils could be evacuees, she now proposed that they all should be. For the places 'could be filled with most advantage by evacuee children'. This 'master' stroke resulted in all financial provision for the school, except for the salary of the superintendent, being transferred from the college to the government to become the responsibility of the National Evacuation Account.

Skillicorn had thus secured not only a valuable facility for the college at minimal cost, she had also won an enhanced reputation nationally for herself by her patriotic action. Moreover, and most importantly for her political strategy for the college, in its provision of additional student places, the nursery school had 'substantially corrected the cut in numbers' which had been imposed on the college by the government 10 years earlier (HCA. Acc. no. ACa 61; Acc. no. ACa. 1320 Acc. no. 1410).

IV

Skillicorn's success in her public role also depended crucially on her ability to wield masculine authority over the community she served. Her professional relationships with her staff were autocratic, brusque and entirely instrumental. As she is reported to have said: 'I am the principal of this college, and I do not discuss my decisions with the staff' (HCA, Acc. no. 1504). All of Skillicorn's actions were subordinated to, and directed towards, what she perceived to be the good of the college as a whole rather than the best interests of individuals themselves. Thus, once she had assured herself that a member of staff was competent, she left her alone to carry out her work undisturbed; incompetent staff, on the other hand, were harassed – some said persecuted – until their work reached the standard that Skillicorn demanded. If it did not, staff were either persuaded to leave or were summarily dismissed (HCA, Acc. nos. 1214; 1406; 1412).

Skillicorn respected people who stood up to her, and usually found a way to satisfy their demands without losing face herself. One member of staff – appointed to revitalise the college's science teaching – threatened to resign unless money was found to modernise laboratory equipment. After a 'short sharp exchange … Skilly patted her side and said she thought the answer was a new science building' (HCA, Acc. no. 1406). (Skillicorn was universally known, but not to her face, as 'Skilly'.) She was a good delegator and could allow others considerable authority within their own particular spheres, provided she judged it to be in the best interests of the college to do so. The powerful personality of Dorothy Westall, the college's domestic bursar, could have provided a threat to Skillicorn's power. But both women, united in their devotion to the college, were able to negotiate around a potentially disruptive relationship to forge one characterised by 'mutual respect' if 'armed neutrality'. Indeed Skillicorn recognised not only Westall's skill in the domestic sphere, in which she took no interest herself, but also her crucial role in wielding the staff, most of whom were residential, into the tightly knit and committed feminine community which contributed so much to the civilised ethos and high standards at Homerton (HCA, Acc. nos. 1405; 1406; 1408).

The masculine impersonality and instrumentality of Skillicorn's professional relationships were not without a darker side, and the 'inexplicable hatred' that she displayed towards some members of

her staff exposed cracks in the masculine construction of her public
role which arguably reflected the thwarted needs of her own femininity. Her victims were always insignificant people whom 'she
trampled on with venom'. One lecturer 'stuck it out with a quiet
sense of humour' but was eventually forced to leave Homerton
after only two years for an inferior post. Skillicorn's cruelty to the
unattractive was balanced by her acknowledged preference for
attractive people (HCA, Acc. nos. 1404, no. 39; 1214; 1410; 1412).
I read this discourse as one of self-hatred, for Skillicorn saw mirrored in unattractive and insignificant women her own lack of
physical attractiveness and her social incompetence. Conversely,
she privileged women who were attractive and popular because
they compensated for her own lacks.

Some members of staff, for instance, were singled out for
Skillicorn's special favour. One of her favourites was described as
'a live wire' whom Skillicorn 'appreciated every moment of'.
Dashing around Cambridge on a motor cycle, she was allowed by
Skillicorn – contrary to all the regulations – to live in the college's
sanatorium with her two godsons who had been bombed out
(HCA, Acc. no. 1412). A few students were similarly favoured, and
the senior student, whom Skillicorn chose herself, was always an
attractive girl (HCA, Acc. no. 1403, no. 36). Skillicorn's rationale
for choosing attractive girls as students was that 'the children will
like to look at her' (personal communication to the author from a
member of staff 1949–55). But another member of staff was more
perceptive:

> Miss Skillicorn was a complex character. She could behave in a
> way that was wounding, and was by no means popular with
> all…I think she was ambitious, and thwarted – partly because
> she was a woman…and *perhaps*?? because she was personally
> unattractive. If only she had had orthodontic treatment as a child!
> (HCA, Acc. no. 1404, no. 39)

V

The skill with which Skillicorn handled her professional relationships in the public sphere was in sharp contrast to her behaviour in
the private sphere. For here she was 'intensely shy' and 'did not

find personal relations easy. She seemed unsure of her self socially' (HCA, Acc. nos. 1410; 1412; 1508). And yet in spite of this noted lack of skill in private relationships, Skillicorn chose her closest companion with the same strategic and tactical skill that she employed in her public life. Importantly, she separated her professional from her private life when she chose Dr Dorothy Sergeant, an influential HMI who had never been a member of her staff (Shorney, 1989: 153), to be her partner. In this way, she avoided any possible conflict between the discourses of gender and power in her intimate life.

The partnership was based on shared interests and mutual professional respect, but its success was due, above all else, to their complementary personalities. Skillicorn was 'anxious and defensive' in the private sphere; she was never at ease socially; and her lack of small talk was proverbial. Sergeant, on the other hand, was warm and relaxed on social occasions, and her support allowed Skillicorn to express the emotionality and 'repressed depth of feeling' which lay beneath her 'gruff exterior' (HCA, Acc. nos. 1214; 1403, nos. 6 and 19; 1405; 1406; 1408). The two women had the means to live in considerable style. They owned a house in Cambridge near the college, and they also had a flat in Homerton's London hostel, Millbrook House. Moreover, they enjoyed an upper-middle-class standard of personal service which was becoming rare in the 1950s. In the principal's flat at Homerton, where Skillicorn lived during the week, she had her own personal maid, Esme, who looked after all her domestic needs. In the holidays, the two women could get right away from Homerton, enjoy the London theatres and relax in the comfort provided by Millbrook's resident house-keeper (HCA, Acc. nos. 1036; 1395; 1404, no. 9).

I have written elsewhere about the nature and importance of homoerotic friendship for women principals (Edwards, 1995). The privacy and discretion with which Skillicorn and Sergeant conducted their partnership, and its upper-middle-class lifestyle, were both important elements in making the friendship acceptable. At Homerton, the relationship was welcomed because it was seen to give Skillicorn the warmth and stability in private which compensated for her isolated and autocratic public persona. One of her former vice-principals gave public, if coded, recognition to the homoerotic nature of the friendship at Skillicorn's memorial meeting in 1979:

> She found it hard to let herself go and yet those of us who knew her great friend Dorothy Sergeant realised that there must be

depths of understanding and affection that she found difficult to bring to the surface. (HCA, Acc. no. 1508)

Skillicorn was heart-broken when Sergeant died suddenly, and in her absence, in 1969. She wrote to a former member of staff with unusual intimacy:

> My dears – I'm afraid my news is sad. Dorothy Sergeant died suddenly and unexpectedly in her sleep on July 28. It has been a shock and sorrow to me as I was away in the Isle of Man. (HCA, Acc. no. 1422)

Moreover, when Skillicorn herself died ten years later, she chose to give public recognition to the friendship. For not only did the two women share the same grave, but the tombstone recorded 'the dear and devoted friendship' which they had enjoyed for nearly 40 years (HCA, Acc. no. 1403, no. 25).

Skillicorn was able to express a feminine discourse of 'understanding and affection' (HCA, Acc. no. 1508) within the private intimacy of her relationship with Sergeant. But the difficulty she found in bringing this discourse 'to the surface' (HCA, Acc. no. 1214) revealed not only the separation of masculine and feminine discourses in the construction of her subjectivity, but also her subordination and marginalisation of femininity in the interests of the masculine power discourse of her public role. Nevertheless, a feminine warmth and sympathy did occasionally surface as part of this public role:

> She was capable of great sympathy in the real crises of life, never sentimental but offering strong support ... she re-organised the timetable of a lecturer so that he could spend some time with his dying wife ... she made advances of salary to those in financial difficulty ... It was characteristic that these acts of sympathy and generosity were undertaken secretly ... Professional austerity and strong feeling existed side by side, almost in separation. (HCA, Acc. no. 1214)

This comment bears striking witness to Skillicorn's doctrine of separate spheres: a separation which was also evident in her relationship with her students. She was usually a remote figure to students and most of them only saw her once in private throughout their college careers for a final interview. Only a few students were singled out for more individual attention 'if they did something special which brought them to her notice' (HCA, Acc. no. 1404, no. 20).

VI

Once she had retired in 1960, Skillicorn began to mix socially with her former students, who were surprised to discover that, now she was no longer principal, she was 'altogether a different person' (HCA, Acc. no. 1404, no. 17). A doctrine of separate spheres was again expressly articulated:

> As a student I saw a formal impersonal 'head of college' figure, only in later life did I get to know her as a warm, friendly, normal person. (HCA, Acc. no. 1403, no. 36)

She enjoyed entertaining her former students and their families to coffee and sherry in the privacy of the Cambridge home she shared with Sergeant; significantly, however, she never acquired herself any feminine domestic or social skills, but instead relied on Sergeant's support to remedy her lack.

When Skillicorn died in 1979, her obituaries in the national as well as the local and professional press extolled the major contribution she had made to women's education (HCA, Acc. no. 239). At her Memorial Meeting, representatives of all sections of the college community remembered with respect and affection 'the many qualities which had made her such an outstanding principal' (*Homerton Association News*, 1979–80). Ruling Homerton had been Skillicorn's world, and she had never properly adapted after her retirement to life in the private sphere. Fate was not kind to her and long before her own death, she had lost not only Sergeant, but everyone else who had been close to her, including her brother and sister and her personal maid, Esme, who had kept house for her. Her twilight years were spent in a local nursing home, still loyally visited to the end by a faithful few of her former students (HCA Acc. nos. 444; 1403 nos. 6 and 36).

Skillicorn's solution to the conflicting discourses of the principal's role was to separate the public from the private as sharply as possible. In her public role as head of the college, she exercised a power wherein masculine discourse made few concessions to the normative constraints of femininity. This marginalisation of feminine discourse in her public role was the key to its success, for it enabled her to ignore not only the feminine shortcomings of her own body, but other feminine imperatives like the desire to be liked which would have impeded her authority. Her masculine exercise of power was also enhanced by the impersonality of her discourse and her single-minded and disinterested pursuit of public good rather than private interest.

The very masculinity of her public role, however, made it difficult for her to enact the feminine discourses she needed to make a success of her life in the private sphere. Skillicorn had tried to overcome the shortcomings of her own femininity by choosing a partner whose feminine skills would make up for her own deficiency. But her failure to acquire those skills herself only exacerbated the 'gnawing feeling of loneliness' (HCA, Acc. no. 444) which overshadowed her life after Sergeant's death. She had indeed sacrificed the private needs of her femininity in the interests of a masculine pursuit of power.

References

Beddoe, D. (1989) *Back to Home and Duty: Women between the Wars, 1918–1939*, London: Pandora
Betterton, R. (1987) *Looking On: Images of Femininity in the Visual Arts and Media*, London: Pandora
Edwards, E. (1995) 'Homoerotic friendship and college principals', 1880–1960, *Women's History Review*, 4, pp. 149–63
——'Revisiting Miss Skillicorn: a journey in auto/biography', *Auto/Biography*, forthcoming
Homerton Association News, 1979–80
Homerton College Archive (HCA) Accession no. 237. Register of Homerton staff
Homerton College Archive (HCA) Acc. no. 239. Obituaries of Miss Skillicorn
Homerton College Archive (HCA) Acc. no. 444. Notes towards an obituary of Miss Skillicorn
Homerton College Archive (HCA) Acc. no. 1036. Interview with member of staff 1961–71
Homerton College Archive (HCA) Acc. no. 1214. Reminiscences of a member of staff 1949–74
Homerton College Archive (HCA) Acc. no. 1395. Interview with a member of staff 1947–54
Homerton College Archive (HCA) Acc. no. 1403. Replies to questionnaire on Miss Skillicorn from students: no. 2, 1935–37; no. 4, 1935–37; no. 6,

1937–39; no. 8, 1939–41; no. 19, 1942–44; no. 25, 1947–49; no. 28, 1949–51; no. 31, 1950–52; no. 36, 1954–56; no. 40, 1958–60

Homerton College Archive (HCA) Acc. no. 1404. Replies to questionnaire on Miss Skillicorn from students: no. 3, 1935–37; no. 9, 1939–41; no. 10, 1939–41; no. 17, 1943–45; no. 20, 1944–46; no. 27, 1949–51; no. 35, 1953–55; no. 37, 1954–56; no. 41, 1958–60; no. 45, 1947–49

Homerton College Archive (HCA) Acc. no. 1404, no. 39. Reply to questionnaire on Miss Skillicorn from a member of staff 1957–59

Homerton College Archive (HCA) Acc. no. 1405. Interview with member of staff 1952–64

Homerton College Archive (HCA) Acc. no. 1406. Interview with member of staff 1955–80

Homerton College Archive (HCA) Acc. no. 1408. Interview with member of staff 1953–75

Homerton College Archive (HCA) Acc. no. 1410. Interview with two members of staff 1943–74, 1952–74

Homerton College Archive (HCA) Acc. no. 1412. Interview with member of staff 1942–46

Homerton College Archive (HCA) Acc. no. 1422. Letter from Miss Skillicorn to member of staff 1949–51

Homerton College Archive (HCA) Acc. no. 1504. Interview with member of staff 1958–83

Homerton College Archive (HCA) Acc. no. 1508. Tributes to Miss Skillicorn at Memorial Meeting, 2 June 1979

Homerton College Archive (HCA) Acc. no. 1533. Papers concerning Miss Skillicorn's early life and background in Manx Museum, Isle of Man. (I am indebted to my colleague Sallie Purkis for carrying out this research in April 1991, and to Ms Anne Harrison, Assistant Curator, and Ms Constance Ratcliffe, Trustee, of the Manx Museum.)

Homerton College Archive (HCA) Acc. no. ACa 61. Reports of Trustees' Finance and General Purposes Committee 13 February 1936; 11 March 1936; 9 March 1939; 24 April 1939; 11 July 1939; 24 October 1939; 22 January 1940; 19 February 1940; 15 May 1940

Homerton College Archive Acc. no. ACa 1320. Principal's reports to Trustees; December 1938, March 1941

Homerton College Archive (HCA) Acc. no. 1892. Correspondence from Henry Lamb concerning Miss Skillicorn's portrait, 1953

Shorney, D. (1989) *Teachers in Training, 1906–1985: a History of Avery Hill College*, London: Thames Polytechnic

Simms, T.H. (1979) *Homerton College 1695–1978*, Cambridge: Homerton College

Stanley, L. (1994) 'Introduction: Lives and works and autobiographical occasions' *Auto/Biography*, 3:1–2, pp. i–ii

9

When Writing the Other is Being True to the Self: Jamaica Kincaid's *The Autobiography of My Mother*

ALISON DONNELL

I write about myself for the most part, and about things that have happened to me. Everything I say is true, and everything I say is not true. (Kincaid in Bonetti, 1992: 125)

He was so sure inside himself that all the things he knew were correct, not that they were true, but that they were correct. Truth would have undone him, the truth is always so full of uncertainty. (Kincaid, 1996: 222)

I

When asked how much of her work is autobiographical, Jamaica Kincaid's stock response is 'All of it, even the punctuation'. However, readers of her work would be well-accustomed to such statements of devious simplicity and complex clarity. They would likewise recognise in the title of her latest work, *The Autobiography of My Mother* (1996), a playful but incisive disturbance in the accustomed use of language. Like the title of this work, two comments which Kincaid has made in interview imply that, for her, the figure of the mother is implicated in the central relationship between writing and the self around which autobiographical works are structured.

My mother used to tell me a lot of things about herself. It's perhaps one of the ways in which I became a writer. (Kincaid in Bonetti 1992: 127)

Clearly the way I became a writer was that my mother wrote my life for me and told it to me. I can't help but think that it made me interested in the idea of myself as an object. (Kincaid in O'Connor 1985: 6)

All of Kincaid's major fictions, to date, have focused on the mother–daughter relationship; a fact which is perhaps more surprising given that she has written in a variety of genres, periods, voices and cultural locations, in order to unravel the politics of colonialism, neo-colonialism and post-colonialism. Although the autobiographical elements of her other works have been noted by many critics, they are given a different status in this work which far more openly courts speculation about how it positions itself on the continuum between autobiography and fiction. In *The Autobiography of My Mother*, Kincaid locates her writing within a genre with a strong tradition of women's writing and feminist criticism, as well as one which consciously brings to the fore questions concerning her own identity as a writer, a woman and an American-Antiguan subject. However, at the same time she forces an immediate dislocation from this generic positioning, signalling that this work is not seeking to define itself unproblematically as a piece of life-writing which takes either herself or her mother as its subject, but as a piece which addresses the multiple imbrications of self, m/other and writing. Both the title of the text and the comments quoted above suggest that ontological, generic and identity boundaries do not hold in the telling of these lives.

It is certainly the case that autobiography's generic seams are not unused to being stretched. The explosion of criticism surrounding autobiography, and particularly women's autobiography, over the last twenty years, has demonstrated that as a genre autobiography can be likened to a restless and unmade bed; a site on which discursive, intellectual and political practices can be remade; a ruffled surface on which the traces of previous occupants can be uncovered and/or smoothed over; a place for secrets to be whispered and to be buried; a place for fun, desire and deep worry to be expressed. Many of the most influential women writers of the twentieth century have chosen to make this bed and some to lie in it too. Virginia Woolf, Zora Neale Hurston, Gertrude Stein, and their more contemporary bedfellows Sylvia Plath, Maxine Hong Kingston and Meera Syal have produced inventive and insightful works from between its covers.

In some senses, it is possible to position *The Autobiography of My Mother* within this tradition of women's autobiography, and citing a few important intertexts may help us to locate the main interests and epistemological concerns of Kincaid's text. Carolyn Steedman's *Landscape for a Good Woman* (1986), in which her own and her mother's life stories are bound to each other in a relationship which not only provides the content of the narrative but also occasions a rethinking about the possibilities of conventional autobiographical modes of telling, is a useful intertext. Zora Neale Hurston's autobiography, *Dust Tracks on a Road* (1942), can also be read as staging questions around the ownership of life stories and the responsibility to tell which are so crucial to *The Autobiography of My Mother*. The most arresting scene of Hurston's autobiography is that of her mother's death and her intuitive interpretation of this event: 'But she looked at me, or so I felt, to speak for her. She depended on me for a voice' (Hurston, [1947] 1986: 87). Maxine Hong Kingston's postmodern, post-colonial autobiography *The Woman Warrior* (1977), which tells a series of stories which both connect Kingston with and remove her from the cultural and discursive community of her female relatives, most notably of her mother, sits well alongside Kincaid's latest work. All three of these auto/biographies share not only the preoccupation with how much our story of the self is involved with our mothers' stories of us and ours of them, but also the concern that 'life-through-story' is never self-present or self-contained.

The idea that stories of the self always connect to stories of others, and that ways of being are enmeshed in ways of knowing, has prompted some critics to question the inevitable collision and conflation of autobiography and biography. Liz Stanley offers a useful definition of such works:

> The notion of auto/biography involves the insistence that accounts of other lives influence how we see and understand our own and that our understandings of our own lives will impact upon how we interpret other lives, maximally it mounts a principled and concerted attack on conventional views that 'works' are separate from lives, and that there can be an epistemology which is not ontologically based. (Stanley, 1994: i)

This notion of the 'auto/biographical', as coined by Stanley, connects with both post-colonial and feminist theories which have sought to reconstruct the subject in an assertion of identity-based

politics and theories of agency, and which have also been attentive
to the idea of the self as a collaborative project in which both others
and language play an active role. In *The Autobiography of My Mother*,
Kincaid conspicuously tests the limits of orthodox Western epistemology, not only (as Stanley suggests) in its organisation of the relationship between lives and works, but also in its models of self/
other relations which crucially inform our understanding of auto/
biographical acts.

Indeed, although Kincaid's work can be usefully approached
through feminist debates concerning women's autobiography (see
Benstock, 1988; Stanley, 1992; Smith, 1987; Marcus, 1994), in this
chapter I wish to argue that in *The Autobiography of My Mother* the
tossing and turning of auto/biography's bedclothes is intrinsically
connected to the ethics and politics of writing the life-story of a
female (post-)colonial subject. The politics of identity has often been
an issue high on agendas of feminist scholarship which, broadly
speaking, has sought to claim a self for women – a different self to
that essential, unified identity-myth bequeathed by liberal human-
ism to the white Western male. To this end, feminist scholars have
involved themselves in the ongoing debates and questions concerning the nature of identity which in more recent years have been
both shaken and arguably strengthened by the interface between
feminist and post-colonial theories. Certainly, the exclusive concen-
tration on gender as a marker of difference has provoked some of
the most fraught and productive debates within feminist theory
this decade, because as Wilkinson and Kitzinger point out:

> This assumption that Otherness is constructed only in terms of
> gender, that Otherness is conferred by femaleness alone, takes for
> granted the primacy of gender in women's lives, and obscures
> other dimensions of power and powerlessness. (Wilkinson and
> Kitzinger, 1996: 4)

Perhaps now least obscured of all other 'dimensions of power
and powerlessness', questions of ethnic and cultural identity have
powerfully shaped feminist thinking in the 1990s, and particular
awareness around issues of representation. It is to this issue which I
wish to address my thoughts on *The Autobiography of My Mother*.
More particularly, I am interested to explore how Kincaid's text
engages with one of the questions at the heart of contemporary

cultural debates about representation within both feminist and post-colonial theory – how can one represent an 'other'?

II

In *The Autobiography of My Mother* this question of representation is implied in the very title as 'how can one tell somebody else's story of the self?' Indeed, the word autobiography in the title may initially encourage us to think of this as a story of the writer's self, to align Xuela, our narrator, with Kincaid, our author, and to read the mother whose autobiography is to be written as that of Xuela – a mother whom we learn died in childbirth. In this reading we would decode the enigma of the proposed 'autobiography of the mother' as a text which seeks to write the story of the unknown mother in order to write the story of the self. However, for those who have read something of Kincaid's own 'autobiography' as revealed in interviews, details of the narrative persuade us to take up the claim that this is the auto/biography of her mother more literally – to read the text as the story of her mother's life which seeks to remember her own dead mother. Indeed, the historical moment of the novel, although not specific, is more that of Kincaid's grandmother who, like the dead mother of this narrative, was a Carib from Dominica.

Tantalised by these partial truths, we cannot be certain who the auto/biographer is this text, or if there is more than one, for if this is Kincaid's mother's auto/biography, then Kincaid is still present as the 'ghost' writer/biographer. What we can be certain of is that writing the autobiography of another necessitates some rethinking around the relationship between self, other and writing. Indeed, it is in the confusion over who speaks, for whom and about whom that our assumptions about the ownership of stories and of selves can be rooted out. The slippage between mothers and daughters, mothers and mothers, fact and fiction, history and literature, autobiography and biography involved in reading *The Autobiography of My Mother* foregrounds those questions of authorship and ownership which are implicit to all acts of writing, but are particularly highly charged with reference to autobiographical works which traditionally authorise themselves by their claims to authentic representation. By refusing to answer these basic demands of autobiography, the text forces us to ask why these questions matter so much and what they reveal about our intellectual and cultural imperatives as readers. Stable truths, origins and identities are all dramatically absent here:

> And your own name, whatever it might be, eventually was not the gateway to who you really were, and you could not ever say to yourself, 'My name is Xuela Claudette Desvarieux.' This was my mother's name, but I cannot say it was her real name, for in a life like hers, as in mine, what is a real name? (79)

In this auto/biography, the failure of representation and of realism give way to ideas of the self which resist the achievement of individuality implied by the act of naming. Bearing the name of her dead mother, Xuela needs to find the self in her story as well as the story of her mother which is embedded in her self. Her subjectivity is marked as both supplement and substitute to her mother's, to which she is joined by a paradoxical and painful 'connection through separation' which is signified by the text's refrain: 'My mother died the moment I was born'.

III

For Trinh T. Minh-Ha, a post-colonial feminist critic, autobiography offers an ideal generic space for an interrogation of such complex subjectivities:

> Autobiographical strategies offer another example of breaking with the chain of invisibility. ... Its diverse strategies can favor the emergence of new forms of subjectivity: the subjectivity of a non-I/plural-I, which is different from the subjectivity of the sovereign I (subjectivism) or the non-subjectivity of the all-knowing I (objectivism). (Trinh T. Minh-Ha, 1991: 192)

However, this confidence in autobiography as an instrument for both representing and constituting alternative models of subjectivity (non-I/plural-I) rubs up uncomfortably against the imperative not to speak for another. Indeed, a reconstruction of female post-colonial subjectivity through autobiography would not only seek to eschew the truisms of 'traditional [male] autobiography: chronological time, individuality, developmental self-hood, myths of origins, the fixedness of identity, bodily wholeness, the transparencies of referentiality, the will to knowledge, the unified self' (Sidonie Smith, 1993: 184), but also to articulate the particular contexts of black and post-colonial life-writing, such as oral histories, embodied narratives and the retelling of ancestral, familial and communal stories of the self.

Such auto/biographies would therefore almost inevitably trespass on the awareness of the potentially oppressive and repressive consequences of making representations of and for an 'other' which have been well-rehearsed in both feminist and post-colonial theory, and which find clear, if extreme, articulation in the words of Sinister Wisdom:

> No-one should ever 'speak for' or assume another's voice … it becomes a form of colonisation. (Sinister Wisdom Collective, 1990: 4)

What is really meant by this injunction? – that no white person can speak for a black person, no straight person for a gay person, no man for a woman, that no one powerful can speak for someone powerless, that no one can speak for another? Does not the insistence on authentic voices with situated knowledge make a false assumption that speaking for is always 'speaking as' or 'talking over', rather than 'speaking of' or 'speaking alongside'? Happier within the protocols of silence than those of risk, it would appear that most feminist and post-colonial critics have been persuaded away from speaking for others. They have been persuaded into 'the sort of breast-beating' which Gayatri Chakravorty Spivak has pointed out,

> … stops the possibility of social change….What we are asking for is that the hegemonic discourses, the holders of hegemonic discourse should dehegemonize their position of the other rather than simply say, 'O.K, sorry, we are just very good white people, therefore we do not speak for the blacks.' (Spivak, in Harasym, ed., 1990: 121)

Paralysed by an awareness that we cannot speak 'as' others, and by the packaged confession of the subaltern other which bolsters the conditions of empowered selfhood, we cannot see any ethical possibilities of speaking 'for' others:[1]

> No need to hear your voice when I can talk about you better than you can speak about yourself. No need to hear your voice. Only

tell me about your pain. I want to know your story. And then I will tell it back to you in a new way. Tell it back to you in such a way that it has become mine, my own. Re-writing you, I write myself anew. (bell hooks, 1990: 151–2)

Clearly, all acts of representation are acts of power, but does that not mean that telling another's story can be empowering too? I wish to argue that Kincaid's fiction gives us an opportunity to understand that there is a way of restor(y)ing agency through representing an other. In *The Autobiography of My Mother*, bell hooks's condemnatory phrase 'Re-writing you, I write myself anew' can be translated into a statement of positive possession of selves previously denied ownership of their own stories. As Kincaid herself has noted:

I didn't know that people wrote, or that it was possible for a person like me from my background or complexion to ever do such a thing. (Kincaid in Birbalsingh, 1996: 146)

Yet, her chosen autobiography does not seek to restore the self of the author to writing, or at least not directly so.

IV

The opening paragraph of the book lays down a potted history of a whole life that is traumatic, yet composed. It is a brief and absolute script of a life in which we are compelled to witness the starkness of both the biog (the plot of the life) and the autograph (the signature of being):

My mother died at the moment I was born, and so for my whole life there was nothing standing between myself and eternity; at my back was always a bleak, black wind. I could not have known at the beginning of my life that this would be so; I only came to know this in the middle of my life, just at the time when I was no longer young and realized that I had less of some things I used to have in abundance and more of some of the things I scarcely had at all. And this realization of loss and gain made me look backward and forward: at my beginning was this woman whose face I had never seen, but at my end was nothing, no one between me and the black room of the world. I came to feel that for my whole life I had been standing on a precipice, that my loss had made me vulnerable, hard, and helpless; on knowing this I became overwhelmed with sadness and shame and pity for myself. (Kincaid, 1996: 3–4)

It is this very composure of the voice which is so unsettling, and the conjuring of a whole life as known and complete which is so intriguing. How can a person know their own beginning and end in such a way as to bring that knowledge to language? Our birth and our death are events and stories which others must tell for us, but here there is no other, just the language of the self. It is a self which speaks the language of beginnings, middles and ends, of looking backwards and forwards; a self which speaks the language of writing and of reading. It is as if before we can read the story of this life, before the textualisation of subjectivity can commence in the more usual way – 'When my mother died' – we must be given a prologue to the relationship between subjectivity, language and memory. It is a relationship in which the self and the story of the self cannot be separated, a relationship whose configuration was frozen at the moment of our narrator's birth and her mother's death.

The first sentence of the novel 'My mother died at the moment I was born' positions the mother as the necessary prerequisite to the 'I', as all mothers are to their birth-children, but the absolute contiguity between death and birth also implies that the 'I' – the identity constructed in the official, colonial language of English, her father-tongue – was created as a consequence of the mother's death. As we read more of Xuela's story we learn how important the death of her mother and her entry into the English language are to this 'I'.

In a Caribbean context, the links with non-colonial cultures are often transmitted through a matrilineal structure, with mothers passing on the voice patterns, gestures, stories and memories of their ancestors. This unauthorised language and knowledge informs the complex constitution of female (post-) colonial subjectivity, often providing a site of resistance and of agency beyond official, public culture. The different texture and value of this linguistic tradition is emphasised in Trinh T. Minh-Ha's eulogy of matrilineal transmission.

The world's earliest archives or libraries were the memories of women, patiently transmitted from mouth to ear, body to body, hand to hand .... The speech is seen, heard, smelled, tasted and

touched .... Every woman partakes in the chain of guardianship
and of transmission. In Africa it is said that every griotte who
dies is a whole library that burns down. (T'rinh T. Minh-Ha,
1989: 121–2)

With her mother's death, Xuela is orphaned from the sensory reality of a body and a language in which the relations of self and other
are not organised around ideas of individuation and hierarchy. But,
unlike Kincaid's other works, *The Autobiography of My Mother* does
not stage a return to the mother's pre-patriarchal, pre-colonial language (see Donnell, 1993; Murdoch, 1990; Natov, 1990), but rather
attempts to negotiate a space of enunciation from within the
English language.

Her entry into this language is an interesting one: 'Until I was
four I did not speak ... I knew I could speak, but I did not want to'
(6). It is easy to associate this refusal of language with the trauma of
her mother's death or the abuses of colonialism, but what is significant here is that Xuela takes control of her memory of language
through this deferred entry. Unlike the conditions of her first birth,
over which she has no control, Xuela elects the birth into the 'I' of
language at a point of conscious knowledge. Unable to remember
her mother's face, she remembers her first words, making a forced
and determined entry into a world in which the pages of her life
had already been written, her 'I' ascribed before she had even learnt
to recognise it.

I learned to read and write very quickly. My memory, my ability
to retain information, to retrieve the tiniest detail, to recall who
said what and when, was regarded as unusual, so unusual that
my teacher, who was trained to think only of good and evil and
whose judgement of such things was always mistaken, said I was
evil, I was possessed – and to establish that there could be no
doubt of this, she pointed to the fact that my mother was of the
Carib people. (16)

Through affiliation to her mother, Xuela is (mis)identified. She is
scripted through other people's 'knowledge' of her mother and it is
a script she is admonished to learn as her own. However, able to
'master' the techniques of 'the language of a people I would never
like or love' (7), Xuela learns to use language to explore the self and

the m/other she knows to exist beyond the assigned subject (and classroom) position of a black/Carib woman. Her insistence on disrupting the flow between colonial knowledge and colonial language marks a resistance to the cultural confines of the 'I' she is assigned. Towards the end of the book, the adult Xuela writes herself a genesis story:

> My life began with a wide panorama of possibilities: my birth itself was much like other births; I was new, the pages of my life had no writing on them, they were unsmudged, so clean, so smooth, so new. If I could have seen myself then, I could have imagined that my future would have filled volumes. (214)

Capturing in the image of an unwritten text the possibility of a life never to be lived, and in the language of cultural domination an identity she could not own, Xuela chronicles a brief moment of her being before entry into the social and cultural script of a patriarchal colonial society. Nevertheless, she must enter the language of this script in order to imagine her life outside it. In the English language which identifies her as other, Xuela is able to re-memory a self – a non-realist self which reconnects her to the stories others have told and will tell of her. Bearing her dead mother's name, she marks the site of loss but also of continuity, she embodies the past as well as the present, the m/other as well as the self. In this autobiography, the 'I' looks backwards and forwards, identifies subject and object, writer and teller in an act of collaborative subjectivity which rewrites the violent individuation of the child. If we ask again, 'How can a person know their own beginning and end in such a way as to bring that knowledge to language?', then this time we can answer that it is by allowing the language of the self to speak the language of others and be spoken by others.

If, as Laura Marcus has suggested, 'autobiography is a staging of memory' (1995: 13), then Xuela's auto/biography, like her memories, are never fully her own. Her stories of her birth, her parents, her childhood, indeed her whole life, are both her own and others' – she does (as hooks accuses) tell other people's stories back to them as if to make them her own. I doubt that Xuela is alone. Most of us claim ownership of other people's memories, sometimes we borrow them from the photographs and stories our parents and relatives tell us, other times we save them up for our children, or we pinch them from our more glamorous or outrageous friends. Often we do not know that we have claimed 'false' ownership for years, often we never find out, nearly always we have to accept that true and false do not have any meaning in the process of discovery. It is why we have borrowed those memories and the uses to which we have put them that are important. Like Xuela, we borrow them to write our own stories of the self; our identities, like hers, are inter-subjective and interconnected, shaped by and shaping other people's auto/biographies.

> This account of my life has been an account of my mother's life as much as it has been an account of mine, and even so, again it is an account of the life of the children I did not have, as it is their account of me. In me is the voice I never heard, the face I never saw, the being I came from. In me are the voices that should have come out of me, the faces I never allowed to form, the eyes I never allowed to see me. This account is an account of the person who was never allowed to be and an account of the person I did not allow myself to become. (227–8)

The penultimate paragraph of the book situates *The Autobiography of My Mother* as an explicitly auto/biographical text (in Stanley's terms), as it testifies to the reciprocal constitution of self and other, lives and works, autobiography and biography. Yet although this parting metanarrative functions as an explanatory narrative for the text as a whole, this state of acute self-consciousness does not offer closure of work, or of text or of identity – it is peculiarly other-directed. Indeed, in Kincaid's text the idea of genres and of identities as mutually constitutive presents us not only with a particular politics of identity around an idea of the self, but also with the ethics of identification around the idea of the other.

It is perhaps not surprising that Kincaid should choose the mother as the figure who answers the question 'who can we speak for other than ourselves?', as it is the mother with whom the thresholds of being are always most confused in the lifelong me/not me affiliation. It is as mothers we experience the continuum of 'being' most acutely and tangibly. Nevertheless, by exploring the poetics and ethics of representing the mother, Kincaid is able to offer a model of representing the other which empowers both the self and that other. It is in Xuela's story that her mother's will be told, and in Kincaid's text that her own mother's narrative will find expression. By exploring the way in which the act of self-narration is negotiated around the m/other, and enabling us to question where the thresh-olds between our own voices and those of others fall, Kincaid dis-turbs the dictum issued by Sinister Wisdom by showing how speaking for another can become a form of decolonisation and dehegemonisation.

As academic and cultural projects, feminism and post-colonialism have both achieved so much in enabling other voices and stories to be heard. However, by only being sensitive to the oppressive conse-quences of representing the other, these movements may be assert-ing, albeit unwittingly, the terms on which other people's stories of the self can be heard and therefore the terms on which we choose to give subjectivity to others. *The Autobiography of My Mother* cautions us that in accepting the injunction not to speak for another we also accept the silence of many.[2]

Notes

1. For me, the execution by the Nigerian government in 1996 of Ken Saro-Wiwa for advocating the cause of the Ogonis was a powerful reminder of the forgotten ethics and politics involved in speaking for.
2. I would like to thank Nicola Shaughnessy for her valuable comments on an earlier draft of this chapter.

References

Bensteck, ed. (1988) *The Private Self Theory and Practice of Women's Autobiographical Writings*, London: Routledge

Birbalsingh, Frank (1996) *Frontiers of Caribbean Literature in English*, London: Macmillan

Bonetti, Kay (1992) 'An Interview with Jamaica Kincaid', *Missouri Review* 15:2, pp. 124–42

Donnell, Alison (1992) 'Dreaming of Daffodils: cultural resistance to the narratives of Eurocentric theory in Kincaid's *Lucy*', *Kunapipi* XIV, pp. 45–52

——(1993) 'When Daughters Defy: Jamaica Kincaid's Fiction', *Women: A Cultural Review* 4:1, pp. 18–26

Harasym, Sarah, ed. (1990) Gayatri Chakravorty Spivak, *The Post-colonial Critic: Interviews, Strategies and Dialogues*, London: Routledge

Hong Kingston, Maxine (1977) *The Woman Warrior: Memoirs of a Girlhood among Ghosts*, New York: Random House hooks, bell (1990) *Yearning: Race, Gender and Cultural Politics,* Boston: South End Press

Hurston, Zora Neale (1947, 1986) *Dust Tracks on a Road,* London: Virago

Kincaid, Jamaica (1984) *At the Bottom of the River,* London: Pan Books

—— (1985) *Annie John,* London: Pan Books

—— (1991) *Lucy,* London: Jonathan Cape

—— (1996) *The Autobiography of My Mother,* London: Vintage

Marcus, Laura (1994) *Auto/biographical Discourses: Theory, Criticism Practice,* Manchester: University of Manchester Press

—— (1995) 'The face of autobiography', in Swindells, Julia, ed. (1995) *The Uses of Autobiography,* London: Taylor & Francis

Murdoch, H. Adlai (1990) 'Severing The (M)other Connection: The Representation of Cultural Identity in Jamaica Kincaid's Annie John', *Callaloo* 13.2, pp. 325–40

Natov, Roni (1990) 'Mothers and Daughters: Jamaica Kincaid's Pre-Oedipal Narrative', *Children's Literature* 18, pp. 1–16

O'Connor, Patricia (1985) 'My Mother Wrote My Life', *New York Times Book Review,* 7, p. 6

Sidonie Smith (1987) *A Poetics of Women's Autobiography: Marginality and the Fictions of Self-Representation,* Bloomington: Indiana University Press

—— (1993) *Subjectivity, Identity and the Body: Women's Autobiographical Practices in the Twentieth Century,* Bloomington: Indiana University Press

Sinister Wisdom Collective (1990), *Sinister Wisdom,* 42:4, pp. 1–6

Smith, Sidonie (1987) *A Poetics of Women's Autobiography,* Bloomington: Indiana University Press

Stanley, Liz (1992) *The Auto/biographical I,* Manchester: University of Manchester Press

—— ed. (1994) *Lives & Works: Auto/biographical Occasions* (double issues) 3:1 and 3:2, i–ii

Steedman, Carolyn (1986) *Landscape for a Good Woman,* London: Virago

Swindells, Julia, ed. (1995) *The Uses of Autobiography,* London: Taylor & Francis

Trinh T. Minh-Ha (1989) *Woman, Native, Other: Writing Postcoloniality and Feminism,* Bloomington: Indiana University Press

—— (1991) *When The Moon Waves Red: Representation, Gender and Cultural Politics,* London: Routledge

Wilkinson, Sue and Kitzinger, Celia, eds (1996) *Representing the Other: a Feminism and Psychology Reader,* London: Sage

10

Self-Image and Occupational Identity: Barbadian Nurses in Post-War Britain

JULIA HALLAM

During the 1950s and 1960s, many women came to Britain from 'New Commonwealth' countries such as Africa, Malaysia and the Caribbean to train as nurses. No records were kept of exactly how many people came or how many stayed, but by the early 1970s some commentators claim that black women formed 25 per cent of the nursing workforce (see Stones, 1972). In spite of their relatively high numbers overall, black nurses have not made inroads into the nursing hierarchy, remaining largely as rank and file members of the profession in low status areas of care such as geriatrics and psychiatry. This has implications in terms of the status of black women in the profession, and in relation to what becomes known about their situation. Absence from both institutional management and the hierarchy of nursing's professional principal organisation, the Royal College of Nursing, has resulted in virtual invisibility, since it is only at this level that research gets done, articles are published and policy debated.

My decision to interview black nurses as part of a broader project on self-image and occupational identity in nursing, stemmed from this continuing omission and invisibility in the official histories of nursing.[1] As a white nurse who would inevitably be interpreting black experience within my own (white feminist academic) frames of reference, I became aware of the epistemological, methodological and ethical issues implicated in such a task. Annecka Marshall and I have argued elsewhere that personal biographical factors play an important role in the production of knowledge (Hallam and Marshall, 1993). Instead of concealing the role of the researcher behind a mask of objectivity, we argue that the shaping and moulding of the experiences of others into forms of knowledge should be an open and discursively self-reflexive process (Hallam and Marshall, 1993: 65). In this chapter, for reasons outlined below, the emphasis is placed on representing the content of the narratives and their place within the institutional contexts of nursing history, rather than the researcher's role in the interpretative process; a brief account of the methodology will serve to outline the approach.

METHODOLOGY

The historian Carolyn Steedman claims that the stories people tell themselves in order to explain how they arrive at the place they currently inhabit 'are often in deep and ambiguous conflict with the official interpretative devices of a culture' (Steedman, 1986: 6). The stories I was told are in deep conflict with nursing's official accounts of the past, but they are not ambiguous. Perhaps this is because they are not celebratory narratives told of and for themselves within their own terms of reference to an audience of their choice, but critical accounts told to a white 'other' who represents official culture and an institutional context. The problems inherent in any research process of mediation, transcription, interpretation and presentation are foregrounded and compounded when the researcher and the researched do not share a common framework of reference. Issues of accent and dialect are an important aspect of these differential power relationships, inscribed not only within the surface level of language use but, in the case of racial difference, within the imaginative frameworks that structure conceptual ideas of the 'other'.[2] My account focuses therefore not on the language or the structure of imagery within the narratives, but on their content. The problems experienced by black nurses arise not from their cultural 'difference' per se, but from the lack of recognition and status given to black nurses within the white profession of nursing because they are black. bell hooks (1992) points out how 'the discourse of race is increasingly separated from the politics of racism'; this account foregrounds the institutional racism that placed many black women (and some men) in low status areas of nursing work in the interests of maintaining a white professional élite.

An important early methodological decision was that I would use the same basic interview framework for all the nurses I was interviewing;[3] I wanted issues of difference to be framed within the interviewees' terms, not according to my own agenda. I therefore avoided asking 'leading questions', particularly on racial issues.

During my initial discussions with potential participants, however, two people informed me that they wanted to use the interview opportunity to raise issues of racism in nursing. We agreed that I would foreground questions on institutional racism as a structuring factor in their careers, and that the tapes would be archived for potential revision by a black nursing scholar.[4] For clarity of analysis and presentation, I have summarised and divided the accounts into three sections. These outline different stages of engagement with nursing's vocational ideal and practices.

In the first section, people discuss their earliest memories of images of nursing, most of which centre on their experiences as children and young women in Barbados. The strongly positive image of themselves as nurses held by this group stems from their early memories of nursing, and its status in Barbados as a highly regarded profession for women.

In the second section, the focus switches to memories of emigration and arriving at hospitals in England to begin training or working as nurses. Here, there is a keen sense of displacement and vivid images of a quasi-military style discipline which was sometimes experienced as demeaning.

The third section concentrates on the more recent past and a growing sense of disaffiliation from the NHS and the institutional frameworks in which nursing is practised. Throughout this final section, the narrators throw some light on the question of what happens to self-image when dominant discourses do not correspond to lived experience; when the gap between personal constructs of nursing identity and the occupational practice of nursing grows ever more unbridgeable.

The sense of outrage felt by the interviewees is not directed at nursing's vocational ideal of self-sacrifice and duty to the patient which is deeply internalised by all the narrators, but at the institution of nursing in Britain, and the practice of nursing within the NHS. The latter in particular is viewed as the villain of the piece for refusing to tackle the racist ideologies inherent within its system of institutional care.

EARLY IMAGES

Early images of nursing tend to have come from female friends and relatives at home in Barbados, some of whom were nurses themselves, some of whom wanted their daughters to be nurses. Playing games pretending to be nurses and doctors was quite popular. Three people wanted to be nurses from when they were quite young. L^5 was most influenced by her godmother who was a midwife:

> She was a very bubbly and loving type of person so she would always come around and see you from time to time and I would see her walk in with this crisp white apron and a little like straw basket over her arm and just go round the village visiting people.

Some people had vague memories of reading books about nursing, but thought that they had not been at all influenced by the images in popular romance stories and magazines. One person commented that doctor nurse romances 'painted a completely different image in the book than what in reality it is' (M). Among this very small group, there was little apparent difference to me between their early images, hopes and aspirations in nursing and those of white interviewees. In Barbados, nursing was viewed as a high status occupation for women; the image of nursing seems to have had a great deal in common with that projected by Britain's most prestigious nursing schools in the London teaching hospitals, which promoted personal qualities of patience, self-sacrifice and service to a higher vocational ideal. It was a difficult profession to enter with limited opportunities for training:

> The nurses there … they were proud. They were proud girls to be nurses. Anybody who got into the nursing profession there were more or less respected and they were proud. (M)

The continuing shortage of nursing staff in Britain throughout the 1950s led to government incentive programmes in New Commonwealth counties such as Africa, Malaysia, and the Caribbean encouraging people to come to Britain to train. These recruitment schemes seemed to offer an opportunity to realise aspirations which might otherwise have remained unfulfilled at home. To train as a nurse in Barbados, you needed to come from quite a wealthy family; for young upwardly aspirant Barbadian women, the opportunity of training as a nurse in Britain seemed an ideal way to achieve a coveted ambition.

RECRUITMENT AND TRAINING

There is no doubt that these personal aspirations were the embers of ambition fanned by nursing recruiters to persuade young women to leave their homes and train in Britain, although the actual mechanisms of the recruitment process are only partially revealed in the accounts below. V was given a copy of a British nursing journal, the *Nursing Mirror*, by a friend; she wrote and applied to three hospitals in the south of England, all of whom accepted her. Rather than going through the formalities of government sponsorship, her parents paid her travelling costs. G and her friends responded to a government led recruitment drive. She remembers hearing about it on the radio, and through the careers service at school. L arrived in England to join her mother, a nursing auxiliary, when she was almost fifteen. She decided that she would become a nurse, and applied for training at a local hospital as soon as she was sixteen. M came to England to join her boyfriend, writing to several hospitals in the hope of starting her training, but she was unsuccessful. She married, had her children and then began working as a nursing auxiliary in the early 1970s.

Many people seem to have been unaware that there were two forms of nurse training available in Britain. In Barbados, only training for state registration (general nursing) was available, and only state registered nurses were employed, therefore becoming an enrolled (bedside) nurse was not useful for anyone wanting to return home. G claims that decisions about who did what training were made in a fairly arbitrary way by Barbadian government employees:

> A lot of us didn't know until we got here. They never let us know over there. And they used to decide – favouritism I guess – who they sent to do enrolled nursing and who they sent to do the general. (G)

G claims that a lot of people ended up in her situation, spending two years training for the roll, who had sufficient educational qualifications for general training. Because she was on contract to the hospital, she had no option other than to complete the two years and get her certificate before she could start her general training: 'I was determined that as soon as I finished, I was going to do my general.' Enrolled nurses had to go back on student pay while general training, and were only allowed six months off the three-year training period for their existing qualifications. This was an added disincentive to take up training for nurses like V who had to support their families, whether they were living in Britain or, as was sometimes the case, at home in Barbados:

> After a few months I was thinking about doing my training but the pay you got was so small I couldn't afford to do my training then ... the wages at the end of the month are only eight or nine pounds.

V shared a room with two other women in a similar situation to herself who had to send money home for the care of their children, and as a result could not afford to give up their auxiliary nursing jobs to train.

Some people commented on the fear and strangeness they felt when they arrived in Britain. G remembers that she didn't like England when she arrived in 1961, and how strange she felt 'because everybody was white'. In conversation after the interview, V told me that she felt as if she was going to be eaten alive by white people when she got off the boat, but that going to the hospital offered a sense of some security. Both V and G started work almost immediately after their arrival at the hospital, only a day or two after they had arrived in England. G found herself in a small country hospital working with eight other black nurses; looking back now, she thinks she was lucky going to Yorkshire because people were very friendly.

One of the significant differences between the training experiences of black and white nurses lies in their social lives. The white nurses recalled how their social lives had revolved around their own cohort groups, and that they rarely mixed with those outside their own set. The positive side of this was the strong bonds forged between women which have been carried into their later lives. Black nurses tended to ignore the peer group hierarchy, bonding across sets and national boundaries to form networks of support:

> I felt strange but it was nice because ... there was eight other black girls there. As soon as they heard the new ones were in they came to introduce themselves. And they were around to let us feel at home. But we were very homesick. (G)

L remembers having a healthy social life:

> There were girls from Jamaica, Trinidad, Bermuda, and there were lots of colleagues from Mauritius and lots from the Caribbean Islands so it was quite interesting.

In addition, there were staff in the hospital kitchens from Greece, Spain and Italy. V remembers a good atmosphere, taking turns in off-duty time to cook food to share with the others, courtesy of a local butcher who used to provide cheap meat for the nursing staff.

Experiences of training were in some ways similar to those of white nurses; people recounted similar stories about their place in nursing's hierarchy, with authoritarian sisters and autocratic medical staff figuring in a comparable fashion. V remembers learning many of her basic nursing skills from one sister in particular, who made no distinction between what she taught to auxiliaries and pupil nurses. G found the sisters somewhat daunting; V remembers one sister who always picked on black nurses, 'she always liked to be shouting at you' but on the whole remembers being treated with respect. M found herself working with a nursing officer who always found fault with the black nurses, rarely with the white: 'I know I'm an auxiliary, I know I'm lower down the scale, but she made me feel so ... oh ... she wasn't nice at all.'

Working with somebody who was determined to find fault was clearly an undermining experience during the early days of training/working, but for this group of women it was the nurses regrading exercise in the mid-1980s that finally undermined them after many years of coping with day to day racial harassment.

REFLECTIONS ON A LIFE IN NURSING

Barbadian nurses had to cope not only with the disappointments of arriving in Britain and finding it a very different place to the idealised conceptions of the 'mother country' they had been taught at school, but also with working in a system of health care that fell well below their expectations. M pointed out how the British system of caring for the elderly in old fashioned and poorly equipped geriatric hospitals seemed quite uncivilized compared with Barbadian standards:

> It was shocking at the beginning. They thought that we – West Indians – were primitive, but when I came to the hospital it was more primitive than what we had.

Although she was wearing the coveted nurses uniform, V initially found nursing work distasteful, she had not expected to be dealing with so many elderly, incontinent people. M recalls that at that time,

> Nobody wanted to work in geriatrics, nobody. I think they wanted people coming to England to work on geriatrics.

M worked with two SENs caring for 52 elderly people on two wards while they taught her basic nursing care; she remained in geriatric nursing for 18 years. A particular milestone for the large black workforce in geriatric nursing was the move for unionisation in 1974/5:

> We had a coloured bloke who came working at the hospital, and he was a charge nurse and he started up the union. Well, there might have been a union before, but nobody came to us ... And it was only when the union came along that the staff begin to increase. (M)

Like the other women interviewed here, M has steered her daughter away from a career in nursing; she feels that the changes in the NHS are making things worse for nurses, who are being asked to do more work for the same pay.

> They haven't said anything about redundancy yet, but what has come up now, they given us part-timers – I work thirty hours a week – this is what I understand it to be, that every nineteen weeks we work one night without pay.

The sense of outrage felt by M at the low value placed on her years of hard work and commitment to the NHS is echoed by the other interviewees. L now works as a staff nurse on a surgical ward after 16 years on night duty in a special care baby unit. Commenting on the fact that foreign nurses were placed mainly on the geriatric wards, L felt that the price paid for this was that they gained only limited experience of medical and surgical nursing, which made it difficult for them to move from the geriatric wards. She sees the nurses regrading exercise in the mid-1980s as something of a victory for those working in this traditionally undervalued area of nursing because SENs were finally given recognition for running wards and being responsible for large numbers of elderly patients. Apart from this small victory for the large black workforce in this area, she thinks it is very hard for a black nurse to move up the career ladder; white nurses dominate nursing management out of all proportion to their numbers overall.

> I think really that black nurses realised that this was happening and that they weren't getting anywhere fast and they opted out. I notice that there aren't as many in nursing.

L is deeply frustrated by the fact that, in spite of achieving state registration and taking extra courses, she has been unable to fulfil her aspirations in nursing:

> I'm the last person to have a chip on my shoulder, but it does seem that once you're black it's ten times harder to move.

She thinks that nursing is less attractive as a career for women these days unless they want to move into management or specialise in an off-shoot area like health promotion. V has spent most of her working life as an auxiliary nurse and is now looking forward to retirement. In spite of years of experience of caring for elderly patients, she has to carry out the instructions of student nurses who are still at college and have very little practical experience on the wards. Her skills and knowledge are ignored, making her feel undervalued and regretful that she didn't do her training:

> You get some young little staff that just come out [of college], maybe I was a nurse before they were born, and, oh, want to push you around, and it makes me feel sad.

V thinks that they're 'trying to do nursing by paper' and that nurses no longer provide the levels of physical care that they used to, even though there are more staff on the wards.

Sometimes you go to the ward, you can't get a cake of soap,
there's no Dettol, there's no Savlon … it's awful. Now the patients
can't even get a slice of bread. There's no breakfast coming out,
no bacon or eggs and I think it is wrong for the old people
because they have worked all of their years and at the end of
their life, they should get treated better.

G worked as a sister on a gynaecological ward for twelve years, and
is now having a rest from the NHS, which she thinks has become a
deeply racist institution. Although she agrees that the nurses'
regrading exercise did benefit some black nurses, it was also used to
discriminate against them. G was the senior Sister on her ward by
many years, but she was given a lower grading (and hence a lower
salary) than her white co-worker. Her tribunal appeal was never
heard. As the cuts in health services started to be severely felt at
ward level, morale amongst the nursing staff fell and tensions
between the staff grew. G decided to take early retirement whilst
she was still young enough to get another job. She can provide
numerous examples of the poor treatment black nursing staff
received during regrading at her hospital and the preferential treatment shown to whites. Like V, G is highly critical of government
policy and the effects that the new internal market in health care
services has at the level of day to day management of patient care:

Patients were complaining that their food was shocking, and the
wards weren't clean because they'd cut back on cleaning and
domestic staff … they expected one person to do the work that
three people used to do. Impossible.

Her views on the changes in the education and training of nurses
are similar to others in this study; that college and degree level
trainings do not sufficiently equip trainee nurses with the skills
they need to be able to do their job. Like other women I talked to,
she hopes her daughter will not take up nursing as a career.

The interviews entirely support Baxter's thesis, namely that black
nurses are endangered unless the health service can prove to those
who remain that the change towards a privatised model of health
care is a change that will value their contribution. To date, this has
not been shown to be the case. The problems of subsuming the experiences of all female nurses under a generalist rubric of development,
change and progress are clear. The social histories of nursing need

to include the contributions that black nurses have made to the profession, and the difficulties that they have had to overcome. As a profession that has been shaped by issues of class, gender and status rather than the possession of a particular, specialist body of scientific knowledge, professional nursing has always been torn between striving for status through education and training and through control of the (largely) female workforce who do nursing work. Both of these projects involve one group of people subjugating an other.

Achieving recognition in the profession has tended to mean specialising in either education or management, leaving those who wished to develop their practical expertise in caring skills without a clear career path once they obtained their registration. The hierarchical structure of the nursing profession was a particularly invidious one for those arriving to train as nurses from Britain's former colonies. Not only did overseas nurses end up working in the least prestigious areas of the health service such as geriatrics and psychiatry which have always been notoriously underfunded and understaffed, but once there, they were caught in a financial trap. For many black nurses, their ambitions to enter the profession as registered nurses ended, cruelly squashed by a combination of low pay, low status and long hours of hard and dirty work.

CONCLUSIONS

Researching the working lives of a group of women whose experiences of nursing life are very different to my own has made me acutely aware of the inevitable problems of interpretation that accompany the research process. A review of the research literature on black nurses working in Britain only serves to further underline the point. For example, Martin (1965) employs a functionalist approach to solving the problem of why black state enrolled nurses were leaving their jobs shortly after the completion of their training. Interviews with around sixty nurses led her to conclude that black nurses were unable to adapt to the discipline of hospital life and as a result of their cultural differences suffered from 'attitudinal aggression' (Martin (1965) in McGuire, 1969). A more liberal interpretation of the facts might have focused on the career aspirations of the group, many of whom were leaving to take up registered nurse training at other institutions.

More recent (feminist) analyses of the working lives of black nurses have tended to counteract the search for individual and group personality traits that predominated in earlier studies, emphasising instead the institutional determinants that position black nurses as victims of an oppressive, racist health care system. For example, Glenn (1992) argues that race and class are integrated elements of gender oppression, illustrating her point with an analysis of stratification in the North American nursing labour force. In relation to numbers of nurses overall, white registered nurses are over-represented in the top grades of the nursing hierarchy, while racial/ethnic women are disproportionately represented in the lower grades of nurses' aid. The institutional care of, for example, elderly white people by black nurses clearly benefits white women, who would otherwise have to shoulder the burden of care. In this interpretation of the situation of black nurses, black women are the victims of not only racial oppression but of a system of social stratification that favours white women.

Two of the women in particular, G and L, used these concepts of oppression as a framing device in their narratives, pointing out how the barriers erected by a white class hierarchy in nursing had effectively halted their careers in the NHS. Accepting these accounts at face value, as transparent descriptions of their working lives, it would be easy to assume that black nurses suffer from low self-esteem and a poor self image. But as I pointed out in the introduction, the language used here is constituted to address a researcher, someone who represents an official institution. It is unsurprising, therefore, to find that personal experience is rendered in a form of address that is publicly recognised, if not officially sanctioned, as that of oppressor and victim. G claims that she can find numerous others to support her testimony who would bear witness to her experience by telling a similar story; L critiques government policy and its effects at the local level. These comments are strategically aimed at the interviewer as an agent of the liberal discourse of equality used within official institutions.

Rather than the interview process throwing light onto the self image of the interviewees, the stories that I heard both illuminated and reflected the image of self I was presenting to others: that of an official, a representative of an oppressive institutional system. The only common touchstone between the interviewees and myself was the framework of beliefs and values that underlies conceptions of good nursing practice: the shared ground of what constitutes a 'proper' nurse. This concept, similarly conceptualised by all the women I interviewed, is centred on a caring image, one that is usually associated with bedside nursing and serving the needs of the patient. The image stresses the emotionally unconditional nature of nursing care, and how it should be given without prejudice to all who are in need of it, irrespective of any personal and social differences between the carer and the cared for. But the nursing profession has been slow to apply these dictates of equality throughout its own internal managerial and professional structures. One result of this is that nursing is a deeply fractured profession, with numerous groups from within nursing and outside it vying to control the hearts and minds of those who do nursing work.

The institutional devaluation of black nurses' working lives and their lack of social status as professional women was a source of anger to all the interviewees, but it was also as a cause of personal grief and sorrow. Recent changes in the organisation of health care services seem to have compounded these feelings; V and M in particular were acutely aware of the effects of the new regime on the most vulnerable members of society, the poor, the elderly and the chronic-sick. While it would be simple to categorise these stories as narratives of oppression, such an analysis oversimplifies both the content of the stories and the manner of their delivery. Without wanting to deny the anguish and despair that institutional racism, with its consequentially unfair working practices and harassment, undoubtedly inflicts on individual lives, the women that I interviewed were aware of their achievements, proud of their skills and mindful of their contribution to the care of some of the most vulnerable members of our society. These stories raise an embarrassing issue for nursing management; the potentially exploitative relationship between those who do the vital work of caring and those who manage care services continues to be one which professional nursing would rather not address.

Acknowledgements

With thanks to G, L, M and V for their thoughts and their time; and Pauline Polkey for her helpful comments on an earlier draft of this chapter.

Notes

1. See, for example, Dingwall, Rafferty and Webster (1988) and Baly (1980).
2. For a more detailed account of this point see bell hooks (1992). Rosalind Edwards (1990) provides a useful focus on the importance of the relationship between epistemology and method in feminist research in 'Connecting Method and Epistemology: a White Woman Interviewing Black Women', *Women's Studies International Forum*, 13: 5, 477–90.
3. I interviewed ten nurses as part of a broader project on self identity in nursing. See Hallam (1996) *Nursing the Image: Popular Fictions, Recruitment and Nursing Identity 1950–1975*.
4. The tapes and transcriptions are deposited in the National Sound Archive, where they constitute the only 'unofficial' accounts of nurses' lives. Other oral histories of nursing have been collated by the Royal College of Nursing under the auspices of the RCN History of Nursing Society.
5. Initials have been used in the interests of confidentiality.

References

Abel-Smith, B. (1975) *A History of the Nursing Profession*, London: Heinemann
Agbolegbe, G. (1984) 'Fighting the Racist Disease', *Nursing Times*, 80, 6:18–20
Alexander, Z. and Dewjee, A., eds, (1984) *The Wonderful Adventures of Mrs Seacole in many lands*, Bristol: Falling Wall Press
Baly, M. (1980) *Nursing and Social Change*, London: Heinemann
Barritt, E. R. (1973) 'Florence Nightingale's Values and Modern Nursing Education' *Nursing Forum*, 7, 1:6–47
Baxter, C. (1988) *The Black Nurse: an Endangered Species. A Case for Equal Opportunities in Nursing*, Cambridge: Training in Health and Race
Box, K. and Croft-White, E. (1943) *The Attitudes of Women towards Nursing as a Career*, Wartime Social Survey, Central Office of Information, London: HMSO
Briggs, A. (1972) *Report of the Briggs Committee on Nursing*, Cmnd. 5115, London: HMSO
Bryan, B., Dadzie, S. and Scafe, S. (1985) *The heart of the race: Black Women's Lives in Britain*, London: Virago
Chua, Wai Fong and Clegg, S. (1990) 'Professional Closure: the Case of British Nursing', *Theory and Society*, 19:135–72
Clarke, M. (1976) *Social Relations Between British and Overseas Student Nurses*, unpublished MPhil, University of Surrey
Cox, M. (1972) 'Problems of Overseas Nurses Training in Britain', *International Nursing Review*, 19:157–68
Dingwall, R., Rafferty, Anne M. and Webster, C., eds, (1988) *An Introduction to the Social History of Nursing*, London: Routledge

Edwards, R. (1990) 'Connecting Method and Epistemology: a White Woman Interviewing Black Women', *Women's Studies International Forum*, 13, 5: 477–90

Gamarnikow, E. (1991) 'Nurse or Woman: Gender and Professionalism in Reformed Nursing 1860–1923', in P. Holden and J. Littlewood, eds, *Anthropology of Nursing*, London: Routledge

Glazer, N. (1991), '"Between a Rock and a Hard Place": Women's Professional Organisations in Nursing and Class, Racial and Ethnic Inequalities', *Gender and Society*, 5, 3:351–72

Glenn, Evelyn N. (1992) 'From Servitude to Service Work: Historical Continuities in the Racial Division of Paid Reproductive Labour', *Signs*, 18, 1:1–43

Hale, S. (1991) 'Feminist Method, Process and Self-Criticism: Interviewing Sudanese Women', in S. B. Gluck and D. Patai, eds, *Women's Words: the Feminist Practice of Oral History*, London: Routledge, 21–136

Hallam, J. (1996) *Nursing the Image: Popular Fictions, Recruitment and Nursing Identity 1950–1975*, Unpublished PhD, University of Warwick

Hallam, J. and Marshall, A. (1993) 'Layers of difference: the significance of a self reflexive approach for a feminist epistemological project', in C. Lubeska and V. Walsh, eds, *Making Connections*, London: Taylor & Francis

hooks, b. (1992) *Black Looks*, Boston: South End Press

Martin (1965) 'West Indian Pupil Nurses and Their Problems in Training', in J. McGuire, ed., (1969) *Threshold to Nursing*, Occasional Papers on Social Administration 30, London: Bell

Personal Narratives Group, eds, (1989) *Interpreting Women's Lives, Feminist Theory and Personal Narratives*, Bloomington and Indianapolis: University of Indiana Press

Pomeranz, R. (1973) *The Lady Apprentices: a Study of Transition in Nurse Training*, Occasional Papers on Social Administration 51, London: Bell

Simnett, A. (1986) 'The pursuit of respectability: women and the nursing profession 1860–1900', in R. White, ed., *Political Issues in Nursing Past, Present and Future*, vol. 2, Chichester: John Wiley pp. 1–17

Steedman, C. (1986) *Landscape For a Good Woman: a Story of Two Lives*, London: Virago

Stones, R. W. H. (1972) 'Overseas Nurses in Britain: a study of male recruits', *Nursing Times*, 9, 7:141–4

Thomas, M. and Morton-Williams, J. (1972) 'Overseas Nurses in Britain. Evidence to the Briggs Committee on Nursing', P.E.P., Broadsheet 539, London

Thompson, S. (1974) 'Overseas nurses deserve better protection', *New Psychiatry*, 9, 3:22–3

Torkington, P. (1985) *Racism in the National Health Service: a Liverpool Profile*, unpublished PhD thesis, University of Liverpool

UK Council for Overseas Student Affairs (UKCOSA) (1971) *Overseas nurses in Britain*, Evidence to the Briggs Committee on Nursing 1972, UKCOSA, London

White, R. (1985) *The Effects of the NHS on the Nursing Profession 1948–61*, London: Kings Fund

11

The Lives of Indira Gandhi

KATHERINE FRANK

Politics, even in the 1990s, is still largely an old boys' club. Women politicians are anomalies with the result that they receive a good deal more media and biographical attention than their male counterparts. Gender – rather than power, influence or statecraft – is the decisive factor in this coverage. No one has ever suggested that Indira Gandhi, the third Prime Minister of India, was a greater leader than the first Indian Prime Minister: her father, Jawaharlal Nehru. Indira Gandhi, nevertheless, has been the subject of nearly twice as many biographies.

In the 30 years since Indira Gandhi became Prime Minister in 1966, 26 biographical studies of her have been published, covering a broad spectrum from scholarly and analytical political studies on the one hand, to gossipy memoirs on the other (see Table 11.1).[1] Most of these biographies have been written by Indians, and more by men than women. At least three were originally authorised or semi-authorised lives (Masani, Moraes, Jayakar) and a great number of Indira Gandhi's biographers interviewed her extensively (Abbas, Drieberg, Bhatia, Masani, Vasudev, Carras, Singh, Moraes, Mehta, Malhotra, Jayakar). She was, in fact, unusually accessible and forthcoming to biographers, especially to women writers like Uma Vasudev and Mary Carras who not only interviewed but also travelled with her. Gandhi, however, fell out with nearly all her biographers before their books were completed and she claimed never to have read any of them.[2] No fully authorised life has been published, though shortly before her death in 1984 Gandhi asked her old friend Pupul Jayakar to write what she intended to be a definitive account.

Reading through the long shelf of Gandhi biographies, distinct types of 'life' recur: hagiographies (Hutheesing, Abbas), profiles (Sen), journalistic accounts written by newspapermen who covered Indira Gandhi for a number of years (Dreiberg, Bhatia, Masani, Singh, Moraes, Tully, Shourie, Malhotra, Gupte), personal portraits (Paul),

152

Biographies of Indira Gandhi published between 1966 and 1992

1966	K. A. Abbas. *Indira Gandhi: Return of the Red Rose*. Bombay: Popular Prakashan.
1967	Anand Mohan. *Indira Gandhi: A Personal and Political Biography*. New York: Hawthorn Books.
1969	Krishna Hutheesing. *Dear to Behold: An Intimate Portrait of Indira Gandhi*. Bombay: IBH Publishing.
1972	Trevor Drieberg. *Indira Gandhi: A Profile in Courage*. Delhi: Vikas.
1973	K. A. Abbas. *That Woman*. Delhi: Indian Book Company. Ela Sen. *Indira Gandhi*. London: Peter Owen.
1974	Krishan Bhatia. *Indira: A Biography of Prime Minister Gandhi*. London: Angus & Robertson. Uma Vasudev. *Indira Gandhi: Revolution in Restraint* Delhi: Vikas.
1975	Zareer Masani. *Indira Gandhi*. London: Hamish Hamilton.
1977	Uma Vasudev. *Two Faces of Indira Gandhi*. Delhi: Vikas.
1978	Ved Mehta. *The New India*. New York: Viking.
1979	Mary Carras. *Indira Gandhi in the Crucible of Leadership*. Boston: Beacon Press. Khushwant Singh. *Indira Gandhi Returns*. New Delhi: Vision Books.
1980	Dom Moraes. *Mrs Gandhi*. London: Jonathan Cape.
1982	Nayantara Sahgal. *Indira Gandhi: Her Road to Power*. New York: Frederick Ungar. Ved Mehta, *A Family Affair*. Oxford: Oxford University Press.
1983	Arun Shourie. *Mrs Gandhi's Second Reign*. Delhi: Vikas.
1984	Swraj Paul. *Indira Gandhi*. London: Heron Press.
1985	Mark Tully and Satish Jacob. *Amritsar: Mrs Gandhi's Last Battle*. London: Jonathan Cape. K. A. Abbas. *Indira Gandhi: The Last Post*. Bombay: Popular Prakashan.
1989	Inder Malhotra. *Indira Gandhi: A Personal and Political Biography*. London: Hodder.
1991	Tariq Ali. *The Nehrus and the Gandhis: An Indian Dynasty*. London: Picador.
1992	Pranay Gupte. *Mother India*. New York: Scribners. Pupul Jayakar. *Indira Gandhi*. New Delhi: Penguin Books India.
1994	Ved Mehta. *Rajiv Gandhi and Rama's Kingdom*. New Haven: Yale University Press.
1996	S. S. Gill. *The Dynasty: A Political Biography of the Premier Ruling Family of Modern India*. New Delhi: Harper Collins Publishers India.

dynasty histories (Mehta, Ali), political studies (Vasudev, Carras, Sahgal, Gill). Interestingly, though contemporary media coverage of Gandhi invariably stressed her unique position as a woman leader, no biographies of her to date have focused on gender. As Rajeswari Sunder Rajan observes, 'Indira Gandhi's historical importance as a woman leader of a postcolonial democratic nation and as an influential third-world political figure has not yet been subjected to extended feminist enquiry' (Rajan, 1993: 103). But although there is yet to be a feminist biography of Indira Gandhi, the fact that she was a woman has had a profound effect on the way she has been constructed as a biographical subject.

GANDHI BIOGRAPHY 1966–92

Politicians are unusual biographical subjects in that lives of them almost always appear long before (as well as after) their deaths, at key stages in their careers. Biographical activity on Gandhi coincided with four distinct phases in her life. The earliest biographies appeared in the late 1960s, shortly after she became Prime Minister, when she introduced radical reforms such as bank nationalisation and abrogation of princely purses and split the Congress Party in 1969. In the early and mid 1970s there was a second spate of books when Gandhi was at the peak of her popularity following the 1971 election and the war with Pakistan which resulted in the creation of Bangladesh. A third wave of lives appeared in the late 1970s and early 1980s after her reputation plummeted during the Emergency of 1975–7, her 1977 electoral defeat and retirement from politics. In the final phase of Gandhi biography, following her comeback in 1980 and assassination in 1984, various writers tried with hindsight to make sense of her crowded and controversial life.

Just as books appeared at these peaks and troughs of Indira Gandhi's career, so did they focus on certain questions and issues. The 1960s biographies, published on the brink of Gandhi's rule, asked 'Who is she?' The post-Bangladesh books hazarded early, and for the most part positive, assessment of her personality and performance. The post-Emergency biographies, in contrast, proffered negative later assessment. Finally, the books published since Indira Gandhi's death – both hostile and admiring – have retrospectively tried to answer the question 'Who was she?'.

Titles are revealing, and those of the biographies of Indira Gandhi written in the 1960s and early 1970s give away their responses to the query 'Who is she?' The journalist K. A. Abbas's *Indira Gandhi: Return of the Red Rose* (1966), an instant biography written less than three months after Indira Gandhi became Prime Minister in January 1966, made it clear that she was her father's daughter, inheritor, even reincarnation. Krishna Nehru Hutheesing's *Dear to Behold* (1969) is a sentimental and uncontroversial account of Gandhi's childhood, married life and years with Nehru from the perspective of a doting aunt. Trevor Drieberg's *Indira Gandhi: A Profile in Courage* (1972), with its echo of Kennedy's famous title, is the first book to consider her politics in detail. In the early 1970s, Drieberg already sees Gandhi's trend towards centralizing and personalizing political power, but he fails to grasp the dangers of her authoritarian leanings.

Drieberg, in fact, is one of the first in a line of male Gandhi biographers who was mesmerised by his subject. The apotheosis of this adoring but not always unintelligent stance appears in Dom Moraes' *Mrs Gandhi* (1980), one of the few adulatory biographies published after the Emergency. Ved Mehta's acidic trilogy on Indira Gandhi and her family, with the ironic titles *The New India* (1978), *A Family Affair* (1982) and *Rajiv Gandhi and Rama's Kingdom* (1994), stands at the opposite pole of this reverential school of Gandhi biography.

Among the early assessment books, Krishan Bhatia's *Indira* (1974) and Zareer Masani's *Indira Gandhi* (1975) are atypically dispassionate. Masani, in particular, casts a cool, penetrating and prescient eye on Indira Gandhi's politics and future. Though he describes her as a 'brilliant politician', he faults her ideological confusion and inconsistency. And writing on the eve of the Emergency, in the midst of grave economic hardship and social unrest in India, Masani portrays Gandhi at a crossroads. He forecasts that either she will move to the left, make alliances with other radical parties and bring to pass fundamental social change, or she will turn to repression and establish a dictatorship with military support. The latter, although without military assistance, is, of course, what came to pass less than a year after Masani's book appeared.

The wide gulf that separates the post-Bangladesh and post-Emergency biographies of Gandhi is illustrated by Uma Vasudev's two books, *Indira Gandhi: Revolution in Restraint* (1974) and *Two Faces of Indira Gandhi* (1978). Only three years separate them, but as

Vasudev says in her Preface to the second, 'between the two books, as between one face of Indira Gandhi and the other, lies a lost connection' (Vasudev, 1978: v). Vasudev is one of the most acute and subtle of Gandhi's biographers and her apparent *volte face* reflected a widespread disenchantment with the Prime Minister in the mid and late 1970s.

In *Revolution in Restraint* Vasudev portrays Gandhi as a leftist, socialist leader, genuinely committed to bettering the lot of the rural masses, eradicating poverty, and maintaining a democratic, secularist state. And in her Epilogue, Vasudev argues that Gandhi 'does not have to resist the blandishment of dictatorship. She just does not want it' (Vasudev, 1974: 532). *Two Faces of Indira Gandhi,* in contrast, tells an unedifying story of political authoritarianism, but Gandhi remains a curiously elusive figure. For, unlike *Revolution in Restraint*, which contains lengthy interviews with Gandhi, her voice is absent in *Two Faces*. What we hear, instead, is a chorus of Gandhi stalwarts, defenders, rejects, and renegades: most of the notable figures who surrounded her, including her son, Sanjay. The book closes, in fact, with a famous interview with Sanjay Gandhi who appropriately, considering his role in the Emergency, has the last word.

Two Faces of Indira Gandhi was the first of a flood of anti-Gandhi books published in the late 1970s and early 1980s. The best of these later assessment biographies is by Indira Gandhi's niece, the novelist Nayantara Sahgal, who published *Indira Gandhi: Her Road to Power* in 1982. Though written by a close relative, this is anything but an affectionate memoir. Drawing on family papers as well as her own memories, Sahgal portrays Indira Gandhi as a withdrawn, suspicious, joyless child who grew into an untrusting, power-hungry and sometimes paranoid adult. The central argument is that Gandhi betrayed Nehru's democratic and socialist principles, created a highly centralised government and party machine, personality cult and dynasty. From the vantage point of the nineties, this vision is highly familiar, but Sahgal's book was the first analytical study of Gandhi as an authoritarian leader and it remains one of the few to explore her relationship with her father.

Since Gandhi's assassination in 1984, there have been three full-scale biographies of her: two by journalists, Inder Malhotra (*Indira Gandhi*, 1989) and Pranay Gupte (*Mother India*, 1992), and the third by Gandhi's friend Pupul Jayakar (*Indira Gandhi*, 1992). Jayakar's, as might be expected, is an almost wholly sympathetic work that includes a great deal of new personal information, especially on

Indira Gandhi's childhood and her relationship with her husband, Feroze Gandhi. Gupte's is an idiosyncratic book, riddled with factual errors and marred by the irritating presence of Gupte himself and several Gandhi 'experts' whom he quotes incessantly to little effect. Malhotra's biography is the most politically detailed biography of Indira Gandhi to date. As a newspaper reporter and editor, Malhotra covered Gandhi for most of her career and was a close friend of her husband. But it suffers from Malhotra's failure to augment his own first-hand knowledge of Gandhi and contemporary Indian politics with valuable published and archival sources.

None of these post-assassination books, then, is definitive. And none is of the scope (or calibre) of Sarvepalli Gopal's monumental three-volume *Jawaharlal Nehru* (1975–84). In part, this is because access to Indira Gandhi's personal and political papers has been, and remains, more limited than access to the Nehru papers. But a more serious problem is that biographies of Indira Gandhi don't come to grips with fundamental issues as they rush to praise or damn their subject. Too often they appear to be cobbled together from memoirs, interviews and old press cuttings. This gives them a kind of ad hoc air. Basic problems such as the distance between biographer and subject, the relationship between the personal and the political in a politician's life, the dangers of mythic and stereotypical representations of Gandhi, and the significance of gender in her life are consistently overlooked or ignored.

WHAT'S IN A NAME? DISTANCE AND IDENTIFICATION

Indira, *Mrs Gandhi* and *Indira Gandhi* are all common titles of Gandhi biographies which reflect the biographer's stance towards his or her subject. So, too, does the way she is referred to in the text though this usually isn't consistent throughout a particular book. She is invariably called 'Indira' or 'Indu' (the name used by her family) in the early chapters covering her childhood, just as Edward Heath is 'Teddy' in the opening chapters of John Campbell's biography of Heath[3] or Harold Wilson 'Harold' at the beginning of Ben Pimlott's *Wilson*.[4] Children, of course, are usually referred to and addressed by their first names. But convention becomes a necessity in the biography of a married woman. It would be absurd to call Margaret Thatcher 'Margaret Thatcher' or 'Mrs Thatcher' when she was growing up in Grantham as Margaret Roberts. And the same holds true for young Indira Nehru in Allahabad.[5]

But what should she be called when she grows up and at the age of 26 years marries Feroze Gandhi in 1942? Indira still? Indira Gandhi? Mrs Gandhi? Authors of academic articles and books seldom refer to politicians by their first names, but surnames alone are rarely used for women – presumably because this would seem discourteous. The most neutral form for women employs *both* first and last names: 'Golda Meir,' or 'Benazir Bhutto.' (This double-barrelled usage is rare for male politicians.)

Few people, however, including biographers, have neutral feelings about Indira Gandhi and so they seldom employ both her names. (Mary C. Carras is a rare exception.) Biographers who were close to Gandhi, and those who want to create a personal, intimate or informal impression, use her first name as Krishna Hutheesing, Inder Malhotra and Pupul Jayakar all do. Nearly everyone else calls her 'Mrs Gandhi'.[6] Sometimes this has chilly overtones, especially when used by hostile male biographers.[7] Certainly 'Mrs' creates a barrier between the reader and Gandhi. Biographers like Zareer Masani and Nayantara Sahgal who use 'Mrs Gandhi' also, of course, reflect the distance they themselves feel from their subject. Less frequently, the formality of 'Mrs' may reflect a sense of awe, even reverence – rather than hostility – as in Dom Moraes' *Mrs Gandhi*.

Moraes' use of 'Mrs' is in fact misleading, for despite his veneration of Gandhi, Moraes feels very close to her indeed. A number of biographers have suggested that their biographies are also covert autobiographies, but few so openly as Moraes. In his Preface, he confesses that while interviewing Indira Gandhi and writing the book, 'I transformed myself for months into a mirror' (Moraes, 1980: xi). Despite the fact that he is twenty-one years younger than Gandhi and from an entirely different background, Moraes insists 'she and I resembled each other … both with an inbred shyness … both with a certain dislike of too much talk and loquacious people; both … with a total tiredness of and total interest in this burning, turning world' (Moraes, 1980: 111). In the late 1970s, Gandhi agreed to cooperate fully with Moraes – an agreement that amounted to authorising his biography of her – and their relationship, he says, became one 'of closeness and care'. This harmony did not last long, but Moraes remained enamoured of and closely identified with his subject even after she had spurned him and his book.

In *Mrs Gandhi*, Dom Moraes exhibits a willed – and ultimately
blinding – identification. Something quite different happened to
Mary C. Carras when she went out to India in 1975 to write a political biography of Indira Gandhi. While working on *Indira Gandhi in
the Crucible of Leadership* over a period of several years, Carras was a
close witness to Gandhi's life. Like Moraes, she interviewed her on
numerous occasions, observed her at work and at home, and travelled with her. On one of these trips they visited a famous temple in
southern India near Madras. In the motorcade, riding in a different
car than her subject, Carras suddenly realised that many of the
people lining their route thought that *she* was Indira Gandhi: the
crowds showered rose petals on the car and 'people clutched at my
hands and nearly yanked them from their sockets.' Then when they
arrived at the temple, Carras (who is a small woman like Gandhi
and apparently was wearing a sari) was again 'mistaken for her and
the cavernous halls echoed with great shouts of welcome. On the
way out, when I preceded her, the enthusiasm of the crowd could
hardly be contained. A number of people broke out from the lines
throwing flowers before me and garlanding me... men prostrated
themselves before me, touching my feet. I was acutely embarrassed
and tried valiantly to lift them up from the damp granite floor, but it
was quite impossible. They were determined to show their affection
to their... "Mother"'. Finally the local Congress party leaders were
able to shield Carras, shouting as they moved forward through the
crowd, that she was not the 'Mother'. Carras made it to the safety of
her waiting car and says that for the rest of the trip, 'I never left the
car and even hid my face' (Carras, 1979: xiv–xv).

Carras was shaken 'by this experience that I shall never forget',
but its significance for her at the time lay in its revelation of the profound and passionate adulation of the people for Indira Gandhi.
Even more startling for the reader of Carras' book, however, is the
extraordinary position she briefly occupies when transcending the
gulf that separates even the most closely identified biographer and
subject, she actually *became* her subject and lived the life she was
observing and writing. Carras's panic in the mob of Gandhi wor-
shippers stems not only from the fear of being mistaken for Gandhi,
but also of losing her objectivity, even her own identity.

This scene in the temple is a kind of metaphor of the process
of biographical identification – an experience that can be both
illuminating and frightening. But after her Preface, Carras renounces
identification. Instead, she stays in the car and hides her face, so

to speak: the rest of the book is an impersonal but impassioned defence of Indira Gandhi as a politician who is committed to social- ist and democratic values and motivated by a drive to achievement rather than power. Though a certain amount of self-projection may underlie this positive vision, Carras is not guilty of the distorting empathy that informs Moraes' book.

THE PERSONAL AND THE POLITICAL

Mary C. Carras' life of Indira Gandhi, Pranay Gupte's *Mother India* and S. S. Gill's *The Dynasty* are the only ones subtitled 'A Political Biography'. In Gupte's case this is a misnomer, and Gill's massive study is actually one of political analysis and assessment rather than biography. Anand Mohan's *Indira Gandhi* (1967) and Inder Malhotra's 1989 life of Gandhi try to encompass both worlds and take as their subtitles the rubric of 'A Personal and Political Biography'. What does such a description – 'the personal and the political' – mean? Very little according to Ben Pimlott, the biographer of Hugh Dalton, Harold Wilson and the Queen. In an essay entitled 'The Future of Political Biography', Pimlott maintains that 'public and private facts...cannot be put in separate boxes. Real life accepts no such partition... "Political character" is always a package in which public and private traits are intertwined' (Pimlott, 1994: p. 158)

Not, however, in Gandhi biography, where the public and the private are usually neatly cordoned off from each other – often by chapter breaks. Mohan entitles one of his chapters 'The Lady Behind the Mask', which tells us among other things, that Gandhi 'paints her toenails, prefers low heels, and uses a light lipstick' (Mohan, 1967: 244). Malhotra's corresponding chapter is 'The Matriarch at Home', in which we learn that Gandhi never exposed her midriff when wearing a sari, and who her alleged lovers were. It is hard to imagine a biography of a male politician with chapters or long pas- sages devoted to his wardrobe, hairstyle, diet, fatherly traits, mas- culine pursuits, and skills as a host; but these are standard in Gandhi biographies, especially in those written by male biogra- phers who seem to feel duty-bound to establish how 'feminine' Indira Gandhi was before going on to assess her 'ruthlessness' as a politician.

The biographical treatment of her marriage is a case in point. Feroze Gandhi, himself an MP with considerable political acumen, had a profound and decisive influence on his wife's political, as well as personal, life. Theirs was a complicated, troubled, passionate relationship with many ups and downs, including political differences, covering a period of nearly thirty years. But most of Gandhi's biographers confine the relationship to a single chapter entitled 'Feroze' or 'Marriage', as if it existed quite apart from – rather than coloured and shaped – the 'rest' of her life.

Another method Gandhi biographers use to splinter private and public is to divide their biographies into the 'personal' years before she became Congress Party president in 1959 or Prime Minister in 1966, and her ensuing 'political' career. As Rajeswari Sunder Rajan notes, gender and authority are thus reconciled 'through the familiar dichotomising of the subject into a private self and a public persona; and here it is the "self" alone that is gendered female' (Rajan, 1993: 116).

This dualistic, compartmentalized way of representing Gandhi seems to derive from a resistance to the idea that women can function as legitimate sources of power. Feminist historians and scholars themselves are often more comfortable writing about subaltern rather than powerful women. Hence the dearth of material on women political leaders.[8] Rajan attributes this to 'feminists' ambivalence towards political power and authority … [and] their opposition to the intrinsic role of the state, and in particular with its repressive and coercive machinery, armed force and the ideology of dominance' (Rajan, 1993: 103). A reluctance to associate women with 'an ideology of dominance' also explains, in part at least, the abhorrence many people felt when a *woman* Prime Minister imposed a draconian Emergency and nine years later a *woman* Prime Minister ordered the military storming of the Golden Temple at Amritsar.

The great irony of this personal–political or private–public way of thinking about Gandhi's life is that she herself almost certainly saw no division between these spheres or indeed thought in terms of separate spheres at all. And this was at once both a great strength and a great weakness. From the time she was a child, her 'private' life was invaded by political activity so that it is scarcely surprising that the boundaries between her own interests and the nation's became blurred. As Jana Everett has observed, 'The phrase coined …"Indira is India, India is Indira" resonated … The Indian people [as she told them] were her children; members of her family were the only people capable of leading them' (Everett, 1993: 131).

CONSTRUCTING INDIRA: ICONS AND MYTHS

The only way gender has consistently figured in biographies of Indira Gandhi has been in her many mythic representations: Freedom's Daughter, Mother India, the Hindu Goddess Durga, Warrior Queen, Iron Lady, and Joan of Arc martyr. But all of these gendered constructions of Gandhi have actually obscured more than they have revealed. They are also, of course, distorting – either diminishing or inflating.

As 'Freedom's Daughter,' Gandhi is portrayed in relation to a larger and more important male figure: her father, Jawaharlal Nehru. This is what Antonia Fraser calls the 'appendage syndrome' in her popular survey of women leaders, *Warrior Queens* (Fraser, 1988: 12). Francine D'Amico prefers the rubric 'political surrogate' to describe women who replace their fathers or husbands as politicians and carry on their programmes and policies (D'Amico, 1995: 22). As Rounaq Jahan and Linda K. Richter have pointed out, the 'appendage' or 'political surrogate' syndrome is the classic career pattern for South Asian women politicians. In India, Pakistan, Bangladesh and Sri Lanka women have come to power either as the inheritors of their fathers (Gandhi, Benazir Bhutto, Hasina Wazad) or husbands (Sirimavo Bandaranaike, Khaleda Zia, Chandrika Bandaranaike Kumaratunge.[9]) Such women, in Richter's words, are only 'accepted as behaving appropriately in politics when they are perceived as filling a political void created by the death or the imprisonment of a male family member' (Richter, 1990: 526). The shadow of Nehru accordingly looms large in biographies of Indira Gandhi, as evidenced in such titles as *Freedom's Daughter, Return of the Red Rose, An Indian Dynasty* and *A Family Affair*. In these books, Gandhi dutifully carries on, measures up to, or betrays Nehru's legacy: she remains defined in the context of his stature.

The portrayal of Gandhi as 'Mother India' – the title of the most recent Gandhi biography, by Pranay Gupte – is perhaps the most potent and enduring of the myths which haunt Gandhi's life, as she well knew. In a 1967 speech she told a crowd of villagers,

> Your burdens are relatively light because your families are limited and viable. But my burden is manifold because *crores* [a crore equals ten million] of my family members are poverty-stricken and I have to look after them. Since they belong to different castes and creeds, they sometimes fight among themselves, and

I have to intervene, especially to look after the weaker members of my family, so that the stronger ones do not take advantage of them. (Malhotra, 1989: 104)

As Rajan notes, 'the acceptable face of leadership is service [because] it denies power [and] stresses sacrifice' (Rajan, 1993: 110). The 'Mother India' card was one that Indira Gandhi played throughout her career by insisting that the only power she wanted was the power to serve, protect, do right and do good. Not that this was an exercise in hypocrisy. There is a good deal of evidence that Gandhi truly believed in her larger-than-life image as Mother India and that she felt a genuine maternal identification with the country. Nehru was the 'father' of independent India; as his daughter *and* 'Mother India,' Gandhi was able to fuse *both* maternal and paternal roles into a single parental figure whose authority might well nigh seem unassailable.

The 'Mother India' myth of Indira Gandhi was the one that ran deepest both within her own and the national psyche, as Carras', Malhotra's and Gupte's biographies all reveal. But after the Bangladesh war of 1971, Gandhi was militarized and elevated into the 'Warrior Queen' in Abbas' and Drieberg's biographies and then into the invincible Goddess Durga in Dom Moraes'. The existence of female gods in Hinduism has long been an explanation for the acceptance of a woman Prime Minister in the patriarchal Indian culture. Gandhi herself was well aware of her semi-divine status in the popular imagination. When Bruce Chatwin travelled with her in 1978, he watched her 'receive' a crowd of a quarter million people come to pay obeisance to her. Gandhi sat on a balcony on a chair placed on a table so that the crowd could see her. 'She jammed a torch between her knees, directing the beam upwards to light her face and arms. She rotated [her]…arms as if performing the mudras of Lakshmi, Goddess of Wealth…"Do get me some more of those cashew nuts,"' she said to Chatwin, '"You've no idea how tiring it is to be a goddess"' (Chatwin, 1989: 326).

But adoration was followed by contempt. When Indira Gandhi was re-elected in 1980, just a year after Margaret Thatcher came to power, both women soon became known as 'Iron Ladies'. The phrase touched a nerve and became in time the title of Beatrix Campbell's study of Tory women, the American edition of Hugo Young's biography of Margaret Thatcher, and of the chapter Fraser devotes to Gandhi, Thatcher and Golda Meir in *Warrior Queens*.

'Iron Ladies' was not a self-chosen image, though Thatcher, after the Falklands, revelled in it. Instead, it originated with Tass, the Soviet news agency, which did not coin it out of admiration. 'Iron lady', as Patricia Lee Sykes observes, 'transforms strength and determination (so admired in men) into rigidity and insensitivity (perceived as flaws in women)' (Sykes, 1993: 225). In Gandhi's case, this negative image was further developed into a vision of her as cold, calculated, ambitious, ruthless, immoral – as seen in Arun Shourie's Ved Mehta's, and, to a lesser extent, Tariq Ali's portrayal of her.[10] The antithesis of a mother or a goddess, Gandhi as 'Iron Lady' is entirely without redeeming qualities and devoid of any sort of emotional reality at all. She is *iron* – not flesh and blood – a human machine.

Indira Gandhi's death, at the hands of assassins on 31 October 1984, shocked even her severest critics, and also reminded nearly everyone who knew anything about her life, that from the time she was a child, Gandhi was obsessed with Joan of Arc. Her childhood impersonation of Joan of Arc on the wide balcony of Anand Bhaven, the Nehru family home in Allahabad, is, in fact, a set piece in nearly every Gandhi biography beginning with Hutheesing who witnessed it at first hand. And it is difficult to find an interview with Gandhi about her early years that doesn't mention this fixation. She always says in such interviews that it was Joan of Arc's death above all that fascinated her. Even a sceptical writer like Ved Mehta hypothesises that when Gandhi authorised Operation Bluestar – the storming of the Golden Temple in Amritsar which led four months later to her Sikh bodyguards' murder of her – she was 'tired of life' and was courting, if not positively inviting, martyrdom. Certainly her life *seems* to come full circle at the end and find its ineluctable fulfilment.

Hence, two of the three biographies published since her death actually begin with long chapters on her assassination, minutely chronicling the last several days, hours, minutes and seconds in Gandhi's life. Malhotra's opening chapter is entitled 'Murder in the Morning'. Writing three years later, Gupte entitles the entire Part I of his biography, 'The End'. It was, of course, horrifying that Indira Gandhi was gunned down in her own garden, by men whose job it was to protect her. It is appalling as well that among the half dozen or so men – bodyguards, aides, secretaries – who walked with her down her garden path, none made any attempt to shield or help her. They all hit the ground or fled.

But Indira Gandhi could not have foreseen and did not orchestrate her own death. Though she had long entertained the possibility of assassination, and seems to have had strong premonitions of death during the last weeks of her life,[11] she could not have predicted how it would happen and how those close to her would behave. Nor is it credible that however 'tired of life' she felt in 1984, that she would choose to act on this feeling by staging a holocaust in the Punjab. In the end, the martyrdom that Indira Gandhi dreamed of as a young girl, was simply an accident when it was achieved. This final 'Joan of Arc myth' of her life is as spurious as all those which preceded it.

GENDER AND BIOGRAPHY

Myths seek to deify or demonize, and this has been their primary function in Gandhi biography. But they have also inadvertently introduced the issue of gender because all these myths – from Freedom's Daughter to Joan of Arc – are stereotypically female ones. Nevertheless, in *Women in Modern India*, Geraldine Forbes rightly says of the plethora of material on Gandhi that it has 'not yet tackled questions associated with the Prime Minister's gender, what this meant to the country, and the extent to which her policies were relevant for women' (Forbes, 1996: 103).

Why is this the case? Most obviously, because the majority of Gandhi biographers have been men. Another reason derives from the fact that Gandhi herself was at pains to dissociate herself from any women's movement and repeatedly asserted that she was not a feminist (Carras, 1995: 56). Too many biographers have taken her at her word, or have wrongly assumed that because Gandhi was not conspicuously committed to women's issues, gender was of no significance in her life and career.

The evidence that it *was* significant – even crucial – is there for anyone to see: in Nehru's autobiography and other writings,[12] in the massive correspondence between Nehru and Indira Gandhi that Sonia Gandhi has edited,[13] in the biography of Gandhi's mother, Kamala Nehru, that Indira Gandhi commissioned and contributed to,[14] in the revealing interviews Gandhi gave to women, including Betty Friedan and Oriani Fallaci,[15] in the autobiographies of countless friends and associates; in the papers at the Nehru Library; in the memories of the many who knew her well who are still alive; in the minds of the millions of women who voted for and believed in her and in those who felt she lied to and betrayed them.

These and many other sources yield information and insights into the significance of gender in Gandhi's life both before and after she became Prime Minister. As an Indian woman, Gandhi lived in a hierarchical, androcentric society and it is revealing to determine when she subscribed to, when she avoided, and when she defied its conventional gender norms. There is no consistent pattern in her behaviour because tradition, accident and personal rebellion all came into play; but by focusing on key events and periods in Gandhi's life we can clearly see how she sometimes adhered to, sometimes flouted, sometimes was trapped by and sometimes escaped socially-constructed notions of femininity and womanliness. In addition, she was acutely aware of others' perceptions and expectations of her as a woman, and these of course had a profound effect upon her behaviour, personality and identity, particularly after she was in office. Indeed, at the height of her power – when she most vociferously eschewed feminism and insisted that she was not 'a *woman* Prime Minister,' but a Prime Minister full-stop – Gandhi was most aware of her highly anomalous position as a woman leader.

In her childhood, young adulthood, marriage and widowhood, the following gender-related areas, in particular, need to be explored: the fact that Indira Nehru was an only child in a politically active family committed to an independence struggle that loosened gender strictures; her parents' unhappy marriage; her mother's feminism; her insistence upon a 'love marriage' to Feroze Gandhi in defiance of her family's and much public disapproval; the tensions in her marriage and the effect upon her of her husband's infidelities; her social and psychological position as a widow. After Gandhi became Prime Minister, it is important to examine her attitude towards women's issues and women in politics (unlike her father, for example, she appointed no women to her cabinet); the effects of her government on Indian women's lives; her position *vis-à-vis* various women's movements; the nature of her populism and her relationship with women voters; and the degree to which gender had a role in her domestic and foreign policy.

Gender is fundamental and inescapable. As soon as we are born, the socialisation process of acquiring a feminine or masculine identity is initiated, and it is a lifelong process. All the biographies that

have been written of Indira Gandhi fail to go back to this fundamental premise of gender. In these biographies she is merely a frac-
tion of a woman – a daughter or a mother or a widow – or she is a
goddess, a man in disguise, a devil or a saint. What is needed now
is a biography of her that is rooted in, but not circumscribed by,
gender – in which the consideration of gender makes us ask more,
not fewer, questions. Questions which enable us to discover more
complicated patterns, more intriguing answers. To explore the issue
of gender is not limiting; it is enlarging. It reveals subtlety and complexity, rather than simplification in a human life. Indira Gandhi,
whatever we may think of her, deserves no less.

Notes

1. Indira Gandhi also figures prominently in the memoirs of contempo-
    raries such as Raj Thapor's *All these Years*, K. K. Birla's *Reminiscences*
    and P. C. Anderson's *My Years with Indira Gandhi*, and in novels by
    Nayantara Sahgal, Salman Rushdie and Rohinton Mistry.
2. Gandhi did read a large portion of Uma Vasudev's *Indira Gandhi:
    Revolution in Restraint* when it was still in manuscript, and made cor-
    rections to, and criticisms of, it. Interview with Uma Vasudev, New
    Delhi, 2 February 1996.
3. John Campbell, *Edward Heath: A Biography* (London: Cape, 1993).
4. Ben Pimlott, *Harold Wilson* (London: HarperCollins, 1992).
5. Almost all married women politicians have taken their husbands'
    names. Benazir Bhutto is a notable exception.
6. In the press, the media and novels, Indira Gandhi collected a number
    of other, generally unflattering, designations: 'Madame', 'that
    Woman' and 'The Widow', among others.
7. In his biography of Margaret Thatcher, *One of Us*, Hugo Young's con-
    sistent use of 'Mrs Thatcher' to refer to his subject contributes to his
    scathing portrait of her.
8. The few worthwhile studies include: Francine D'Amico and Peter R.
    Beckman, eds, *Women in World Politics* (London: Bergin & Garvey, 1995);
    Michael A. Genovese, ed., *Women as National Leaders* (London: Sage,
    1993); Laura A. Liswood, *Women World Leaders* (London: HarperCollins,
    1995).
9. Both parents of Chandrika Kumaratunge, the current President of Sri
    Lanka, led the country before her. Her father was Prime Minister from
    1956, until his assassination in 1959. Her film-star politician husband,
    Vijaya Kumaratunge, was also killed by assassins in 1988. Her mother,
    Sirimavo Bandaranaike, was Prime Minister between July 1960 and
    March 1965, and again from May 1970 and July 1977. In 1978,
    Sri Lanka changed to a Presidential system of government. Currently,

Sirimavo Bandaranaike is Prime Minister, while her daughter holds the more powerful executive position of President.

10.   The 'Iron Lady' also lies behind Salman Rushdie's fictional portrayal of Gandhi as 'the Widow' in *Midnight's Children*. See my article, 'Mr Rushdie and Mrs Gandhi', *Biography*, 19, n. 3 (summer 1996), 245–58.

11.   Sonia Gandhi writes of her mother-in-law's strong sense of imminent death in the autumn of 1984 in *Rajiv* (London: Viking, 1992).

12.   Jawaharlal Nehru, *Autobiography* (London: John Lane, 1936). *The Discovery of India* (Calcutta: Signet Press, 1946). *Glimpses of World History* (Allahabad: Kitabista, 1934–5). *Selected Works of Jawaharlal Nehru*, eds M. Chalapathi Rau, H. Y. Sharada Prasad and B. R. Nanda (Delhi: Orient Longman and NMML, 1992). *Selected Works of Jawaharlal Nehru* (second series), ed. S. Gopal (Delhi: Orient Longman, NMML, 1984).

13.   *Freedom's Daughter: Letters between Indira Gandhi and Jawaharlal Nehru 1922–39*, ed. Sonia Gandhi (London: Hodder, 1992).

14.   Promilla Kalhan, *Kamala Nehru* (New Delhi: Vikas, 1973).

15.   Betty Friedan, 'How Mrs Gandhi Shattered the Feminine Mystique', *Ladies Home Journal* (May 1966). Oriana Fallaci, *Interview with History* (Boston: Houghton Mifflin, 1976).

References

Abbas, K. A. (1966) *Indira Gandhi: Return of the Red Rose*, Bombay: Popular Prakashan

Abbas, K. A. (1973) *That Woman*, Delhi: Indian Book Company

Abbas, K. A. (1985) *Indira Gandhi: The Last Post*, Bombay: Popular Prakashan

Ali, Tariq (1991) *The Nehrus and the Gandhis*, London: Picador

Bhatia, Krishan (1974) *Indira: A Biography of Prime Minister Gandhi*, London: Angus & Robertson

Carras, Mary C. (1979) *Indira Gandhi in the Crucible of Leadership*, Boston, Mass.: Beacon Books

Carras, Mary C. (1995) 'Indira Gandhi: Gender and Foreign Policy,' in *Women in World Politics*, ed. Francine D'Amico and Peter R. Beckman, London: Bergin & Garvey

Chatwin, Bruce (1989) 'On the Road with Mrs G,' in *What Am I Doing Here?* London: Picador

Dabari, Raj and J. Dabari (1983) *Indira Gandhi's 1028 Days*, Delhi: R. & J. Dabari

Drieberg, Trevor (1972) *Indira Gandhi: A Profile in Courage*, Delhi: Vikas

D'Amico, Francine (1995) 'Women National Leaders,' in *Women in World Politics*, ed. Francine D'Amico and Peter R. Beckman, London: Bergin & Garvey

Everett, Jana (1993) 'Indira Gandhi and the Exercise of Power,' in *Women as National Leaders*, ed. Michael A. Genovese, London: Sage

Forbes, Geraldine (1996) *Women in Modern India*, Cambridge: Cambridge University Press

Frank, Katherine (1996) 'Mr Rushdie and Mrs Gandhi,' *Biography*, 19, no. 3: 245–58

Fraser, Antonia (1988) *Warrior Queens*, London: Mandarin

Gill, S. S. (1996) *The Dynasty: A Political Biography of the Premier Ruling Family of Modern India*, New Delhi: HarperCollins

Gupte, Pranay (1992) *Mother India: A Political Biography of Indira Gandhi*, New York: Scribners

Hutheesing, Krishna (1969) *Dear to Behold: An Intimate Portrait of Indira Gandi*, Bombay: IBH Publishing

Jahan, Rounaq (1987) 'Women in South Asian Politics,' *Third World Quarterly*, 9, no. 3:848–70

Jayakar, Pupul (1992) *Indira Gandhi*, Delhi: Penguin Books

Khilnani, Niranjan M. (1989) *Iron Lady of Indian Politics*, Delhi: H.K. Publishers

Malhotra, Inder (1989) *Indira Gandhi: A Personal and Political Biography*, London: Hodder & Stoughton

Masani, Zareer (1975) *Indira Gandhi*, London: Hamish Hamilton

Mehta, Ved (1978) *The New India*, New York: Viking

Mehta, Ved (1982) *A Family Affair*, Oxford: Oxford University Press

Mehta, Ved (1994) *Rajiv Gandhi and Rama's Kingdom*, New Haven: Yale University Press

Mohan, Anand (1967) *Indira Gandhi: A Personal and Political Biography*, New York: Hawthorn Books

Moraes, Dom (1980) *Mrs Gandhi*, London: Jonathan Cape

Paul, Swraj (1984) *Indira Gandhi*, London: Heron Press

Pimlott, Ben (1994) 'The Future of Political Biography,' in *Frustrate Their Knavish Tricks: Writings on Biography, History and Politics*, London: HarperCollins

Rajan, Rajeswari Sunder (1993) *Real and Imagined Women: Gender, Culture and Postcolonialism*, London: Routledge

Richter, Linda K. (1990) 'Exploring Theories of Female Leadership in South and Southeast Asia', *Pacific Affairs*, 63:524–40

Sahgal, Nayantara (1982) *Indira Gandhi: Her Road to Power*, New York: Frederick Ungar

Sen, Ela (1973) *Indira Gandhi*, London: Peter Owen

Singh, Khushwant (1979) *Indira Gandhi Returns*, New Delhi: Vision Books

Shourie, Arun (1983) *Mrs Gandhi's Second Reign*, Delhi: Vikas

Sykes, Patricia Lee (1993) 'Women as National Leaders: Patterns and Prospects,' in *Women as National Leaders*, ed. Michael A. Genovese, London: Sage

Tully, Mark and Satish Jacob (1985) *Mrs Gandhi's Last Battle*, London: Cape

Vasudev, Uma (1974) *Indira Gandhi: Revolution in Restraint*, Delhi: Vikas

—— (1978), *Two Faces of Indira Gandhi*, Delhi: Vikas

Part III
Writing

Representing Women's Lives: the Life-History Project

12

A Good School Revisited

MARY EVANS

This title is, I have to admit, literally untrue. I have never been back to my school, and the last look that I took as I walked down the drive was precisely that – a last look. I remember the feeling of that July afternoon: that the school and I had somehow made peace with each other and even if I had no wish to return, then at least I did not leave with only harsh memories. Even so, the memories were clearly harsh enough, and when I came to write *A Good School* (1991) it was a surprise to me, and obviously to some readers, how angry I still was with the school. Speaking about the book recently I suddenly felt furious – there seemed to be no good reason for this, and yet it was an emotion too powerful to be left uninvestigated. The investigation is the theme of this paper.

The school in question, and the school which was the setting for *A Good School*, was an excellent girls' grammar school in a prosperous commuter suburb on the fringes of London. The school was housed in its own, properly built and maintained, solid brick buildings and contained designated space for the sciences, art and domestic science. There was a swimming pool, extensive playing fields and well landscaped gardens. There was not a mobile classroom in sight, nor did any of the paintwork, external or internal, look in need of repair. Six hundred girls, in navy blue gabardine, arrived every morning – wearing hats and without so much as an earring between them to detract from the entirely uniform dress code of the school. When we arrived at school we changed into our indoor shoes, hung up our blazers and went to our classrooms before filing into the assembly hall for the daily service of thanks. This order of life was one which I followed for seven years, and it was never at any time different in any way. There were no strikes, no disruption, no absconding pupils, indeed nothing except one untimely and tragic death to mark out the years. Looking back on those years now, it is impossible not to see them, as a parent, as enviable years in which education was able to proceed with little interruption. My own children have gone to 'good' state schools, but even these 'good' schools in a middle-class village and town in Kent have mobile classrooms, rotting buildings, occasional unruly pupils and – very occasionally it has to be said – striking staff.

But for all this contrast, which is hardly great or dramatic, my own assessment of my children's and my own education is that my children are being better educated in precisely the sense which I think I longed for as a teenager. What I could not articulate then, indeed I had no understanding of it, was a desire for difference, for plurality and for diversity. A source of envy which I could identify at the time was longing for an education more like my brother's: an education which had clearly some understanding of the possibilities of the disturbance of thought. Later, at university, this vague and inarticulate feeling was translated into something truly respectable in academic terms and was called critical inquiry and debate. I also learnt ideas about the functions of great art to upset and challenge. These were not possibilities of which we were informed as we plodded our way through *Jane Eyre* and *Mansfield Park* and were taught to see these texts as confirmations of the rewards of good behaviour and generally abiding by the rules.

The rules were not, of course, just the written school rules which we were told about in our first year. The rules which mattered were rules about conformity and obedience and learning the limits of creativity and originality. It was that, I now think, which so enraged me and made me so jealous of what I perceived as the Elysian fields of my brother's education, going on just a few hundred yards from me. In his school, I fondly imagined, boys were encouraged to think and to challenge. Indeed, through the emphasis which that boys' school placed on the classics there was an engagement with some of the passions and the pleasures of life. It was, inevitably, a fantasy, but contained enough truth to make me look back, even now, with envy. In that boys' school, a highly regarded and old established Head Master's Conference grammar school, boys were being taught the legends of Oedipus and the events of the Trojan War. Many – like my brother – gave up at the first irregular Greek verb, but others – and this we knew by the sixth form – were becoming fluent in something more than a dead language. They were becoming fluent in the great themes of civilisation, themes in which men participated.

Now, as I write this, I begin to be able to name, and to explore, those feelings of some thirty-five years ago. Central to that experience of school was, I now think, a feeling of emotional and political impotence. How was I ever to claim a place, indeed make a place, in the public world, if we were taught in ways which seemed set on its eternal evasion? I wondered, and I remember this vivid wonder, if we were all expected to go through life like Fanny Price in *Mansfield Park*, forever waiting for our moment through a change in the circumstances of others, but never creating those changes through our own agency. Fanny is not, I also now know, the passive and patient heroine we learned about but in fact an active creator of her own fate. But this reading, which owes an enormous amount to feminism and a literary criticism which allows the text to be disturbed, was some way away from the school syllabus of the 1950s. Female agency had not yet been named, let alone discovered, in most educational practice. Even if we were (very fully) encouraged to do well in education, there seemed to be a lurking sense of unwritten boundaries, of how far could we go without destroying the whole edifice of learning and education.

So what now emerges for me out of this retrospective exercise is a sense of the fragility and the limits of the education which we were given. It was almost, and this I am sure had a great deal to do with its rejection by many of its pupils, devoid of contact with anything which we experienced as reality. The only 'real' subject of the school – and the one most obviously related to everyday life – was domestic science. Yet this subject, and its teacher, was regarded as a joke by the pupils. The poor woman had to face the snobbery of her colleagues in the staff room, who quite clearly took the view that cookery and needlework were something to do with servants and the lower classes, and the wilful incompetence of the pupils for whom domestic science was a chance to talk in class and eat raw cake mixture. Nobody took the subject at what was then GCE 'Ordinary Level' and the mere idea of Advanced level in the subject would probably have been regarded as comic. Over in the boys school, it has to be said, the mundane would receive much the same treatment: woodwork was regarded with as much derision as domestic science and nobody in either school managed to abandon their cultural prejudice about the making of the material world. As a lesson in binary oppositions, this education could not have been more vivid; food was an appropriate matter to study when it was raw (as was wood) but once cooked it was removed from serious study. In a bizarre way, it was the natural world and nature which was being celebrated whilst culture was denigrated.

In this hierarchy of matter, two lessons were apparent: class was closely related to the academic standing and prestige of a subject and so was gender. Woodworkers were not middle class, even though they were, at least, men. But in this instance of educational distinctions, masculinity could not save woodwork from its class associations. The systems of class and gender cast their long shadow over the school and affected, I now realise, almost everything we did. (I say 'almost' here because the school was in no sense sealed from the outside world, and the times were just about beginning to change.) Yet in describing these systems it is not enough to say that they were there, they also have to be delineated in their detail, their inconsistencies and their contradictions.

Of the two systems of the social order in the school – those of class and gender – it is difficult to say which was the more influential. Both were certainly all-pervasive. Everything we did, from the shoes we wore, to the way we held our cutlery, was infused with class expectations and class codes. What was appropriate was essentially middle-class behaviour, but behaviour which was defined by speech, deportment and what can only be described as attitude. It was a middle-class world which had a very sharp sense, in particular, of what was *vulgar*, a word which carried precise connotations of low class, common and generally unacceptable. It was a real form of boundary control between us, our families, our peers and our world and the hordes outside. These hordes did not value education, thought only of money and were inclined to make rude jokes. What was so different about those days were two aspects of English cultural life which have now dramatically changed: one was the public attitude to the making of money and the other was the toleration of other subcultures.

On the first issue – the public attitude to the making of money – it is largely part of the legacy of Thatcherism that the possibilities of commerce have come to be a part of the school, indeed the academic, curriculum. In the 1950s and early 1960s I lived amongst people who had clearly made – if not great amounts of it – then at least enough money. But the attitude to money was to say the least, hypocritical, and through its very hypocrisy, provided a fertile breeding ground for Thatcherite ideas. Thus the general view was that it was perfectly acceptable to be well provided for, but to set out to make money, indeed to think about it, was something that well brought up people did not do. The package was one which has been remarked on by many writers about English culture: the contempt for trade but the love of the profits of trade being an organising principle. Growing up above the shop in Grantham taught Mrs Thatcher hard and brutal lessons in reality – lessons which she then had to temper at her school and at Oxford. Indeed, when I think of that girlhood and mine I think of its contrast in terms of the experience of cultural patterns. Mrs Thatcher was born knowing the ideas which Marx propounded theoretically – that people make their living (in fact stay alive) through their involvement in the process of production. Her grammar school – and certainly by her own account Oxford University – attempted to educate her away from this single lesson. The failure of both these institutions to shift an attitude to money learned, literally, at her father's knee was to become apparent in a political agenda and a publicly endorsed attitude to those without money.

The circumstances in which I – and most of my contemporaries – grew up, were less harsh than those Grantham years over the shop. We were well provided for, and did not have to prove our right to be at grammar school, or later at university. It was, as the Water Rat was to say in *The Wind in the Willows* of the river bank, very much *our* territory and a world to which we belonged. In a way which made absolute sense of the idea of cultural homogeneity, the home and the school were one. The school could expect support from parents (indeed the parents were united in their support for the various requirements of the school's uniform) and there were no uncomfortable discrepancies to deal with of manners and morals. The assumptions of the world outside (or our part of the world outside) and the world inside were similar and consequently made the organisation and policing of behaviour a straight-forward matter. In the late 1960s and the 1970s it is apparent that English culture took issue with the ordered life of schools: the publication of the Oz magazine *School Kids* issue, Lindsay Anderson's film *If* and the various controversies surrounding the publication of sex education material were all instances of the ways in which the so-called 'permissive' culture of the 1960s and 1970s began to challenge the accepted authority of middle-class schools. Long hair, the wearing of jewellery, the control of extra-curricular activities all became flashpoints in the differences being articulated between generations and – eventually – between classes and races.

So the first point of tension, the first break in the peaceful life of many schools, came in terms of differences between generations. A youth culture was invented just as I left school for university and with it came the whole panoply of different clothes, music, language and eventually behaviour for people of different ages. But as soon as this culture was invented, it was rapidly redefined in terms of class, gender and race. In terms of my generation, the difference can be illustrated in terms of loyalties to different popular music: to identify with the Beatles (prior to Yoko Ono) was to identify with white British culture which was in many ways safe. To identify, on the other hand, with the Rolling Stones was to identify with a transgressive culture, with traditions located in the Black population of the United States and with ideas which had little place in conventional society. The Beatles were 'safe' enough to be awarded the MBE; nobody ever suggested that the Rolling Stones should receive the same ritual appropriation.

In reviewing, even briefly, these shifts in youth culture in the late 1960s and 1970s one aspect of the changes becomes particularly apparent. It is that crucial to the rethinking of cultural expectation for adolescents and young adults was a change in sexual *mores*. When the Rolling Stones sang about satisfaction it was an explicit reference to the possibilities of sexuality; by far from the first time that anyone had mentioned sexuality in song, but significant as the beginning of explicit references to sexuality in a mass cultural form. Thus sexuality was far from being made public for the first time in the 1960s (Philip Larkin was absolutely correct in his ironical reference to the 'invention' of sexuality in the 1960s) but the codes surrounding it changed in two vitally important ways. First of all, moral discourses about sexual behaviour shifted. (About this there is a considerable literature, some of which takes issue with the whole idea of permissiveness and argues that what happened was a prioritisation of *male* sexual interests.[1]) Premarital chastity was, for example, no longer advocated as an ideal, let alone practised as reality. Sexual compatibility and sexually explicit behaviour were often endorsed, and what Barbara Ehrenreich has described as 'recreational sexuality' was widely accepted.[2] Second, the language of sexuality changed: sexually explicit language become part of public discourse and a vocabulary of sexuality became a taken-for-granted part of everyday speech.

This digression into territory which has been widely explored is made here in order to contextualise my sense of the changes which have occurred at, and out of school between the 1960s and the 1990s. I have already mentioned that my sense, and my experience (although emphatically not an experience which I would for one minute claim as general) was of a close relationship between home and school, accompanied by a sense of inarticulate frustration at the areas of life, ideas and possibilities which the school, and the education it provided, did not give voice to. Clearly, that sense of the 'unsaid' was shared by many of my generation, for whom the lyrics of the Rolling Stones and the permissions increasingly given in the written and spoken word were very welcome. But when I now consider the possibilities allowed by these changes in the culture I am deeply sceptical about the degree to which there is a real increase in open discussion rather than a distracting shift in the vocabulary of discussion. Indeed, the argument could be taken further to the point where the suggestion is voiced that the cultural changes of the last twenty years have obfuscated rather than illuminated issues about power and control in education, and indeed the organisation of English social life generally.

In an earlier part of this paper I spoke of our education in English literature at my grammar school and our instruction in such standard classics as *Jane Eyre* and *Mansfield Park*. When we read these (and both are still being read by later generations of school children) we were very properly told about the cruelties of the early nineteenth century to children and – especially in the case of *Jane Eyre* – the humiliations imposed upon the poor and the powerless. Our attention was not drawn to the erotic possibilities of the relationship between Jane Eyre and Rochester, and we were instructed in the reading of the novel in terms of its potential for teaching self-discipline and self-control. What was interesting about this reading was that it always endorsed the moral certainty of Jane Eyre: we were not encouraged to admire the hideous Mr Brocklehurst or the cruel Mrs Reed. Our attention was directed towards Jane Eyre as a sturdy upholder of her own self-esteem. Now in one sense this reading was highly acceptable: Jane Eyre *does* endorse female agency, and those nineteenth-century critics who condemned the novel as subversive knew very well that Charlotte Brontë was furiously concerned to give women moral equality with men. So in that sense, our teachers were entirely correct to praise Jane Eyre and to offer her – and the novel – to us as an illustration of what women could achieve in terms of the development of their own self-hood. But what was never confronted in this reading – and very much part of the question about social ambiguity around the issue of femininity – was that even while Jane Eyre's sturdy independence was endorsed, her subversive attitudes were marginalised.

It is probably a commonplace of the teaching of literature in schools that teachers may not wish to dwell too often, or too thoroughly, on the subversive possibilities of literature, lest they encourage these tendencies in their pupils. Thus I wish to argue that the shift towards more 'accessible' literature on the school curriculum is part of a recognition – albeit tacit – of that commonly made remark among literary critics that 'all great literature is critical literature'. *Jane Eyre*, in the same way as *Mansfield Park* or *Hard Times* thus offers a complex challenge to teachers and schools: on the one hand the structure and resolution of fiction ('Reader, I married him' is, after all, a closure of certain ambiguities) suggest and endorse the confirmation of the conventional; while, on the other hand, they question and challenge the order which they are apparently re-enforcing. *Jane Eyre* and *Mansfield Park* can be read as treatises about the vindication of 'good behaviour'. At the same time, they can also be read as powerful, and potentially subversive, accounts of women negotiating particular positions with powerful institutions and/or individuals.

The subversive possibilities of these novels was, I think, what I saw and what was a central part of their allure. I could not, in those days, articulate any sense of the subversive or transgressive in literature. I doubt if I knew the terms. But what I did recognise was that more was going on in *Jane Eyre* and *Mansfield Park* than simply narratives of female struggle and resolution though heterosexual marriage. The emphasis of the teaching which I received was on the possibilities of overcoming difficulties and on the value of stoical endurance. What was equally important in the case of *Jane Eyre*, was the implicit assumption of social progress: England in the 1960s, we were told, had become a kinder place to children. Thus, the link was made between Jane Eyre's progress and progress in society as a whole. That heady optimism, of a society which still largely endorsed the progressive expectations of the Welfare State and the post-Second World War settlement, was part of the reading of *Jane Eyre* which we were offered. Reading the novel now, it is impossible not to read it in the light of Foucault's reinterpretation of the concept of post-Enlightenment 'progress' and the profound scepticism with which it is nowadays commonplace to interpret historical and social change.

But the 'stories' of the novels which we read (and Austen and Charlotte Brontë were accompanied by Dickens, Thackeray, and Elizabeth Gaskell) were the most crucial part of the readings offered. 'Knowing the plot' was held to be essential to the understanding of the novel and in one sense that was obviously important. But 'knowing the plot' – in the sense of knowing exactly who marries whom – contains numerous normative assumptions *about* the plot and it is that point – of questioning the order of narrative – that I now regard as an important theme in both my education and education generally. Moreover, I would now argue that those shifts towards more 'accessible' literature are part of a recognition by schools and teachers that the great narrative fiction of English literature is – as the exam questions suggest – always critical literature. In a society which is more unsure about its moral cohesion (and this would certainly be true of Britain in the 1990s rather than the 1960s) it is difficult to continue to 'read' great fiction with quite the same heady optimism as we then read the classics.

Thus, what I would suggest is that what I now recognise in my education is an example of the working out of women's relationship to knowledge and writing which has been articulated by writers such as Kristeva, Irigaray and Harding.[3] All these authors, in different ways, have argued that there is no such thing as gender neutral language – or knowledge. This potentially revolutionary, and deeply radical idea, has been part (and a very crucial part) of academic feminism of the 1970s: what is generally described as 'second wave feminism'. The writers mentioned above are by no means the only women who have contributed to this debate, but what they share with others is the refusal of the taken-for-granted assumption that the tradition of written knowledge and culture is one which presents a universal position. Kristeva *et al.* have argued that in post-Enlightenment culture women and femininity have both been marginalised by a culture which has been dominated by men. Kristeva recognises the great 'feminine' writers (such as Joyce and Proust) but she sees them as part of a contested space in literature between male and female discourses of understanding. As Toril Moi has written of Kristeva:

> If 'femininity' has a definition at all in Kristevan terms, it is simply, as we have seen, as 'that which is marginalised by the patriarchal symbolic order'. This relational 'definition' is as shifting as the various forms of the patriarchy itself, and allows her to argue that men can also be constructed as marginal by the symbolic order, as her analyses of male avant-garde artists have shown.[4]

The richness, and diversity, of Kristeva's work (and that of many other feminist writers on literature) cannot be adequately represented here, but what I have come to recognise, in reading Kristeva is that the appeal of 'masculine' education, which I so deeply envied as an adolescent, was associated with ambivalence about the female condition – obviously mine in particular – and the construction of womanhood and femininity which we were being encouraged to endorse. My understanding of the school's culture was that femininity had to be 'organised' in a way which included the acceptance of a patriarchal judgement and wisdom and yet excluded the endorsement of the 'feminine'. Thus my experience of education was that we were being encouraged to accept the place of women as 'angels in the house' – the 'good' women of Mansfield Park and Thornfield Hall. As such there were real limits being set on the possibilities of women's lived experience. In this context the question of endurance and stoicism were obviously elements to be emphasised in *Jane Eyre* and *Mansfield Park*, and what was not to be emphasised were the challenges of Jane and Fanny to patriarchal authority. Hence the paradox of my fantasy about the value, richness and sheer excitement of 'male' education: in my imagination this education would in some sense rescue me from what seemed to be offered to women – an explanation of the world in which only acceptance and patient endurance were possible and in which female agency was always questionable. In short, what attracted me was the prospect of masculine agency – the idea fixed in my adolescent imagination was that 'men' could act and define and order the public and private space in ways which women would not.

In this context – that of inarticulate dissatisfaction with the model of femininity being offered to me – the 'masculine' had a considerable appeal. My teachers did not point out to me (indeed, at that point no one could have done so) the internal ambiguities in the texts studied: I did not learn about the theoretical implications (in terms of what Kristeva has called *jouissance*) of the absence of positive mothers in *Jane Eyre* and *Mansfield Park*, nor did I learn about the ways in which Jane Eyre herself challenged – through the erotic – the phallic power of Mr Rochester. We passed rapidly over those passages in which Jane sadistically threatens Rochester with the withdrawal of her love and moved instead to the firmly institutional morality involved in the rejection of Rochester's offer of bigamous marriage and illicit heterosexuality. It was not suggested that the negotiation of heterosexuality is *in itself* problematic: it was only problematic in Charlotte Brontë and Jane Austen because the individuals concerned had inadequately understood its proper social organisation.

We were therefore drawn to the inescapable conclusion – and a conclusion inescapably linked to the progressive assumption of the post-war consensus – that proper social arrangements and appropriate institutional mechanisms could organise the inherent confusions and contradictions of sexuality. In a sense which I now regard as fundamental, I would argue that our education assumed rigidly modernist values that have clearly been fragmenting throughout the twentieth century. In terms of the English literature syllabus, this view was apparent in the endorsement of narrative and, most importantly, narrative as closure and resolution. The origin of this form of fiction (and its anti-femininity and its part in the marginalisation of Women) was not identified. But what came across in the teaching was an extraordinarily debilitating refusal of the feminine which encouraged many of my contemporaries to seek either (or both) the authority of the male symbolic order or explicit, socially constructed femininity. The feminine *as difference* was a position which it was too difficult to articulate.

These words are written – as the cliché goes – less in anger than in sorrow. The education my good school gave to me was, in many ways, valuable in entering the entirely patriarchal world of higher education. But my relationship to that world remained problematic until my biography and general history reached a coincidence where ambiguity in social and sexual relations became possible, and thus a liberating rather than a restrictive possibility. Those great texts which we studied (in my view so unsatisfactorily) can now be reread in terms of the choices and the spaces which they open up for women. The rejection of this great tradition, in favour of more facile and/or accessible literature, offers not a liberation for contemporary adolescents but a debased version of the restrictive readings which we were offered. Thus, just as we reach the point where we might begin to understand the richness of complexity, it is removed in favour of simplicity and confirmation. The conventional, I would argue, remains the enemy of education. Its nature may change, but the good school still needs to challenge its incursion into understanding.

Notes

1. See, for example, Sheila Jeffreys, *AntiClimax* (1990), London: Women's Press.
2. Barbara Ehrenreich, *The Hearts of Men* (1983), London: Pluto Press.
3. For the extensive selection of Kristeva's work, see *The Kristeva Reader*, ed. Toril Moi (1986), Oxford: Blackwell. Luce Irigaray's most frequently cited articles in 'The Sex Which is Not One', repr. In Elaine Marks and Isabelle de Courtivron, eds, *New French Feminisms* (1981: 99–106), Brighton: Harvester.
4. Toril Moi, *Sexual/Textual Politics* (1985; 166), London: Methuen.

References

Ehrenreich, Barbara (1983) *The Hearts of Men: American Dreams and the Flight from Commitment*, London: Pluto

Evans, Mary (1987) *Jane Austen*, London: Tavistock

—— (1991) *A Good School*, London: Women's Press

Jeffreys, Sheila (1990) *AntiClimax: A Feminist Perspective on the Sexual Revolution*, London: Women's Press

Shaw, Jenny (1995) *Education, Gender and Anxiety*, London: Taylor & Francis

Steedman, Caroline (1986) *Landscape for a Good Woman*, London: Virago

Wilson, Elizabeth (1980) *Only Halfway to Paradise: Women in Post-War Britain, 1945–1968*, London: Tavistock

13

The Most Difficult Door

CATHERINE BYRON

Be wary, but don't fear the darkening street.
I give you this, my opened map of flight.

The Most Difficult Door
(Rumens 1987: 67–9)

The first and only week that my Irish grandmother and my English grandmother spent together in the house of my childhood was early in the summer I turned thirteen. Thirty-seven years later, I remember it as the only still point of my shifting, shifty genetic inheritance and of my ambiguous nurturing. 'Mongrels', my brother and I used to call ourselves. We were so very conscious of belonging to neither the Ireland our mother came from, nor the England of our father. We were growing up in Belfast, chief city in the country of neither parent, Northern Ireland, and within a social and intellectual community where it was assumed we were Protestants. We were in fact practising Roman Catholics. Well, three of us were; my father was argumentatively agnostic.

Looking back, it seems extraordinary that our two grandmothers had not met before. There were unimpeachable reasons why neither of them had made it to our parents' wedding, but I feel sure that the ceremony itself, if not the union, would have offended them both if they had been there. A Roman Catholic marriage service, but with no Nuptial Mass? Neither would have been happy. For the two women were, even for the period, unusually fervent holders of their own highly coloured and dramatically opposed beliefs. My father's mother was a deeply religious strict Methodist, the wife of a headmaster, from England's south coast. My mother's mother was a deeply religious Roman Catholic who had run, almost single-handed, her husband's small farm in East Galway. What on earth would they make of one another when they met at last, for the first time, eighteen years after their son and daughter's wartime marriage? They would be under the same roof at long last. That was, however, in the province that was the unaccommodated relict of the centuries-long conflict between their countries and their faiths.

The house itself, in a cul-de-sac called Holyrood, was jerry-built late Victorian; the tell-tale orange dust of dry rot fungus kept coming to light in new places, and the hallway was particularly prone to its invasive threads of mycelium. The early summer that my grandmothers came, the hall floor was not, as usual, having new planks pieced into it. My mother was relieved. It was bad enough that the two women, both in their seventies, had to go all the way up to the guest room on the top floor, which with the turns and half-landings meant four substantial flights of stairs. For my brother and me the attic storey was far snugger than our draughty first floor bedrooms, and in every way more desirable. The guest-room had what my mother called a queen-sized bed, almost half as wide again as our narrow singles. We were never, ever, allowed to sleep in it. I dream that I do, sometimes, even now.

My parents were that classic courtship couple, a doctor and a nurse. They were brought together by the war in London's time of greatest peril, and then their city centre hospital was evacuated into the country. They fell in love for keeps there, cycling along the deeply leafy lanes of Buckinghamshire. When they married in a nearby (Catholic) church in 1943, were they sad, or secretly relieved, that neither of their mothers was there? My father's mother was ill with heart trouble. My mother's mother could not leave either farm or Ireland, not during what the Irish government called 'The Emergency' – elsewhere known as 'The Second World War'. It would take those 18 years before the two women set eyes on each other for the first – and last – time. How utterly astonished both my parents were when they did finally meet, and loved each other immediately. They stayed on together in Holyrood – did they really share that queen-sized bed? – for more than a week. The joint visit was unplanned, unexpected, and a complete success.

'The really glorious moment was when the two of them were sitting side by side, watching the wedding of the Duke and Duchess of Kent on that first television we had. How they both adored a royal wedding!' my mother told me, marvelling still at that common ground between them when she spoke of it a month later, a year later; speaks of it even now when she is older than they were when it happened.

Four years on, though, from that legendary, healing week, things were very different. It was within days of my English grandmother's sudden death in London. I found my mother in distraught tears that were different from her initial grief and shock.

'Can you believe it?' she asked me. 'I've just heard it from the solicitor. Granny has left Ian Paisley money in her will.'

'What? Ian Paisley?'

'Well, not by name. But she's left it to his organisation. "To help in the good fight of the Protestant Truth against the Church of Rome." And I loved her. I thought she loved me. I thought she'd accepted me as her daughter, despite the religion. Now I feel I hardly knew her after all.'

It was one of the very few occasions in my life when my mother could not find the words that would hold together the wound in her that was her 'mixed marriage'.

Through all the Belfast years our home was a microcosm of our parents' bifurcated life, its uneasy balance of power and appeasements. How expert we the children became in the subterfuges and the well-chosen silences that kept our father sweet. For he was understandably bitter about the promises he had been forced into making by the Church in order to marry my mother: that any children were to be raised and schooled as Catholics. We worked very hard to minimise his day-to-day awarenesses and hurt. My mother first and then my teachers – all nuns from Ulster homes – schooled me expertly in what Seamus Heaney has called 'the government of the tongue'. Sometimes I think that my friends and relations who have grown up in the South, the Twenty-Six Counties, the Republic, whatever you want to call it, have no idea how beleaguered and placatory and colonised a version of Catholicism we Northerners were raised in – men as well as women.

Then it all came to an end. My brother and I returned one July from our respective religious boarding schools, and found the carpets already lifted, the furniture already sent for crating or to the salerooms. There were faint shadows on the walls where pictures and plates had hung. We were moving, we were told, to London.

In that blessed, baggy house, all the impossibilities and tensions of our parents' unlikely coupling had been, somehow, contained. The strangeness for both of them of living in a half-alien place with smouldering sectarian tensions that half-matched their own had – I think, I guess – made their own split loyalties more manageable. After they left Belfast, and settled uneasily into a tiny just-built town-house in the London suburbs, things were difficult between them for a long time. I left home soon enough to escape the worst of it. I even took the radical step of marrying when I was still only nineteen, and a student, to ensure that I got away completely. The oddest thing of all, looking back, is that I married an Englishman, and buried all my Irishness, and my plans to be a writer. I forgot a great part of my self, like so many other young women who have come over from Ireland, South or North, down the decades of this century. Irish women have been experts in assimilating, intermarrying; in burying both the shame and the pride of coming from Ireland.

So I married my Englishman – who was in fact, as we later discovered, half-Irish – and, in an out-of-sequence version of the Sleeping Beauty story experienced by many more women than me, I fell asleep. At my prince's kiss I began a sleep that took away my country, my poetry, and a large part of my self.

When I woke up, I was ten years into my marriage.

1977: THE FIRST AWAKENING: NIGHT FLIGHT

I wake from the nightmare, terrified.
'Army! Open up!' Soldiers are crashing first their fists and now the heavy butts of their guns against our front door. The panel near the lock is beginning to split, splintering inwards. I am back in the hall of Holyrood, and in the midst of an army raid. What or who are they after?
       'Number sixteen! Open up!' the soldiers cried.
       But our house was number four ...
         I was trapped in the wrong house
            the wrong dream
        and soldiers kept on banging
           at that unknown door. (Byron, 1993: 47)

I am writing it down, catching it, trying to hold it steady. It arches away from my grasp like a landed fish. In the nightmare I'm home, I'm in Belfast – and yet it's not right, somehow it's not right. Only when the soldiers call out 'Number sixteen!' do I realize that I'm not in 4 Holyrood. The house in the nightmare is then instantly unfamiliar, very grand, and decorated entirely in bright shades of orange. The poem that appears on the scrap of envelope I've scrabbled round for beside the bed is almost automatic writing. It is the first poem I have written for ten years.

The place where I have woken is Avonbank, a small farmhouse twenty miles south of Glasgow, in the southwest of Scotland. Here I am with my husband and two small daughters, plus six goats, two pigs, twelve laying hens and one crazy cockerel. I must shake off both terror and the shreds of sleep, and get up. So many living creatures rely on me here. 'Always the *I can't wait* of stock and farm' (Byron, 1993: 29). This is not quite the tough economy of subsistence farming that my Galway grandmother struggled in, but it's tough none the less. No time or space in my heart to think of the Belfast I have never once returned to: no space even for taking in, really taking in, the doorstep shooting of a relative, an uncle by marriage, who was murdered two years since when he answered a knock on his door, just a street away from my ur-house, my Holyrood.

This is the third year we have lived in the West of Scotland. The baked goods trouble me. They are too like Belfast goods: thin freckled potato cakes to pan-fry for bacon and egg breakfasts, soft triangular soda farls, wax-wrapped loaves of sliced white pan. Other things are unsettling too: the segregation of schools and of children into Catholic and Protestant; the announcements in the local press of Orange Lodge meetings; the very accents and cadences of Glasgow speech. Dead ringers, too often, for Belfast.

We have so little cash to spare, but on just one day each year I insist on leaving the farm and the children, and going alone into Glasgow, to the bookshop where I will spend the day deciding which paperback I will take back to Avonbank as my essential ration for the year ahead. The first year I bought Seamus Heaney's *Door into the Dark*. This year I bought his *North*. Is it his words that have entered my dreams and turned them into nightmares? Or is it my dreams that have made me open to his words? My brain is so scrambled by babies and animals that I only read the children's books these days. Heaney's poetry is the one grown-up text I can cope with. Strange to remember, dimly, that I took two degrees at Oxford before dropping out, turning off, mucking in.

My Galway grandmother, hearing that we keep goats, is deeply ashamed for us. When she was farming, only the landless kept goats. They could graze them on 'the long acre' – the roadside verges. It was all the grazing they had.

'Ah, they must have fallen on hard times, God love them,' she writes to my mother. When my mother comes up from England to visit us, she laughs at the way we play at farming. I think I am being very radical, but what does that word mean? Perhaps I am

literally returning to roots, rather than making new ones. And I'm
not even very good at it. My husband and I learn how to handle
our goats and hens from books. We were not, like her, brought up
to farming. Our animals again and again have a hard time of it
through our well-meaning, townie ignorance.

That nightmare gives me the first poem. Later I title it 'Night
Flight to Belfast'. But I will get no closer to writing another until
four years have passed: when we have left the farm, and left the
west of Scotland.

1981: THE SECOND AWAKENING: DRIVING NORTHWEST

It is breakfast time in the English Midlands, early September. My
daughters have settled into the new school year. There is a week
before term begins at the Art College where I've got a part-time job.
I say – to all three of the family, out of the blue – 'I think I'm going
to drive to Ireland today.'

Last week I noticed – where? – that the ferry fares to Ireland fall
to the winter rate today. I've also noticed on a map that the trunk
road we now live near, the A5, goes northwest from here across
England and Wales, straight to Holyhead: the ferry port for Dun
Laoghaire in Dublin Bay.

'I'm going to drive to Donegal.' The plan is unfolding as I speak.
I have never spent a night away from the children before, but the
time is suddenly right. My husband is so astonished he agrees, and
the girls are surprisingly calm. I promise them I'll be back for the
weekend, see them all off to work and school, fix afterschool child-
care with my neighbour, and start throwing clothes and a sleeping
bag into the car.

It is thirty-six hours later. I am standing barefoot on my beloved
Narin strand in southwest Donegal. The westering sun is lost
behind lowering rainclouds driven towards me by equinoctial
gales, but I know the exact line of its fall into the Atlantic: between
the isles of Iniskeel and Aranmore. I am alone on the rainswept,
windswept strand, my chief mother-landscape all through childhood. I'm going to pitch my pup-tent on her dunes, and sleep with
my ear against her intricate sward. Tomorrow I'll wake at first light
to walk her sands of pounded shell and bone.

And already I'm jotting down lines, finding words that move like
live creatures on the pages of my notebook. At first I'm writing of

my own return, of the seventeen-year displacement since I was last in this place – at seventeen years old. The symmetry both delights me and appalls: my life halved – or doubled? Quickly, so quickly the pressure becomes unstoppable, I know what I want to write, and the words, the lines, whole poems well up from some long-untapped source in me. I keep having to huddle, my back to the gale, in hollows of the dunes in order to take down my own dictation. I am voicing the Irish landscape's own layered witness to the past. I am speaking the unrecorded and disregarded herstory of my grandmother's rural generation of women. These are the two themes that will be at the heart of my first book, *Settlements*: the sequence that is in my grandmother's voice, 'Galway', and the sequence that gives the book its name, about the making and remaking of the land itself.

In the next four years I will write, and eventually share, then gradually publish, many of these poems. In October 1985 I will hold the first slim copy of *Settlements* in my hands, amazed. This book will be of my mother's, and her mother's, Ireland: the Republic, the Free State whose bloody birth they both witnessed. As I rejoice in the rain on Narin strand on that blessed September day in 1981 I cannot yet conceive of returning to my own differently troubled Ireland – to Belfast. Sure, haven't I far too much of the matter of the South to deal with first, to keep me circling, distancing – delaying?

I will not dare to make that journey until 1987.

AUGUST 1988: THE THIRD AWAKENING: FINISHING OUT OF STEP

January 1987. Belfast. Everything white under snow. In all my imagined returns to the city of my childhood, there was never *snow*! Such an uncommon weather in that damp sea-city, where one season trickled rainily into the next. Or so I remember it. And did the hills always hang this close over the west of the city – or is it that their out-of-the-ordinary whiteness leans on perspective?' (Byron, 1992: 153)

Bless, me, Belfast, for I have sinned: a sin of omission. It is twenty-three years since last I walked your streets.

And now it is August of the year after that brief, strangely cloaked return. I have written the body of my first prose book, astonished still at my staying power, I who love poetry for its brevi-ties, its gaps, its silences. How did I ever produce the tens of thou-sands of words, the fourteen *chapters*, for heaven's sake, of this manuscript? There is still one last chapter to write.

It was Seamus Heaney's words that finally brought me home to Belfast, by way of St Patrick's Purgatory. His twelve poem sequence 'Station Island', published in 1985 in the collection of the same name, was the irritant that got me back over the Border from my mother's and my grandmother's Ireland, and north into my own. Crazily, I footstepped his virtual pilgrimage to St Patrick's Purgatory by doing it for real myself, last summer. First of all, in the January, I travelled to Lough Derg in the remote and unpicturesque hills of southeast Donegal, and gazed across its chill waters at the hibernating miniature city that is the Purgatory, Station Island. There were months to go before the start of the pilgrimage season, when from June to August pilgrims would crowd onto it, day after day, on their overlapping three-day 'stations'. I was trying to imag-ine my own intended 'station' – on a literary quest, not a Catholic one, I assured myself. I had been haunted by the odd feel to the feminine absences Heaney was clearly – unclearly? – trying to artic-ulate within his predominantly male-peopled poem. Was it some-thing about the place itself that had unnerved him, I wondered, that stone island set in fresh waters, pre-Christian haunt, perhaps, of the goddess? Last summer, and in the seasons of writing since, I have found much bleaker reasons. I have finally lost patience with Heaney's accounts of the feminine, whether in terms of the land, or the spirit; even – especially – in terms of the real women and men who walk on, or away, in his poem 'Station Island'.

In January 1987 I gazed, none the wiser then, but eager for the quest, across Lough Derg's waters. Then I simply drove northeast across Donegal to my aunt's house in Derry. There, I was one mile over *that* Border. The next day – how come it was suddenly so easy? – I drove on, due east, to Belfast. Automatic driving. A flying, snowbound stopover.

And now I am back again, a year and a half later. This time I have driven slowly from the south on a different trajectory, up from the Mourne Mountains through County Down. My slowness comes from terror and longing, for this time I am planning to go *all* the way home, back to Holyrood, the house of my childhood. On Down's switchback roads I realise that I have never been a dri-ver on these roads. I left just days after I reached the legal age for a licence. So it is all the more important that I walk the last stretch home – though not barefoot, as I was on Station Island.

Belfast without snow. And on my own … I park the car as near the city centre as I can, and walk across the square through crowds as anonymous and absorbed as those on Station Island's lake-bound piazza. At the far end I keep on walking, out from the centre but still within the city, walking south to the house I grew up in …

My house is empty. It's a student house now, unused through the long vacation. So I can walk right up to it, and look through every ground floor window, through the letter box, into the yard. I am hungry to see it, but brace myself for the hurts.

The hearths of my old home are not just cold, they have hard-board tacked over them. The plaster mouldings of its cornices are gap-toothed. Each room looks like a waiting-room. Or a boiler-room. The backyard is partly demolished, its bricks a rubble of red and the flaking whitewash of countless springtime fresh coats. There has been no whitewashing now for many springs … (Byron, 1992: 244–5).

While I am sitting on my backyard's crumbling wall, the thump of an explosion sends a shiver through the atmosphere. Not so very far away, I think, as if I am used to this. I am unsurprised. As I walked south out of the city, I had noticed, with only a mild curios-ity, the traffic slowly seizing up in both directions, and the thick throb of ever more helicopters overhead. More thumps. This is the day set for the extradition of Maze Prison escaper Robert Russell from the Republic to the North. It sounds as though West Belfast is exploding with anger and despair. And yet I feel detached, as if I'm not here, not *now*, on the twenty-sixth of August 1988. I am back in August 1964, on the day when the last contents of 4 Holyrood were crated up, and the container taken off to the docks for shipping to England.

In Belfast *I* am the ghost, the unquiet shade stranded, like Heaney's men, in lack of acceptance and lack of understanding. A seven-teen-year-old takes so little and so much into exile. I have never, I realize with a shock, been an adult here. My forced leaving of Belfast twenty-four years ago is an unfinished story. It snags me continually in its over-and-over-again stuck record of grief. How to go forward from that repetitive and finally uncreative nostalgia?

My returns to Ireland's west have been, I see now, those of a child running to its mother for simple consolation. I have sought there the landscape of my childhood's delight, and also a more subtle and spiritual comforting. Last summer's experience at Station Island has indeed pushed me, rude and unprepared, into Experience, and made me turn away in puzzlement from the 'mother' that I now see with adult eyes ... (Byron, 1992: 246)

I realise with fear, but also a dawning relief, that I may not always need – want? – to write only about Ireland.

1992: THE FOURTH AWAKENING:
WRITING THE PATERNAL LINE

My father, my mother and I are walking along the grey shale of Charmouth beach on England's south coast. A mile to the west, behind us, is Lyme Regis, the town of Jane Austen's *Persuasion*, and of John Fowles' *The French Lieutenant's Woman*. For my father it is his Eden, the enchanted boyhood place he lived in until he was eleven. It has taken until now for me attend to his shy plea back in 1985, when *Settlements* came out: 'Isn't there anything in the story of *my* side of the family that you might want to write about?' No, Dad, has been my unspoken, unvarying reply. My matter is Ireland. My *mater* is Ireland. But here we are in Dorset, walking his child-hood lanes, peering through a high hedge at the house that he grew up in, well inland.

Oddly, he is more interested in the house that he *didn't* grow up in, and hurries us back to the sea. He is not sure of the number, but it was one of a row of eighteenth-century fishermen's cottages just up the hill from the Cobb, Lyme's famous and spectacular harbour.

'My mother was so sure it would fall down into the sea,' he tells us, 'she wouldn't let my father buy it. But – it's still here, seventy years later!' He is utterly astonished that so much of the Lyme Regis he remembers has not been washed away.

This stretch of the Dorset coast has a tendency to slip into the sea. Its unstable shale cliffs are a fossil hunter's dream. To many, the name Lyme Regis means fossils, and Mary Anning – who in 1810 at the age of eleven found a complete ichthyosaur on Charmouth beach – is more famous than Austen or Fowles. But my father, though he was to become a scientist, was not encouraged to follow her example. Far too dangerous. His mother was – despite the steel corset of her faith – always dreading what might be lost, rather than welcoming what might be found.

And so we are walking along Charmouth beach, under its unbuilt-on, unsecured cliffs, and my father is terrified that my mother and I will be caught in a landslip. We, heedless beach-combers, are fossicking happily in the slithered shale at the cliffs' feet, alert for ammonites. We soon find several small, glittering beauties, and then feel ready to stop ignoring my father, who has been gesticulating all this time from near the sea's edge, wanting us to join him at that safe distance. We walk on together as a three-some along the shoreline.

A muffled bang. I instinctively raise my camera from a huge ammonite glistening in a sea-pool, and photograph the tiny land-slip as it happens. About two hundred yards away, stones and small boulders are bowling down to the sea, and a puff of dust goes up above the cliff face. Two walkers, startled, dodge to one side. The effect on my father is astonishing. He is like a small boy, thrilled and even triumphant.

'Mother was right! You see! She was right!'

The blown-up print of my snapshot will be the best present I give him in years. I am suddenly immensely curious about this woman.

1997: WRITING AS A FORM OF LEAVING

It took me a quarter of a century from the date of my physical departure to leave Ireland for real, but that same quarter century did not see me putting down a new taproot into English soil. 'As a woman I have no country. As a woman I want no country' (Woolf, 1938: 96). Yes indeed. But Virginia Woolf also told us to think back through our foremothers, advice that I still find it very difficult to disentangle from their countries when I try to think back through mine.

I'm researching my English grandmother's life now. I'm wary and circumspect, but I'm warming more and more to her testy dis-senting tradition, her intransigent pacifism, her disdain for the bourgeois niceties of her sisters. Recently my father has given me the prison letters she and his father exchanged when she was interned for much of 1940 in Holloway Prison. She was arrested without warning, during the Battle of Britain, for noisily preaching pacifism when so many other pacifists – including Virginia Woolf – had reluctantly renounced it in the face of Hitler's barbarism. My English grandmother, the more I find out about her, is difficult, intolerant: no martyr, and an uncomfortable role model in interesting ways I never imagined when, say, my mother felt so betrayed by that bequest to Ian Paisley's co-religionists. I feel increasingly drawn to her.

I am no longer just my mother's daughter, my maternal grandmother's granddaughter, in the place where it matters: my writing. Ireland was for years a sort of romance with me, a slowness, a sweetness – however bloody my subject-matters. My too-close, barefoot reading of Heaney's 'Station Island' confirmed a gut feeling that nationalism, Catholicism and the gender distortions they fostered in the North of Ireland were sickening, not sweet. I was ready to leave.

I am conscious already how much tougher – in my head and under my tapping fingers – I will be on Winifred, my father's mother, than I was, in my starry-eyed thirties, on Catherine, my mother's mother, the one I was named for. I have no idea what I will make of Winifred's – and my – England. In my fiftieth year I'm into the fascination of what's difficult. One day I may even be clear enough of country to see Catherine, too, uncanonised. No rush, though.

References

Carol Rumens (1987) *Selected Poems*, London: Chatto & Windus
Catherine Byron (1992) *Out of Step*, Bristol: Loxwood Stoneleigh
—— (1993) *Settlements & Samhain*, Bristol: Loxwood Stoneleigh
Seamus Heaney (1969) *Door Into the Dark*, London: Faber & Faber
—— (1975) *North*, London: Faber & Faber
—— (1984) *Station Island*, London: Faber & Faber
Virginia Woolf (1938) *Three Guineas*, London: Hogarth

14

Digging Up Tangled Roots: Feminism and Resistance to White Working-Class Culture

VAL WALSH

If it is true that we can only look from a position of (relative) safety/ confidence/power, it is no surprise that I came to the life history process after my father's death in October 1990, and a three-year period during which I experienced a sudden and sharp sense of my own mortality. Life, health and professional circumstances had combined to create a crisis of confidence and meaning.[1] In 1993, I found myself simultaneously letting go of my institutional academic position (if not my academic identity), and starting my life history.[2] Later the same year, at a women's art exhibition entitled *Women Remember/Women in Conflict*, I encountered the work of artist Irene Runayker.[3] Written across one of her mixed media images, I read:

> In times of bereavement and broken dreams, our camouflage frays, decays and our history shows through. (*The Forty Five Stars*, Taoist text, cited in Runayker, 1994)

Life history process was precipitating a sense of opening rather than closure, expansion rather than contraction and withdrawal, hope rather than depression. This was academic work, but also an important part of my personal recovery and renewal.

Encouraged by other feminists to speak auto/biographically as a woman from a white working-class background, I realised that I had hitherto largely failed to examine my relationship with my class background. In particular, I had neglected the dimension of

class in relation to my feminism for too long, not really engaging it
critically as a feminist issue. Class was where my primary politics
was: that is, my class consciousness and class allegiance, and I had
failed to grasp its *gendered* significance, and therefore its political
significance within academic and socio-political debates, which
increasingly concerned me as a feminist.

This chapter draws on the early stages of my life history. The
agencies of class, gender and feminism within the processes of intimacy and estrangement, friendship and hostility, in the father/
daughter, daughter/father dyads, are central to the hybrid purposes of the narrative, which hovers at the conjunction between
psychotherapeutic discourses – explanations and goals – and the
socio-political. At a crossroads we have to choose one direction,
one way. At a conjunction we may experience synchronicity and
integration, as well as confusion and fragmentation. We find new
ways, not just back and forward, but of being in the here and now,
supported rather than burdened by what has gone before. The
chapter is in four sections: (i) Working-class hero/father and his
companion daughter; (ii) The father-daughter dance; (iii) The threat
of female agency; (iv) Moving beyond resistance?

WORKING CLASS HERO/FATHER AND HIS
COMPANION DAUGHTER

I grew up in the 1940s and 1950s on the largest council estate in the
world, amid other white, working-class families. A former local
Deputy Librarian described Dagenham as 'probably the most
solidly working-class district in the world – including Moscow'!
(Greenslade, 1976: 14). It is not surprising then, that as a girl and
young woman I saw myself as working class (as 'ordinary'), with a
politics firmly connecting me with these roots. But this early sense
of class allegiance was political, not social, and developed in the
context of my relationship with a father who was a committed
Socialist and trade unionist. At the time, I had nothing with which
to compare working-class culture; I was unaware of the significance
of my mother's different class background; and my father provided
the strength of class politics as part of my upbringing. I believe
these factors to be influential in my achieving class consciousness
as a young person which was not marked by shame.[4]

My father, Stephen Cadywould, was proud of his 'Cockney' identity. A boy from Stepney, East London, he left school at fourteen. He educated himself via evening classes in his twenties and in his thirties while working as an engineer in the Royal Air Force, which was when I first knew him. After the war, he returned to work as a top colour printer in London. He was elected Assistant Secretary of the London Printing Machine Branch of what became SOGAT, as I started grammar school in 1953, and in 1962 he was elected Secretary, a post he held until his retirement in 1972. My father provided a role model for me in relation to the public world of work and politics. He encouraged and supported me without stint throughout my schooling, telling me that 'Education is one thing they can't take away from you'. As a working-class socialist, he attached importance to education as a means to social, economic and political understanding, and as preparation for employment. He once told me that if I ever got the chance I should study economics. This suggests that, at the time, he did not view me as stereotypically female (and therefore incapable of understanding economics), but as his firstborn. His expectations during most of the 1950s were not yet obviously gender-differentiated. I felt no pressure to conform to a set of values he held. At home I learned to talk and question freely and without fear. Discussion with both my parents was a prominent feature of my upbringing.

My father told me about his childhood in the East End, of infant mortality, poverty, ill-health and premature death; and of unemployment, trade union activism, and anti-fascist demonstrations. It was a story of hardship and struggle, of audacity and determination in the face of employers and the ruling class. He was clearly a leader. For me as a child, his was a narrative of class agency and resistance, with no sense of class shame. On the contrary, there was pride and self-esteem (see Fox, 1994: 64). In this he was both conforming to the master narrative of resistance in working class fiction, and diverging from it in his lack of shame (ibid.). During this period I related to him not as a man, but as my father. I was daughter to my own working-class hero. And I had the makings of a 'natural companion' (Goulter and Minninger, 1994: 29), that is, 'a creature like himself' (ibid.), who would enjoy and care about the same things as he did. For example, my father took me to public meetings, and my social and political concerns at the time mirrored his own. I saw him as a political man, a man of principle: a fighter for causes; a defender and protector of other men (working as he did in

an all-male environment); a strong and determined man, deserving
my respect, who also loved and respected me.

When I was about thirteen, however, I began to *judge* my father
in his role as my mother's husband, from the new vantage point of
our common identity as women. He became less father, more
(mere) man in my eyes. This woman-identified stance was also (in
view of my mother's different class background) a shift in *class*
positioning, which I was unaware of at the time. This shift from
daughter to young woman, and father to man; and from father-
identification (back?) to mother-identification, was a turning point,
and a significant landmark for my latent and later feminism. I therefore identified with my mother as female, before feeling the full
impact of society's messages about femininity. I was also facing my
father's growing ambivalence towards formal education as I moved
through adolescence and towards a female identity which was, in
part, a consequence of both that education and my upbringing. In
the late 1950s, as I became more knowledgeable and articulate (and
older), my father's unequivocal support turned to dismissiveness
and put-downs: behaviour I now recognise as defensive, perhaps a
function of fear. 'Book-knowledge', he said, 'cannot compare with
the School of Life, and is no substitute.' (Feminists, too, have emphasised, even prioritized, experience over theory!) I was left wonder-
ing, in my late teens, just how old I had to be for my concerns and
arguments to carry any weight with him. When would my knowledge be my own, as opposed to second-hand? (He died about thirty
years later, without our achieving this accommodation.) I was embrac-
ing and succeeding within a world of formal education which he
had left at fourteen. Entering art school at eighteen in East London,
then three years later moving away from home to study in southeast London, the unforeseen had happened. I had slipped into the
public world and beyond his grasp.

My father had been a significant point of reference for me as a
girl. I had developed confidence in the context of our relationship,
emanating from our long walks and talks together on the coast and
surrounding countryside where the family spent weekends and
holidays. As I acquired other points of reference outside home (personal, educational, social), he must have felt his authority as father
and as working-class man undermined. I now realise that an important aspect of this dynamic was the fact that his masculinity, and
the authority vested in it, was predicated on my *femininity*: that
combination of innocence, ignorance and compliance which had,

ironically, played no part in my upbringing or education. After encouraging me as he would a boy, he now faced his need for my continuing *dependence* as daughter, and there was nothing in his background or experience to prepare him for this dilemma. He had not imagined or understood the consequences of education for a girl; and he failed to anticipate that it was not a neutral, technical process of 'development', but had class and gender consequences which would challenge us both.

Did my father feel additionally beleaguered because I was elder sister to a brother who showed less motivation in those areas which linked me to my father, such as politics and current affairs, and less interest and facility in learning and debate? Was he uncomfortable that it was his daughter, not his son, who followed him as politically active, demonstrating and speaking at meetings and on street corners? Did he come to feel that his 'natural companion' should have been my brother? My evident political passion and commitments during my teens and twenties echoed his own as a young man in the 1920s and 1930s, but I suspect that his sense of pride and identification was later mixed with feelings of ambivalence because I was not his *son*.

My father could encourage me while I was a child, and feel empowered by this. My mother's early snapshot of us, taken in our backgarden and captioned 'Val with her dad!', celebrates this relationship (Figure 14.1). I am held securely aloft, like a trophy. This is a classic father/baby daughter pose: the strength (and gentleness) of the father are displayed. The daughter 'crowns' the father's identity, and in turn is expected to feel valued and special. My mother intensified this effect, when she had the photograph reprinted and enlarged, cropping my father from the waist, and making the image horizontal rather than vertical. The result emphasised my father's arms and head as human cradle for my small body. But I am not smiling, and I do not look confident. My gaze is uncertain, perhaps denoting reluctance, even resistance, to being 'manhandled' in this way. Yet this was an important picture to both my parents: the enlargement was pasted onto painted plywood and hung on the wall.

So my father could encourage me as a girl, but only up to the point where my articulacy was something for him to take pride in, as an extension of his own verbal skills. When he began to experience my voice as 'talking back' (hooks, 1989), his pride was displaced by ambivalence. But this is not only personal stuff, since we

Daddy's Girl (*c.* 1944)

are also talking about the sexual politics of speech and authority. As bell hooks has made clear:

> In the world of the southern black community I grew up in, 'back talk' and 'talking back' meant speaking as an equal to an authority figure. It meant daring to disagree and sometimes it just meant having an opinion. (hooks, 1989: 5)

I identified strongly with these words when I came across them in 1991, recognising both my own stance as a girl and woman, and why it constituted such an affront, not just to authority figures, but also to some peers, including women, who choose (even now) not to 'talk back'. My father had, by his example, encouraged me to be principled and brave, and had been influential in creating a context and a political awareness which facilitated my 'talking back'. But he had not anticipated finding himself on the receiving end. He was disconcerted. Certainty was replaced by defensiveness. My educated identity, my incipient adult status as a woman, my inchoate feminism, combined to widen the gulf between us: I was no longer daddy's clever girl. And I had thought I was doing so well…

THE FATHER-DAUGHTER DANCE

Barbara Goulter and Joan Minninger offer six dysfunctional scenarios of 'the father-daughter dance', which they see as not only historical but also as archetypal (Goulter and Minninger, 1994: 10). The Pygmalion and companion daughter resonate for me. The father mentors the daughter, distant dreams become reality, he cannot bear to let her go (Goulter and Minninger, 1994: 96). In such a scenario, the daughter who gets on with her own life will surely stand accused of betrayal, while herself feeling betrayed by the turnabout in her relationship with her father.

Goulter and Minninger see the establishing of separate identity between father and daughter to include 'transforming the father from a love-object to a like subject, from an object of idealization to a human being' (1994: 90). But 'human being' is a term which obscures the power relations and social formations which appear to be so central in my own account, as a multiple marginal. The authors seem oblivious to the psychic and social repercussions of class (see Fox, 1994; Sennett and Cobb, 1972; Spence, 1986, 1995; Steedman, 1993), and their text demonstrates unselfconsciously heterosexist assumptions about women's lives after father. The concept of (internalised) *oppression* is missing. Moreover, the *politics* of women's speech and authority is overlooked. For example, my own attempts in my teens and early twenties to relate to my father as 'like subject' rather than 'love object' (Goulter and Minninger, 1994: 90) – that is, to 'talk back' as I had been encouraged to do as a child – became part of the problem and were resisted. Having been my father's 'love object', I failed to make the transition to 'like subject'. At this moment of crisis, my father's working-class masculinity failed him (and me), leading him to feel uncomfortable with my developing identity as a woman. White working-class culture shifted from being my cradle, to feeling, if not a prison, certainly a bed of nails. Did I, then, 'go too far in separating' (ibid.)? My sense of responsibility does not extend to guilt here, not least because, in a patriarchal society, women's guilt is a feminist issue. 'The relation between social formations and structures of feeling' (Fox, 1994: 14) threads through critical auto/biography, and points to the inadequacy of considering only one or the other: social formations or structures of feeling. Just as there were no feminist contexts in the late 1950s and early 1960s to support and inform a working-class girl's coming to form as a woman, there was no context (for example, other concerned working-class men/fathers) which would have helped my father reflect on his classed masculinity. Again, this is not simply a private matter or personal failure:

> Our notions about what a girl should be and how a father should raise her have changed more over the last fifty years than over the previous hundred and fifty, or the thousand and fifty before that. (Goulter and Minninger, 1994: 27)

Though politically active since a boy, my father's Socialism could not help him in relation to questions of subjectivity, gender power relations, and how to father a budding feminist daughter! His Socialism was so implicated in his working-class masculinity, it could be seen as part of the problem. The narrative resources for a white working-class man in relation to his own classed masculinity and sexuality have been, and still are, practically non-existent or very limited. And while as father and daughter we both lacked the means for politicising our dilemma, as a female in the post-war years, I was benefiting from early equal opportunities models of educational practice (see Walsh, 1997). These would help me survive, in some measure, the avalanche of sexualised pressure to be feminine, which was to follow from the 1960s. As a result of women's movements and feminisms, from the 1970s I would encounter and become part of a richness of narrative resources available to women, even, gradually, to women from working-class backgrounds (see *Feminism and Psychology*, 1996). In the meantime, my move from girl to woman contradicted those norms of masculinity which had earlier served as role models and markers of value for me. It became clear that achieving in terms of those criteria, as a female, was not at all the same as if I had been male.

My father's latent sexism and misogyny, previously masked by his working-class, socialist enthusiasm for his first-born and for education, now surfaced. If I had been male, he could still have claimed me in his own image (which some of his male relatives continue to do to this day). As a woman, I was not this comforting extension of himself, but something more complex and disturbing – more 'other'. Becoming educated, I was also in my mother's image, and specifically so, when like her, I became an art student. Did this, I wonder, serve to remind my father that when he first met the woman who became his wife and housekeeper, mother to his (*sic*) children, she was a double scholarship, educated woman with a (lower?)middle-class background.

Perhaps I inadvertently stirred the roots of his own dis-ease, so deeply buried: his own class and gender conflicts and turmoil, his own sense of bereavement, loss, even shame? When he died in 1990, his life companion for nineteen years after my mother died, told me of his sense of repeatedly being 'left' by women: his abandonment by his sisters who died very young; his feeling that his adored mother preferred his irresponsible elder brother (from whom my father remained estranged after the death of their mother at forty, when he was eighteen). His first wife (also middle class) died in her late twenties, when he was thirty-two, and my mother (his second wife) died of cancer at fifty-nine, after thirty years of marriage, when he was sixty-three. His companion confided to me that she herself had come to fear dying before him, thereby adding herself to the list of women who had 'left' him behind and, she implied, let him down! Hearing this, my first thoughts were that the fact that his sisters, mother and two wives had all died *prematurely* seemed to have escaped him, except in terms of the consequences for himself. Perhaps he had carried unresolved grief from these early bereavements forward into later life as internalised anger at the unfairness of life.[5] Or was the subtext that he could not hold on to these women, could not fully control them? If he saw their various 'departures' as acts of (wilful?) abandonment, he could also construe their behaviour as defiance. I trembled at what all this meant for me, as his only daughter. I had had no inkling of the possible significance of these female precursors for our relationship. How little support there was (and is?) for men, particularly working-class men, in dealing with personal crisis, emotional trauma, bereavement and loss, in ways which do not undermine their 'proper' manhood.

THE THREAT OF FEMALE AGENCY

The father's anger [is] an expression of his frustration and fear of losing her, while the daughter's anger expresses her determination to run her own life. (Goulter and Minninger, 1994: 140)

Without a sexual politics, and in the absence of a political framework for understanding how we were positioned as daughter and father, woman and man, we could only experience this process of estrangement as personal rejection, personal attack. So what was political and structural, was experienced as wounding, even calculated. Without, for example, Giddens' idea of structuration –

> that social structure and individual action are inextricably linked and that human beings can draw on information and experience to transform the structures that organise them. (Swain, 1996: 20)

– my father and I were embedded in the structures of power we needed to transform and transcend. To defend himself from my growing separate identity and power, my father pathologised me: the 'good girl' was fast becoming the 'bad woman'. He could not bear to lose his responsive and attentive little girl. (Without her, who was he?) Whereas, in order to be 'me', I had to leave her behind (see Gilligan, 1995). To do this, I had to escape. Having been the companion daughter to the well-intentioned Pygmalion father, before I left home at twenty-one, I was more the yearning daughter to the lost father (Goulter and Minninger, 1994: 32).

> In this relationship, the father abandons the daughter, either by outright desertion or by rejection, remoteness, or neglect. (Goulter and Minninger, 1994: 32)

The power struggle between father and daughter is complex. Historically, 'the patriarchal father was the most powerful member of the household whereas the daughter was the least powerful' (Goulter and Minninger, 1994: 25). However, the balance of power shifts when 'the daughter feels that she has less to lose than the father does because she is more willing to sacrifice the relationship' (Goulter and Minninger, 1994: 140).

So I was the one to put actual geographical distance and time between us in my twenties. To become adult and subject, rather than simply older, involved my developing feminist consciousness and commitment. This too was unforeseen by either myself or my father. Yet he was not authoritarian as a parent, or violent, and I experienced his loving care and attentiveness as a girl. I owe him a lot. But as I grew older, he wanted to continue as Father, a figure of authority and respect, beyond reproach or criticism: my working-class hero. I wonder now whether my educated status and identity came to trigger shame in him? A class shame which had hitherto remained internalised (and invisible to me as a girl and young woman), and not part of his public persona. Did he mistake my departure for contempt rather than pain?

In describing her own experience as a girl and young black woman, bell hooks points to what are still common conditions for women in patriarchal societies:

> The punishments I received for 'talking back' were intended to suppress all possibility that I would create my own speech. That speech was to be suppressed so that the 'right speech of woman-hood' would emerge. (hooks, 1989: 6)

Because my experience as a child, at home and at school, was so very different from this, it was bewildering to discover further down the line, that for me too, 'there was no "calling" for talking girls, no legitimized rewarded speech' (hooks, 1989: 6). I had been deceived. I had, after all, developed a facility which would, in a patriarchal society, bring punishment, censure and loss, and would be taken as a mark of my insubordination as a woman, rather than as a sign of future stardom! The influential study by Broverman et al. (1970) showed that, on the one hand, in clinical judgements of mental health those personality characteristics identified with a 'normal healthy adult' were almost identical to those identified with a 'normal healthy male'; while on the other hand, those identified with a 'normal healthy female' differed markedly from both lists. Female cannot therefore be equal, neither can she be valued as different: she is intrinsically 'defective' and shameful. And if a female manifests 'gender' hybridity in these terms, she is presumably either unclassifiable or pathological. Is maturing as a female in a patriarchal society an oxymoron, a contradiction in terms? We may mirror male attributes as best we can; or fulfil our 'feminine destiny' and remain infanticised all our lives; or, as feminists, be stigmatised as 'deviant'.

MOVING BEYOND RESISTANCE?

I grew up on a working-class estate where the existence of class structure was largely denied and 'intellectualism' was suspect (Greenslade, 1976: 161). So my own home/class background was doubly 'different' within its experience of, and concern with, education and politics. I was grounded, from the start, in different soil from most of my peers, and perhaps most significantly, from other working-class girls and women on the estate. While the attainment of 'positive freedom' is linked with the achievement of class consciousness within the discourses of class and politics (see Fox, 1994: 15), class consciousness 'as we understand the term, is primarily a masculine conception' (Cronin citing Zweig in Fox, 1994: 40).

This may help to explain why, for two reasons, as I moved from girl to woman my class consciousness failed to bond my father and myself. First, as a woman, it was not something I was supposed properly to have; and second, it did not help me in understanding gender from a classed position. This is women's experience (Fox, 1994: 196): *it is what we need to understand*. If it is true that 'we need a more flexible set of concepts to address the contradictory pressures of class and gender in working class literary productions' (Fox, 1994: 23), it is also evident that those contradictions are sourced in people's lives.

By acquiring 'masculine' class consciousness as a girl and young woman, I was unwittingly intensifying my difference from other working class women, who, according to Zweig:

> ... were less proud of being working class, more aware of its deprivations. The result was a different form of class awareness – less aggressive and self-satisfied, more bitter and, in a sense, more pecuniary. (Zweig in Fox, 1994: 40; see also Steedman, 1993)

With a father who was first a skilled manual worker, then a trade union official (and being one of only two children), I was also a member of 'the respectable working class' (how I hate these intra-class distinctions). I did not directly experience working-class depri-vation, poverty and criminality, and did not encounter the middle classes in numbers, socially and professionally, until I was into my twenties. These factors shielded me for a time, and may have con-tributed to both my early shame-less class identity, and my growing sense of difference *within and from* white working-class culture. The roots of class and gender ambivalence seem clear.

Further, because of my father's class identity and socialist poli-tics, and then the way in which my younger brother was bound into white working-class culture when he too became a printer at sixteen, increasingly for me, class was gendered. White working-class culture meant: men/masculinity/male/dominance/my father.

And these were tangled, instrumental, and oppositional factors for my development as a woman and a feminist. Our easy-going rapport as father and daughter when I was a girl became an unresolved power struggle. Moving to overt confrontation in my late teens and early twenties, it descended into suppressed anger and silent longing once I cut all contact after my mother died, when I was twenty-nine. Eleven years later, when my daughter was four years old, it was the (outwardly confident and successful) angry daughter who renewed contact with the anguished father (Goulter and Minninger, 1994: 33). Neither of us realised how much buried anger and anguish we had been carrying around in the intervening years, as the former warring father/daughter (Goulter and Minninger, 1994: 140). A degree of reconciliation was achieved, which according to his companion did wonders for him. It was, she said, as if a cloud had been lifted from him. He was changed.

The photograph taken in 1983 in my father's Essex garden, records this sense of relief, and hope. In bright sunshine and against a backdrop of roses in full bloom, we testify to this 'new start'. It is an image that memorialises what we momentarily achieved. It also constructs the ideal, imaging the dream of intimacy, acceptance and harmony – both lost and yearned for. As 'family snapshot', it hides the complexities of our relationship over time (see Spence, 1986; 1995; Spence and Holland, 1991), including the hurt and pain of estrangement.

My daughter benefited from the attentions of her 'new' grandad. Watching them together over the eight years of their relationship, I was reminded of the early years of my own relationship with my father: our walks and talks and jokes, as we gently sparred with each other. The photograph I took of my eleven-year-old daughter and her grandad (Figure 14.3), walking ahead of me up a hill, arm-in-arm, sums up their companionship, six months before he died suddenly of cancer.

I realised, with emotion at the time, that part of his intense pleasure in this relationship was the opportunity to relive those happy times we had shared as father and daughter, when I was Anna's age. It was his chance to 'go back' to before things went wrong. It was also a reminder of how much he had loved me then, and (I knew) how much he had missed me since. This relationship offered me a new way of relating to my father, relatively uncontaminated by our struggles as father and daughter. During this period

Father/Grandad, Daughter/Mother, Daughter/Granddaughter

Steve and Anna in Tuchan, France, April 1990

I referred to him either as Steve, or in his new role, as grandad. Never as 'dad', my father. But:

> With healing from trauma, you can't scoot around it, you actually have to go through it if you want to move beyond it. (Trenshaw, 1996: 37)

So much remained unsaid, undiscussed, from those painful transitional years, and from the later years when I saw my mother descending into depression, before being diagnosed in 1967 with terminal cancer. So my father and I were unable to renew and build on our early friendship. We could not achieve equality as adults, without reopening old wounds and exposing hidden injuries. It has been a combination of life history process, including life history work with other women (Walsh, 1998), and shiatsu treatment and training,[6] which has begun to make these memories and emotions accessible to me during the last four years. The weaving and interplay of life history processes and holistic body-work have, for example, allowed hurt and anger to surface. This offers the possibility of understanding. These energies and insights, in turn, fuel creative process (see Morley, 1995; Walsh, 1996), which opens up opportunities for letting internalised anger go as a determining factor in my life.

Anger has been variously described and explained, not least as a 'natural' emotion, for example as 'the natural response to frustration' (Goulter and Minninger, 1994: 129). It has also been called 'the psychological equivalent to pain' (Colburn in Goulter and Minninger, ibid.). It is clear that the social formations at work here, and the structures of feeling which attend them, are inextricably entwined. For example, the anger referred to above is, *properly and understandably*, both personal and political: implicated in my identity as a woman from a hybrid white-working-class background, and imbricated in the development of my feminist identity. My anger is both gendered and classed, and has multiple, tangled roots.

I am beginning to think that becoming a woman and a feminist has been more significant than either my education or professional identity in dislocating me from a sense of continuity and ease with my class roots. This process may have started earlier than I imagined: that is, before I had the language and concepts of feminism. For before I had the language and concepts of feminism, I had the longing to be, the impulse to try, the sense of personal integrity and right to respect bequeathed me by my parents, which I would carry forward, sometimes with less than welcome consequences. My initial class-consciousness both obscured and devalued my mother's status and meaning in my life, and thus failed to include and account for our identities and experiences as *women in a patriarchal society*. I needed feminism and feminist friendships for that.

In these challenging scenarios, it is obvious how women's conceptual resources are rooted in and work with our emotional resources, both in and through our lives and works (Walsh, 1996). Faced with life's contradictions and oppressions, a woman – this woman – needs the warmth of friendship and feminism to keep her going! Without the knowledge and courage our feminisms afford us, women are likely to remain subjugated, at the very least tamed: domesticated for patriarchy. Many of us will blame ourselves for our 'failures' and 'inadequacies', that is our 'difference' from men. The category 'woman' functions within and for patriarchy, but the category feminist – however problematic, contested and tenuous at times – is something which continues to be of our own making. Retained as a process, I believe it can help women move beyond camouflage, beyond resistance, towards a healing place and sustainable relations.

Acknowledgements

I am grateful to the following women for their personal and critical engagement with this text in process: Dr Jean Hardy, Dr Chris Mann, Julie Matthews, Dr Louise Morley, Dr Helen Pearce, Dr Pauline Polkey and Jo Stanley. In their mix of vigorous reactions written in the margins (such as, 'Yeah!' – 'Ouch!' – 'Stop being so damn private!'); their probing and insightful comments and questionings; and in their attentiveness to the position of the reader, they echoed the text's hybridity. This mix of toughness and tenderness has been a vital spark for me.

Notes

1. In 1990 my life fell to pieces, and continued to fall to pieces for the next three years or so. The sudden death of my father in October

1990 was tightly sandwiched between the collapse of two key, long-standing relationships. At the time I was a senior lecturer in higher education. That autumn saw higher education institutions across the country over-recruiting, to the extent that in some there were not enough rooms or furniture to go round. At the same time, the new managerialism was gaining ground. Virility culture (Walsh, 1994a; 1994b) was becoming fashionable (and, in my institution, routinely wore a black bra). Institutional upheaval was accompanied by newly institutionalised vindictiveness, which engulfed and polarised students and staff. Many of these had previously worked alongside each other, with some degree of apparent mutuality, compatibility and purpose. Suddenly, bullying was routine and 'smart': the mark of power. Men cried; senior male members of academic and non-academic staff were physically removed from campus (and their posts), while others were publicly and routinely harassed and disparaged at meetings. Female non-academic staff frantically attended stress-management sessions after hours or took sick leave. (For an alternative version see Gee, 1994.) Within these new structures I was an anomaly (and irritant): the only Course Leader of both the only all-women interdisciplinary degree programme team in the institution, and an interdisciplinary Applied Social Science option, 'Gender and Society'; as well as a specialist contributor to another interdisciplinary degree programme. I was a long-standing equal opportunities and feminist activist and one of three Consultants within the new Equal Opportunities Unit (and still battling, this time inside the structure set up to implement equal opportunities throughout the college). I had been an active and executive member of my NATFHE branch for many years, and had represented both the institution and the union during the PCFC negotiations in London in the lead-up to the restructuring of the sector. Then, after twenty joyous years teaching in higher education (including extensive teamwork and collaboration with colleagues; a record of innovation and course development; and with enthusiastic student evaluations spanning my years and Courses in the institution), I found myself in the eye of the storm. In 1992, as my smiling photograph went up in the main corridor (along with the other Equal Opportunity Consultants, as part of the publicity for the unit), I was heading into grievance procedure and industrial tribunal. The irony was lost on management!

2. Writer and historian Jo Stanley prompted me to start this process in February 1993, with a view to contributing to the life history strand of the Women's History Network Annual Conference at Central Hall, London, November 1993. Some of this material was also presented at the BSA Study Group on Auto/Biography Annual Conference, December 1994, University of Manchester.

3. The international exhibition, Women Remember/Women in Conflict took place in the Great Hall, at the Albert Dock, Liverpool, in October 1994. It was closed down by the financial director of the Albert Dock Company, because of the 'offensiveness' of one piece of work (a life-size, naked self-portrait) which he said would upset the public. The organisers and artists refused to remove it. With another woman,

I attempted to mediate with him. His bullying behaviour at this meeting was another dose of virility culture in action. I told him that if we had not been representing other women, we would have walked out immediately. Women picketed outside the Great Hall, collecting signatures in support of the show continuing, uncensored. We took it in turns to guard the show overnight, as we feared for the exhibition's safety. One night, while women pickets slept on the cobbles outside the Great Hall, just feet from the shiny black depths of the dock waters, two uniformed security guards stole the petition sheets from their sleeping bodies. This resulted in more uproar and bad publicity for the dock company, and a further reminder for women of what we are up against on a daily basis. Representing ourselves is still taboo. Shame-less women are clearly threatening to men in suits.

4. Pamela Fox has discussed shame theory (1994: 10–20) in her desire to reclaim the term 'shame' for cultural studies of class and gender: for scholars 'searching for nuanced, respectful approaches to class cultural forms' (Fox, 1994: 10). She argues that to do this, 'shame needs to be dislocated from its exclusively psychoanalytic or anthropological frames of reference' (ibid.).
5. I am grateful to sociologist Helen Pearce for this further insight.
6. Shiatsu is body-work based on Eastern healing practices. It works with touch: acupressure points (tsubos) and meridians (channels of Energy which run throughout the body), using movement, pressure and stretches to improve balance, flow and connection in and with the whole self and its environments.

References

Broverman, Inge K., Broverman Donald, Clarkson Frank E., Rosenkrantz Paul S. and Vogel Susan R. (1970) 'Sex-Role Stereotypes and Clinical Judgements of Mental Health', *Journal of Consulting and Clinical Psychology*, 34:1, pp. 1–7

Feminism and Psychology (1996), 6:3

Fox, Pamela (1994) *Class Fictions: Shame and Resistance in the British Working Class Novel 1890–1945*, Durham and London: Duke University Press

Gee, Ruth (1994) 'Survival is not Compulsory' in Weil, Susan, ed., *Introducing Change 'From the Top' in Universities and Colleges*, pp. 131–40, London: Kogan Page

Gilligan, Carol (1995) 'The Centrality of Relationship in Psychological Development' in Blair, Maud, Holland Janet and Sheldon Sue, eds, *Identity and Diversity*, Milton Keynes: Open University Press

Goulter, Barbara and Minninger Joan (1994) *The Father-Daughter Dance*, London: Piatkus

Greenslade, Roy (1976) *Goodbye to the Working Class*, London: Marion Boyars

hooks, bell (1989) *Talking Back: Thinking Feminist – Thinking Black*, London: Sheba Feminist Publishers

Mahony, Pat and Zmroczek Christine, eds (1997), *Class Matters: 'Working Class' Women's Perspectives on Class*, London: Taylor & Francis

Morley, Louise (1995) 'Measuring the Muse: Feminism, Creativity and Career Development in Higher Education' in Morley, Louise and Walsh Val, eds, *Feminist Academics: Creative Agents for Change*, pp. 116–30, London: Taylor & Francis

Runayker, Irene (1994) 'Forty Five Stars for Peace', acrylic on paper, with sepia photocopied photographs, *Women Remember/Women in Conflict*, The Great Hall, Albert Dock: Liverpool

Sennett, Richard and Cobb Jonathan (1972) *The Hidden Injuries of Class*, New York: Knopf

Spence, Jo (1986) *Putting Myself in the Picture (A Political Personal and Photographic Autobiography)*, London: Camden Press

—— (1995) *Cultural Sniping: The Art of Transgression*, London: Routledge

Spence, Jo and Holland Patricia, eds (1991) *Family Snaps: The Meanings of Domestic Photography*, London: Virago

Steedman, Carolyn (1993) *Landscape for a Good Woman: A Story of Two Lives*, London: Virago

Swain, Harriet (1996) 'And now for my next trick…' Interview with Anthony Giddens, *Times Higher Education*, p. 20

Trenshaw, Katheryn (1996) 'Breaking the Silence'. Interview by Satish Kumar, *Resurgence*, November–December, 179, pp. 35–7

Walsh, Val (1993/4) 'Virility Culture Invades the Colleges', *Everywoman*, p. 38, December–January

——(1994) 'Virility Culture: Academia and Managerialism in Higher Education' in Evans, Mary, Gosling Julie and Seller Ann, *Agenda for Gender* (discussion papers on Gender and the Organisation of Higher Education), University of Kent at Canterbury, Women's Committee, pp. 1–10

——(1996) 'History/Theory/Practice: Moving from Death, Through Breath, Towards Co/Creativity'. Presented at the Women's Studies Network (UK) Annual Conference, Feminisms: Past, Present and Future, University of Glamorgan: Wales

——(1997) 'Interpreting Class: Auto/Biographical Imaginations and Social Change' in Mahony and Zmroczek, pp. 152–74

——(1998) 'Women Academics of White Working Class Origin: "Strangers" in Paradise? Or Just "Other"? *Auto/Biography*, vi:1+2, pp. 59–66

15

The Swashbuckler, the Landlubbing Wimp and the Woman in Between: Myself as Pirate(ss)

JO STANLEY

In writing a cultural history *Bold in her Breeches: Women Pirates Across the Ages* (Stanley, 1996), I found that despite my denials of any desire to be a lethal robber, I actually wanted to be what a woman pirate symbolises. Through the lives of Ann Bonny, Mary Read, Granuaile and others, I was covertly exploring my boldness, sadism, propensity for outrage and appropriation. What does it mean to me to sail away and swashbuckle? To psychically pull on breeches when faced with an enemy? To admit/deny my desires to stay (safely) ashore and assured in my frocks?

The 'ss' attached to 'pirate' here reflects the gendered and diminishing writing up of these fetishised desperadas. But what were they 'actually'? What am I, in 'being' them, doing for me in the name of feminist history? What in me am I recuperating? And in claiming to retrieve some 'mariners who happened to be female' from the tyranny of Sexy Devil status, in what ways am I writing out their actual extraordinariness?

MEANINGS

What is a pirate? The *Oxford English Dictionary* definition is one who plunders on the seas. But the now-mythical pirates in Western culture give such characters another meaning: historical swashbuckling heroes who are fitting stars for Hollywood movies such as *Blackbeard the Pirate* and *Captain Blood*. That meaning is at variance

216

with what today's sea bandits actually are to wary maritime insurers, protective unions, and anxious shipowners. They are young, often ex-military, South East Asian men who sneak up to oil tankers in their high-powered inflatables. They climb silently aboard in flip-flops and T-shirts, heist the crew's credit cards, rob the safe, and pick up any quickly resaleable electronic goods in 20 minutes, preferably while the crew are sleeping.

The role of pirate gained further meanings in the last two decades when feminists revisioned themselves in history as cross-dressing desperadas. Some of the characters in Julie Wheelwright's *Amazons and Military Maids* or Ellen Galford's novel, *Moll Cutpurse*, could be played by Madonna or Tina Turner. Mid-1990s' movies such as *Bandit Queen* and *Cut-throat Island* (starring Geena Davis as the pirate heroine) put that pleasure on the big screen for all to gaze upon. A piratess as feast?

I see the interest in violent outlaw women as partly uchronic. In Alesandro Portelli's terms, such re-presenting and re-seeing can – in some cases – be a version of that 'great literary form of refusing existing history: uchronia' (Portelli, 1990: 151). These tales offer a representation of what might have been – in this case, if only women in the past had had more power and freedom. Stories and movies of women desperadas offer readers exciting knowledge of their own potential in a similar way to the sometimes fabulous narratives of Portelli's Communist interviewees, 'contrasting a desirable world to an existing one and by claiming that it is only by accident it did not come into being, the uchronic hypothesis allows the narrator to "transcend" reality and refuse to identify himself and be satisfied with the existing order' (Portelli, 1990: 151).

This ties in with another meaning of piracy. In analysing the meanings of the 40 robbers in the story of Ali Baba, therapist Verena Karst saw the figure of pirate as expressing the presence of the denied needy, desiring and even thieving side of ourselves. She had a deeply inhibited woman client who dare not accept anything she was offered. The client 'dreamed the following dream: "I have a pirate ship under my command. I sail along the Côte d'Azur in the pirate ship and plunder and steal whatever I like. It feels great." In dreaming this, it becomes clear to this woman that she too had wishes and longings that she would like to fulfil without too much exertion' (Karst, 1996: 53). Such theft also, as Karst points out, indicates the low self-worth of the robber, who desires to have more than others in order to feel that someone else is worse off. To long to say 'Open Sesame' (or 'Stand and Deliver') and get our goal is to mistake the principle of having wealth for the truer satisfactions of being rather than possessing (see Karst, 1996: 64).

MOTIVES

I wrote *Bold in Her Breeches* just after I had finished editing Jo Spence's collected works, *Cultural Sniping: The Art of Transgression* (1995). The significance of that experience was that I had lived for two years with the huge (cover) image of Jo leering through a stocking mask taking aim with a lethal crossbow. She was playing, seriously and joyously, at being an outlaw who uses violence to get her desires, including social justice. To assure myself that one day my long editing labours would indeed become the thing that she and I desired – a proper book that would have a political effect – I created my own mocked-up version of the potential cover and stuck it in front of the computer. (Our desire was achieved, but through daily grind and not by one afternoon's piratical appropriation on a sunny ocean.)

As feminist historian and lover of style, I wrote my history of women pirates in that feminist context, in 1993. I wrote it not because I was interested in exploring sassy lady devils in pants, but out of a pragmatic pedagogical desire. I seized on women pirates as a popular way to say to a greater audience what I have been saying for a decade with my academic work on women's maritime history (primarily stewardesses and female domestic staff on liners): women worked at sea.

PROCESS

The book was a fairly light-hearted by-product of that mainstream work. I conceived it while writing about the moral duties of sober shipboard matrons who escorted emigrant women to the colonies. The historical research was relatively easy; I sat at Greenwich or Kew looking at old documents and piecing possible viewpoints out of popular texts such as *Love Stories of the Pirates*, *Sodomy and the Pirate Tradition*, *The History of ye Pyrates*.

But there were times in Manila, while researching modern piracy, when I was terrified. I ducked out of confrontations with the criminal underworld that might have made good stories about women and modern piracy but … Yes, I found I was not prepared to die for my writing. I was wimp not hero: yes, just another lone woman who wanted to be safe in a world of frocks and fun, not overwhelming pistols. I was too scared to don the metaphorical breeches to challenge that violent masculine culture.

THEN CAME THE QUESTION…

Bold in Her Breeches, when it came out in Spring 1995, had extensive publicity. It quickly reached number four in the best-seller list at Silver Moon, Europe's biggest feminist bookshop. HarperCollins' limo pulled up at my house day after day to take me to Broadcasting House to transmit four or five programmes at a time on pirates. Every interviewer – from Vanessa Feltz while having her breasts plaster cast on air, to Kiwi DJs at tiny radio stations, to a *Big Issue* feature writer – asked the same question: 'Did you write about women pirates because you really wanted to be one, Jo?'

Speaking in balanced, responsible mode I gave the Appollonian answer (Hillman, 1993: 36–40): 'No, not really, because I think they were probably psychopaths. I don't want to kill people. And I don't think ordinary seafaring workers should be murdered while doing their daily jobs. I like the *idea* of being a woman pirate but I think the *reality* would have been distressing: weevilly biscuits and wet bedding; peer group pressure to be violent; the boredom of keeping daily company with moronic hoodlums.' (I prefer, as I wrote in my preface, to stay home eating Yorkies in my heated water bed.)

That's what I said. But increasingly I felt able to acknowledge to myself – not least while dressed as pirate under the encouraging gaze of feminist friends – that I could give a Dionysian 'yes' in reply. Yes, I love to take, to play, to dare, to be irresponsible, to be violent. Yes, I could, I see, get off on a sadistic ego trip as a vicious swashbuckler. Yes, I am interested in the bold masculine archetypes in me I have for too long disowned but kept appearing in my dreams: the yacht engineer and the army captain, the handsome exiled violinist and the tyrant. And then there is the much more complicated truth that sits – no, lumbers and darts – in between this split: the woman who seeks to be neither wimp nor pirate, but seer.

PIRATICAL POLARITIES

I experienced the media interviewers as asking me the question in the tradition of Western metaphysics: binary pairings in which the pirate figure (as daring but loveable prince of a little light-hearted misrule) is admired. By contrast, people who dare not leave home on land for the sea, dare not transgress nor take what is not theirs, dress boringly, and fear to challenge others for what s/he wants are that shameful thing: conformists out of cowardice. As Derrida shows, the structurally dominant one of the pairing depends intimately on the subordinate term being defined as opposite (Derrida, 1976: 26). In this case, the landlubber/wimp is clearly the less attractive position.

It is an enduring split and of great fascination to students of the human psyche. Jungian Polly Young-Eisendrath (1984) works as therapist with couples using the model of hag and hero, the beautiful prince versus the hag/nag/Terrible Mother (implicitly someone who thinks people should not venture and not have fun). How can they relate to each other better? Similarly, how could Robert Louis Stevenson's Dr Jekyll be interesting if it were not for the terrible Mr Hyde, and vice versa?

So how could I have answered 'No' wholeheartedly? To do so would have been to state myself as boring. Equally, how could I answer a wholehearted 'Yes'? The hero/prince is too large for life. He excites envy and therefore brings danger; he is unrealistic about his own ability to deal with danger. He thinks he is charmed. I do not want to take such injudicious risks.

The question is, of course, more complex. For one thing, neither the pirate nor the wimp is wholly autonomous or at ease in that milieu. Both are spectacles, presented to be judged by others. For another thing, pirates were only exciting outlaws in the eyes of certain beholders.

LE QUESTION

For months after *Bold in Her Breeches* came out I found I kept asking myself the question urgently, but in French: 'Moi, pirate?'. I couldn't understand why that accent, that formulation. Then I realised, it is being asked by someone foreign to me, someone who doesn't know me, a someone whose language 'I' don't know or claim not to know. But it is I who am asking it, of me. Am I obfuscating the answer? 'Milord, je ne comprend pas le français. Qu'est ce qu'elle dit?'

Is it simply that the problem is that when others ask the question of me, they seem to ask it from a foreign position: that of a person who believes that a pirate is the voluptuous female counterpart of Errol Flynn? My difficulty in replying is that all my research, by contrast, leads me to think of pirates in another tongue to that discourse. Thinking as social historian, pirates signify seafarers who suffered privation and may also have inflicted cruelty while working on slave vessels; they were jobbing seafarers who switched to different types of shipping when necessary. They were petty crooks who were alienated and irresponsible; 'criminals' constructed by an unjust society. I also think of them as diverse. My history of women pirates spans the entire world and twenty-five hundred years, moving as it does from Artemisia in 480 BC, to pirates' accomplices such as Susan Frani in the 1990s. There is no one such entity, a woman pirate, any more than there is one such entity: a seaman, or a woman writer.

Or is the problem in being able to formulate an answer caused by something else to which I am still foreign, whose language I don't yet speak?

SILENCE IN COURT

It may be partly affected by no woman pirate in history having spoken for herself according to records. (If they did not, how can I?) No piratess has authored an extant autobiography. The accounts of their cut-throat careers and swooning amours (lesbian and heterosexual) were created by others: male, non-pirates, often in a judicial position. When in 1720 the most notorious women pirates, Ann Bonny and Mary Read, were challenged to speak in their own defence at the Jamaican court of St Jago de la Vega, they faced a jury of privileged planters. The only woman who spoke about them was a native of the island: Dorothy Thomas (Trial Transcripts PRO C0137/ 14/ XC 18757). She testified against them. And the printed records of the Anglo-American piracy trials of this period (now stored snugly within the Colonial Office records at Kew) all claim that in trial after trial the pirates remained mute when asked by the court what they had to say for themselves. If that claim is true, it may mean that they chose to exercise the right of silence knowing that injustice would anyway prevail. Or possibly these real pirates too may have had trouble with the non-pirate's question: 'Do you like being a pirate, do you want to be one?'

The only proper answer might be 'What does it mean to you, Mi Ludd?'. Or even, 'By whose authority do you presume to ask me?'. Or even 'We've all got ter make a living, guv'.

Now today, musing at home in a tropically hot bath, I consider prosecuting parts of myself – benignly – for wanting to be a woman pirate. What woman would not want the power to satisfy her desires? My court testimony would be long and voluble. In the tradition of women's court testimony (see for example Cohen in Kadar, 1992: 83) my heavily determined narrative would cast me as well-intentioned victim of circumstance.

As judge, I let myself off because I see piracy has been necessary for my survival. 'Yes, I sometimes need to be a pirate, Mi Ludd, but as for *wanting* to be one ...' I also do not want to disavow the self who likes to stay at home daydreaming and cooking, painting and hiding with the phone unplugged. Nor can I divest myself of the self who has the wisdom to see what piracy means.

I could also let myself go free – sentenced to a life of pleasure and met needs – on the grounds that I go a-pirating as part of my own seeking of political justice. The process of justice being, as Jane Flax argues 'one of the ways individuals manage the strains of being simultaneously public and private, alone and in relation to others, desiring and interdependent' (1993: 341). On a collective level (and some writers such as Rediker (1987) have seen pirate ships as communes), Flax argues that 'justice is one of the ways groups manage the strain of mediating between the individual subjectivities of which they are composed and objectivities such as limited resources, past traditions, and the consequences of past decisions and practices which those individuals did not create but to which they must respond' (1993: 341). As such, I can see that many of the times I have acted piratically I have acted for the common best and perhaps in the only way I personally knew I could.

WHAT A PIRATE IS MADE OF

Perhaps I could answer the key question ('Would you have liked to have been a pirate, Jo?') better if I look in detail at what being a pirate implied. First of all, the past tense is important. The stereo-typical – or even archetypal – pirate is the Anglo-American sort. He sailed in the late 1600 and early 1700s and often risked capture but never faced the gallows. He liked his love affairs with fine-rigged local ladies and always ended up marrying the most spirited one on the island. This alliance was permitted because – lo and behold! – he turned out to be a scion of her privileged class after all and not at all a prole in need.

Such a version offers this working-class female no room to enact aspects of myself. But there are certain things the stereo/archetypes did that allow me to insert my fantasies. Firstly, a pirate is stereo-typically made of a heroic desire for justice. He is a merry man of Sherwood who just happens to be operating on the high seas and not under the green trees; his life's pleasure is to take from the rich to give to the poor. I like the notion of being a profitable adventurer, of acquiring enough doubloons and pieces of eight to buy what I want. As the only feminist movie of women's piracy, *Madame X: An Absolute Ruler*, (Ulrike Ottinger, 1977), has it, the job offers the rare chance of getting the world, gold, love and adventure at sea. All of these I desire. Mixed up with the desire for loot for me is the desire for justice for us all.

Political psychologist M. Kent Jennings (1991: 198) points out that social psychology finds there are, broadly speaking, two approaches to justice as motivation for action. On the one hand, simple self-interest: I as individual accrue advantage from behaving in a just manner, i.e. distributing wealth more equitably to the deserving poor, including me in my below-income household. On the other hand, there is the more impartial justice, that is, behaving in a way that 'does not rest on personal advantage. Acting to reduce unjust distribution is a good in and of itself' (Jennings, 1991: 198). And I see that as socialist I am interested in taking not only for me but for those around me who are also in need.

Secondly, there is the chance of roving the ocean. On Aegean fer-ries and private boats on the sunlit Caribbean, I discovered the extreme pleasure of being at sea, and the sense that I would do any-thing to stay on it. In fact pirates seldom roved the seas at will, but sought intelligence as to what ships were worth heisting and set out after them deliberately. A pirate ship was always a working one, a place of constant graft not lazing about sunbathing as if it were a cruise. I plead guilty to a desire to roam the seas more idly, as non-worker, and with no pressure to fulfil the goal of plundering.

Jo Stanley: female pirate

Thirdly, there is the opportunity of dressing in fancy clothes, as pirates notoriously did when they went ashore. So, like the upper-class eighteenth-century women who played in transvestite masquerades dressed as pirates (Castle, 1986: 64), I plead most definitely and guilelessly guilty of the desire to dress in scarlet velvet breeches, fine hats plumed with the most gracious of ostrich feathers, a brocade waistcoat, lace ruffles at my wrist and neck, a frogged velvet jacket, and a parrot as matey as my cat sitting on my shoulder. And yes, having wielded so many theatrical cutlasses in photo calls, now I know I would happily spend my days armed with a sword whose balanced weight and cutting abilities were as familiar a companion in trouble as my own personal alarm is now. These comforting clothes are those in which I could never be mistaken as someone to be messed with. This pirate garb, especially the trousers in which I am not female – are a label that says 'Keep off! I've got power'. A masculine message: 'I'm an Exotic Other who cannot and will not be expected to conform. I'm also a flash git – admire my cloth'. On the other hand, I also plead guilty to inordinate love of my landlubber's dressing-gown and guilty to daily donning of Lycra leggings and trainers for ease. Yes, I am guilty of ambivalence and conflicting desire.

What else is a pirate figure made of? He–she makes people walk the plank. This punishment – which serious maritime historians such as Rediker (1987) and Cordingly (1995) doubt ever existed – means that I can terminate the people who irritate me. I can high-handedly dispose of these commanders of opposing vessels and continue to tread the boards of my own and their ship unchallenged, as possessor. I can outrage and appropriate, backed by my cut-throat crew. So speaks the pirate prince, proudly. But my hag fears punishment for such sinning and has no crew. And my wise woman fears the imbalance; that violence must result from this impudent and imprudent violence.

THE OTHER QUESTIONS

Other questions are far more urgent to me than 'Would you have liked to have been a pirate, Jo?'. They are about dealing responsibly with the making public of histories. They are as follows: 'Why can't you write fiction about these women, Jo?'. This question matters because I always have written novels and short stories and plays about the real women I have researched. In the case of the women pirates, I felt that they had been constructed into something so fictive that my job was to create a more plausible fiction, a 'truth' as I saw it. It was almost, but of course not quite, a reversal of my usual process.

The second question is: 'What am I, in "being" them, doing for me in the name of feminist history? What in me am I recuperating?'. I am exploring myself. And in claiming to retrieve some 'mariners who happened to be female' from the tyranny of Sexy Devil stereotypical status, in what ways am I writing out their actual extraordinariness? This is a serious point. There were many times when I felt I was trying to 'normalise' the women, to present their psychology and social situations in such a way as to make their careers explicable, to exonerate them from my own notional charge that they were, in some cases, psychopaths. I was also trying to protect them both from men's sexual objectification of their bodies and from my own dismal fear that they might have been all-too-frequent victims of shipboard gang-bangs; the hags and not the heroines of the Jolly Roger'd vessels.

CONCLUSION

At the end of all this struggle to understand my answers to the question 'Would you have liked to have been a woman pirate Jo?', I remain nonplussed at the question. 'Quoi?' At the heart of my fluctuating desire to enact the pirate archetype might be the simple need to have someone legitimise my desire, to say 'You can have what you want. There's no need to heist anything, steal anything, act against people to wrest it off them.' The need to self-actualise, as in Maslow's illuminating hierarchy of needs, is less urgent than the physical needs (food, shelter, rest); social-affectional needs; self-esteem and dignity needs (see Chowning Davies' discussion, 1991: 397).

But actually, in the complex capitalist world where my desires are in themselves offensive to those who seek to hold power for themselves, the odds on being offered satisfaction are slight. The odds on being approved of for having such wants, are even more slight. Anyway, approval is not the point.

At my best – at the calm, beautiful and wise site within me where neither the hag nor the prince, the landlubbing wimp nor the bold pirate in me are obsessionally present but also not dangerously absent – I can approve my own desires. I can even respond to their refutation with the 'amiable dignity' that is one definition of mental health. I can sit metaphorically on deck sunbathing, eating chocolate, eyepatch disguise off, listing my needs and desires pragmatically *alongside* the strategies for ensuring they are at least partially met. A pirate at rest, a pirate who can cope. A pirate who is happy enough to go on to create from the ocean of life whatever stories her wandering heart desires.

In writing about the lives of women pirates I have written about desire. This essay's subtext has therefore been about the polarities between desire's legitimisation and satisfaction on the one hand, and opportunistic, illegitimate seeking of satisfaction on the other hand. If an essay is about desire, it is necessarily an essay about power too. And maybe it is also an advertisement for the need for wisdom; for the hag's insistence and reclusiveness and for the pirate prince's strategic cutlasses.

Maybe I do want to be a woman pirate more than I do not. I have to be one, metaphorically, if I want equal rights and justice (not to mention velvet leggings, chocolate, books from Silver Moon, enough money to be nomadic and enough electricity to heat the water bed). But I'd rather not have to fight in this way for those; I'd rather they were my – and everyone's – just deserts.

References

Castle, Terry (1986) *Masquerade and Civilisation: The Carnivalesque in Eighteenth Century English Culture and Fiction*, Stanford: Stanford University Press

Cohen, Elizabeth S. (1992) 'Court Testimony: Self and Culture in the Making of Text', in Ladar, ed., *Essays in Life Writing*, Toronto: University of Toronto Press

Cordingly, David, ed. (1995) *Life Among the Pirates: the Romance and the Reality*, London: Little, Brown

Davies, James Chowning (1991) 'Maslow and the Theory of Political Development; Getting Down to Fundamentals', *Journal of the International Society of Political Psychology*, 12:3

Derrida, Jacques (1976) *Of Grammatology*, G. C. Spivak (trans.), Baltimore: Johns Hopkins University Press

Flax, Jane (1993) 'The Play of Justice: Justice as a Transitional Space', *Journal of the International Society of Political Psychology*, 14:2

Galford, Ellen (1993) *Moll Cutpurse: Her True History*, London: Virago

Garber, Marjorie (1993) *Vested Interests: Cross-Dressing and Cultural Anxiety*, London: Penguin

Hillman, James (1993) *Healing Fiction*, Woodstock: Connecticut

Jennings, M. Kent (1991) 'Thinking about Social Injustice', *Journal of the International Society of Political Psychology*, 12:2

Kadar, Marlene, ed. (1992) *Essays in Life Writing: From Genre to Critical Practice*, Toronto: University of Toronto Press

Karst, Verena (1995) *Folktales as Therapy*, New York: Fromm International

Kristeva, Julia (1984) *The Revolution in Poetic Language*, Margaret Waller (trans.), New York: Columbia University Press

Madame X (1997) *An Absolute Ruler/Madame X Eine Absolute Herscherin*, eds Ulrike Ottinger/Tabea Blumenschein, West Germany, 1977, Exportfilm Bischoff, Isabellastr. 20, D-800, Munich, Germany

Portelli, Alessandro (1990) 'Uchronic Dreams: Working-class memory and possible worlds' in Raphael Samuel and Paul Thompson, eds, *The Myths We Live By*, London: Routledge

Rediker, Marcus (1987) *Between the Devil and the Deep Blue Sea: Merchant Seamen, Pirates and the Anglo-American Maritime World, 1700–1750*, Cambridge: Cambridge University Press

Spence, Jo (1995), *Cultural Sniping: The Art of Transgression*, London: Routledge

Stanley, Jo (1996), ed., *Bold in Her Breeches: Women Pirates Across the Ages*, London: Pandora

Wheelwright, Julie (1994) *Amazons and Military Maids: Women who Dressed as Men in the Pursuit of Life, Liberty and Happiness*, London: Pandora

Young-Eisendrath, Polly (1984) *Hags and Heroes: A Feminist Approach to Psychotherapy for Couples*, Toronto: InterCity Books

Index

Abbas, K. A., 155, 163
  Return of the Red Rose, 162
Academy, 64
academic, xiv, xv, xvi, 23, 25, 37, 40, 56,
  80, 81, 96–107 *passim*, 109–21
  passim, 197–8 (n. 1), 211
  community, 56–7, 96–107 *passim*,
    109–21 *passim*, 197–8 (n. 1)
  interdisciplinarity, xiv, xvi, 80, 81
  marginalisation, xv, 37, 38, 40
  Research Assessment Exercise, 37
Africa
  Nurses to NHS, 137, 140
Aguilar, Grace, xvi, 81, 83–5, 86, 89, 90,
  92
  *Home Influence, A Tale for Mothers and
    Daughters*, 84, 91
  The Spirit of Judaism, 83
  *The Vale of Cedars or The Martyr: A
    Story of Spain in the Fifteenth
    Century*, 93 (n. 4)
  The Women of Israel, 83
Ali, Tariq, 164
Ali Baba, 217
alienation, 39, 40
Allan, Mary, 113
Anderson, Anna (Grand Duchess
  Anastasia), 5–8 *passim*
Anderson, Elizabeth Garrett, 70
Anderson, P. C.
  My Years with Indira Gandhi, 167 (n. 1)
'angel in the house', 97, 182
Anti-Sweat Shop Organisation, 63
Anning, Mary, 194
Artemisia, 221; *see also* pirate/ss
Austen, Jane, 83, 180, 183, 194
  Fanny Price, 175, 182
  Mansfield Park, 174, 175, 179–82 *passim*
  Persuasion, 194
autograph, 130
autobiography, xiii–ix *passim*, 12, 14, 16,
  23–5 *passim*, 29, 30–2 *passim*, 55, 56,
  64, 96, 99, 100, 106, 123–8 *passim*,
  130, 133, 134, 158, 165, 221
  Anglo-Jewish, 26
  as research, 23–6
  intellectual autobiography, 24
  see also life-stories; life-writing;
    personal ethnography

auto/biography, xiii–xix *passim*, 12–13,
  14, 16, 22, 24, 29, 31, 34, 38, 44, 52,
  56, 70, 71, 110, 125–9 *passim*, 133,
  134, 197, 203
  auto/biographical practice, xiv, 61–79,
    80–94, 96–108, 109–22, 123–36,
    137–51, 152–69
  auto/biographical theory, xiii, xiv,
    xvi, 3–21, 22–33, 34–43, 44–58
  auto/biographical writing, xiv, xv,
    xix, 173–184, 185–196, 197–215,
    216–28
  collective, 38
  see also autobiography; biography;
    life-history; life-stories; life-
    writing; personal ethnography
Auto/Biography, 29
Autobiography of a Shirt Maker, 61–79

Babbage, Charles, 102, 106
Bagley, Alec, 36
Bakunin, 76 (n. 5)
Bandaranaike, Sirimavo, 162, 167–8
  (n. 9)
Bandit Queen, 217
Bangladesh, *see* Gandhi; India
Baranowski, Mr, 27, 28
  see also Poland
Baxter, C., 146
Beatles, The, 178
de Becker, Madame Stuart, 12
Beckman, Peter
  Women in World Politics, 167 (n. 8)
Beer, Gillian, 62
Bell, Currer, Ellis, and Acton, 86
  see also Charlotte Brontë; Emily Brontë
Belloc, Bessie, 70
Bhatia, Krishan
  Indira, 155
Bhutto, Benazir, 162, 167 (n. 5)
  Big Issue, 219
binary pairings, 220
biography, xiii, xiv, xviii, 5, 8, 10, 12, 16,
  17, 20, 24, 29, 31, 74, 75, 97, 100, 127,
  130, 134, 137, 152, 154, 155, 157–60
  passim, 164, 165, 166, 183
  feminist biography, 14, 16
  and science, 5, 8